LEE BOO
OF BELAU

LEE BOO
OF BELAU

A Prince in London

Daniel J. Peacock

South Sea Books
Pacific Islands Studies Program
Center for Asian and Pacific Studies
University of Hawaii

University of Hawaii Press
Honolulu

Library of Congress Cataloging-in-Publication Data

Peacock, Daniel J., 1919–
  Lee Boo of Belau.

  (South Sea books)
  Bibliography: p.
  Includes index.
  1. Lee Boo, d. 1784. 2. Oceanians—England—
London—Biography. 3. Palau—Princes and princesses—
Biography. 4. London (England)—Social life and
customs—18th century. 5. Wilson, Henry, d. 1810.
6. Antelope (Packet) I. Title. II. Series.
DA676.9.023P43   1987   942.1'05'0924   [B]   86–27258
ISBN: 978-0-8248-3230-8

*This book is dedicated
to the late Nevil Dickin,
rubak of London, to the
rubaks of Belau, and to
mechas Shirley Greene Peacock
and the women and children of Belau*

CONTENTS

ILLUSTRATIONS

MAPS

EDITOR'S NOTE

This volume is the first of a new series entitled *South Sea Books* published jointly by the University of Hawaii Press and the university's Pacific Islands Studies Program. The title was suggested by Mr. Stuart Inder, former editor and publisher of *Pacific Islands Monthly,* and was adopted because it has a very special historical meaning. As J. C. Furnas noted in his *Anatomy of Paradise,* the term "South Sea" originated in a misconception: "The isthmus of Panama so twists that Balboa first saw the Pacific south of him, whereas two-fifths of it actually lay to the north." Nonetheless, from that time in 1513 for the next two hundred years or so, the "South Sea" meant the Pacific to most Westerners. The term "South Seas" came much later, along with all of its romantic connotations.

South Sea Books will include works of general interest that deal with the islands and peoples of the Pacific Ocean, and the current volume is an appropriate beginning. The focal character is Lee Boo, the talented son of a paramount chief in the Belau Islands, who was taken to London in the 1780s. Lee Boo's escort and mentor was the English Captain Henry Wilson whose vessel, the *Antelope,* had been shipwrecked on Belau's reef. The tale is well told by the author, Daniel Peacock, who served as an educator in Belau and elsewhere in the U.S. Trust Territory for over two decades. It is evident that Peacock cares about the young Belauan who was never to return home. However, Peacock goes beyond Lee Boo's story to tell us about others whose lives were touched by this island ambassador of over two hundred years ago.

The School of the Pacific Islands, Inc., a nonprofit, educational corporation, played a crucial role in seeing this volume to press and launching *South Sea Books* by providing a subsidy for the production costs of *Lee Boo of Belau*. I wish to personally extend my appreciation to the Board of Trustees of the School of the Pacific Islands, Inc., for their consideration of Peacock's work and the attention they gave to his manuscript when it was still in the review process. The four members of the board have shown a deep interest in the peoples of the Pacific, particularly Micronesia; they are: Larry Janss, Edwin Janss, Steven Davenport, Jr., and Michael Newman.

ROBERT C. KISTE

PREFACE

This is not a work of fiction. Lee Boo lived. He was born in Belau—the islands the English called Pelew—the westernmost islands of Micronesia. His life ended in London, thousands of miles from his Pacific island home. The circumstances that led him to England, his life in London, and the events that followed as a consequence of his death two hundred years ago are the subject of this book. May it honor his name and that of his people.

May this book also inspire latter-day Lee Boos to reflect on their own lives and record what others may wish to know before it is too late. Had Lee Boo lived out his years in his own islands, at least some of his wisdom and insights might have been passed on to later generations in traditional ways. But having never returned from the greatest adventure of his life, he left no legacy. Instead, others who knew little of his language and culture have written of him and of the events that took him from his islands and into a broader arena. In doing so, they could not avoid the use of conjecture. Despite such difficulties and the limitations of available resources, what follows is faithful to all that my research has revealed to have been recorded. Footnotes have been shunned in favor of occasional citations within the narrative, but, for the sake of readers who seek more information, more extensive notes, lists of sources, and an annotated bibliography have been appended.

The Islands of Belau

The English were the first to describe the Belau Islands in any detail, and for a hundred years or more their maps described them as the

Pelew Islands. But to the Spanish, whose claim to them and to all of the Caroline Islands was upheld by Pope Leo XIII in 1885, they were the Palaos. To the Germans who bought them from Spain in 1899, they were the Palau-Inseln. The Japanese, who ruled them between World Wars I and II as part of the mandated islands under the League of Nations, knew them as Palau or, sometimes, Para Shoto or Parau-Jima. And to the Americans who administered them after World War II, as one of the six districts constituting the Trust Territory of the Pacific Islands, they were the District of Palau.

To the present-day descendants of Lee Boo's brothers and sisters these islands are now, as they always were, Belau, and they are governed as the Republic of Belau by the people of Belau (although the "Palau" spelling is frequently used).

Given these varying contexts, the proliferation and garbling of the spelling of island names was inevitable. For example, although Lee Boo always spoke of Belau, Captain Wilson knew the islands as Pelew, and John McCluer, with greater accuracy, called them Palou. To minimize confusion, the spelling "Belau" is generally used, except in quoted material. However, "Pelew" and other English spellings have been retained where appropriate, for example, Coorooraa for Koror and Oroolong for Ulong.

Similarly, for personal names, including that of Lee Boo (which would be spelled differently in Belau today) I have used the spellings found in the accounts of Keate, McCluer, Delano, and the other sources upon which I have had to rely as the only written record of the events described here.

ACKNOWLEDGMENTS

Unlike Captain Wilson and his crew, my voyage began in Belau and ended in London. My closest colleagues then (1953–1958) were Alfonso Oiterong, who was to become Vice President of the Republic of Belau, and the late David Ramarui under whose direction I worked for many years after we both found ourselves at Trust Territory Headquarters on Saipan. I owe to them what understanding I have of things Belauan. In my first year in Belau my mentor was William Vitarelli whose creative talents inspired my own. From a distance, but a close presence, Director of Education Robert Gibson gave me confidence in my writing, and at my side for most of my time in Belau, Harry Uyehara was a reliable informant and co-worker. It was Harry, along with Hera Owen, who guided Belau's Museum into existence, thus encouraging my own interest in Belau's past. But the Belau years were first and foremost a family experience for us as have been most of our travels within Micronesia and most of our voyages beyond.

In 1961, having moved to Pohnpei, my wife, Shirley, and I, along with our daughters Karen and Paula, made our first trip to London. An article describing how we found Lee Boo's tomb was solicited by Richard J. Umhoefer, editor of the *Ponape-per.* Later, Raymond Ulochong of Belau, then working at Headquarters, asked that the article be reprinted in the *Micronesian Reporter.* The response was more than I could have imagined. It inspired me to learn more. Comments and letters from Micronesian students were particularly poignant. I especially want to acknowledge the letter I received from Dr. Anthony Polloi, who wrote from the Fiji School of Medicine.

While in Pohnpei I was given a copy of E. M. Forster's "Letter to Madan Blanchard" by linguist Ed Quackenbush. This eventually inspired a summer-long stay in London by which time our family included our son, Daniel Lawrence. But the sustained effort of researching this book did not begin until after my retirement in 1980. It began in Hawaii where I used the university's outstanding collections at the Hamilton Library. Here I received the help of many kind people including, notably, Renée Heyum, curator of the Hawaii and Pacific Collection, along with Lynette Furuhashi and Karen Peacock of her staff. At the Bishop Museum where, in earlier years, I had gained inspiration from the anthropologists I had known best in the field (in Belau), Roland and Maryanne Force, I was guided to the Lee Boo signature by Librarian Cynthia Timberlake. During this period of research in Hawaii I received the first of many letters from Nevil Dickin in London. He had been put in touch with me by the Reverend Nicholas Richards, rector of St. Mary's Rotherhithe, who has obliged me with patience for many years. Nevil had begun research into the Lee Boo story and wanted to compare notes. The comparing and sharing went on for some time, first by correspondence, then together in London after Shirley and I went there to put the finishing touches on this book.

In London Nevil Dickin and I visited the haunts of Lee Boo, Captain Wilson, George Keate, and many a lesser character related to the story. It was a joyful experience and I owe Nevil as much for his friendship as for his findings, valuable though they have been to this project. Even after Nevil became seriously ill his interest never waned. If he thought of a question or a comment after I had visited him at the hospital and reported on my progress, he would sometimes send messages to me in the hand of his friend Jack Ritchie, who has my thanks.

Among others who assisted me in London I want to single out particularly Mrs. Dorota Starzecka of the Museum of Mankind whose kindness toward us and whose assistance merit more than a mere thank you. I am also more than thankful to Graham Binns who read my manuscript and to Diana Athill who, at Mr. Binns' request, read the manuscript and provided kind words of encouragement and advice.

In Rotherhithe, in addition to that of the Reverend Nicholas Richards, I received help from Mary Boast and Bernard Nurse, both then librarians at the Local Studies Library. Paul Woodhead, prime mover behind Rotherhithe's Lee Boo Bicentennial, Dave Slater who directed the pageant, and Robert Tedman who designed and illustrated the bicentennial booklet, deserve special mention.

It would be impossible to name all of the people who assisted me at each library and museum in London. I can at least express gratitude to them collectively and offer my thanks to the governing bodies that maintain these marvelous institutions—particularly the British Museum and Library. It is a delight to rub elbows there with patrons from so many areas of Britain and the world. But not all of my research was done in London. There were excursions throughout much of England in search of the *Antelope,* the Wilsons, and others, the most memorable of which was our day in Colyton with Nevil Dickin as guests of Ann and Alan Jones at Oroolong House. I hope they will welcome this book into their home as warmly as they welcomed us.

Now that this voyage has ended and I can reflect on what may have been missed, I wish I had had with me the Belauan poet, Val Sengebau, the Belauan historian Katherine Kesolei, and the Micronesian historian Francis X. Hezel, S.J. Were that possible I am sure nothing would have been missed. I hope their friendly counsel will be reflected in what I have written. Similarly, I hope Dirk Ballendorf and his colleagues at the University of Guam will find this book useful.

Finally, I want to express thanks to Robert Kiste who made the essential decision to publish this book; and to Linley Chapman, his careful and knowledgeable manuscript editor; and to Sae Kusaka and Barbara Trapido, who did the cartography. I also thank photographer Takumi Tashima, and, at the University of Hawaii Press, all who helped with so many details, especially editor Kathleen Matsueda.

1

LETTER TO LEE BOO

JAMES BOSWELL, in his *Life of Samuel Johnson,* quotes Dr. Johnson as having said in sorrow, "We shall receive no letters in the grave." Johnson is said to have spoken these words shortly before the death of Lee Boo. Although these two people were worlds apart in life, only the River Thames separated them at the time of their death. Johnson, master of the English language, wrote and received his ample share of letters within his long and illustrious lifetime. Lee Boo, in his short span, did not. This book begins, then, with a letter to Lee Boo.

DEAR LEE BOO,

You are not forgotten. In fact, no lad from a Pacific Island was ever better remembered.

There was Omai. I wonder if anyone ever told you about Omai? He was ten years ahead of you, making him the first Pacific islander to visit London. He could hardly have been forgotten—gone, but not forgotten. He was returned to his islands by Captain Cook. Within eight years of his departure a London theatre presented a play about him. But London staged two plays in your honor. Omai died in obscurity, unhappy and disillusioned. You died with friends around you, so loved by your hosts, the Wilsons, that they buried you in their family plot. We are told that "a great concourse of Parishioners thronged the church" that December day in 1784 when they buried you in St. Mary's churchyard.

Your friends at the East India Company provided the tomb erected over your grave. Brook Watson wrote the epitaph. Remember peg-legged Watson who lost his leg to a shark? He was a member of Parliament when you knew him; he went on to become Lord Mayor of London. You would have been proud of him, as he was of you. He wrote the lines:

> Stop, Reader, stop!—let Nature claim a Tear—
> A Prince of *Mine,* Lee Boo, lies bury'd here.

And many a tear has been claimed, including those of the great poet Samuel Taylor Coleridge who is said to have wept at your tomb before entering these lines in one of his poems:

> My soul amid the pensive twilight gloom
> Mourn'd with the breeze, O LEE BOO! o'er thy tomb.

Many more lines of poetry have been written in your honor, but also, more notably, a book. Your friend George Keate, who visited you so often at the Wilsons' home on Paradise Row and asked you so many questions, recorded the story of the shipwreck and the experiences of Captain Wilson and his men while they were with your people in the islands they called Pelew. His book, *An Account of the Pelew Islands,* was printed many times in many editions and translated into many languages. Even the Americans in their new United States printed it. Some printed just that part of the story that explained where you were from, how you got to London, your life with the Wilsons in Rotherhithe, your fine character, and finally the courage with which you faced death. That book, which they called your "history," became recommended reading for school children all over England and in America as well.

Mr. Keate's young daughter, Georgiana, remembered you. Fifteen months after your death she was able to paint a portrait of you from memory. It took its place in her father's book along with that fine portrait of your father, the Abba Thulle, done by Mr. Devis. Many others have tried to draw pictures of you, people you never met and people who lived long after you had died.

More than one hundred years after your death the East India Company remembered you again and had a fine memorial plaque placed on the walls of St. Mary's Rotherhithe in honor of you, your father, and the people of "Pelew" who were kind to the shipwrecked men of the *Antelope.*

Then, in 1907, the Reverend Edward Beck, rector of St. Mary's, wrote a book about his parish of Rotherhithe in which he devoted an entire chapter to you and your father. As a result of that book, a London street was named in honor of your father, a street that is just a few steps from your tomb. You knew it as Neptune Street; it was renamed Rupack Street. "Rupack" was thought to be the only appropriate Pelew Island word for king. Just as it was assumed, understandably but incorrectly, that your father was "king of the Pelews," it was also assumed that you must have been a prince and it is as "Prince Lee Boo" that you are remembered.

But no matter how you may have wished to be addressed, your hosts in England would have called you a prince, for they observed that you behaved like a prince. Even the distinguished writer E. M. Forster found reason to describe your princely conduct. Sitting among the books of the London Library at St. James's Square nearly a century and a half after your death, he wrote an essay contrasting your life in London with that of Madan Blanchard, who stayed behind in Pelew. How appropriate! You understood the importance of books from the first time you saw them, and you loved the park at St. James's.

Although a copy of Keate's book was given to Abba Thulle when the East India Company sent word of your death, it has long since fallen victim to the vicissitudes of time and the tropics. But other copies have found their way to your home island and copies are available today at the public library in Koror. In fact, Daniel Ngirairikl translated the book into your own language and it was then read, chapter by chapter, over Koror radio. But there is more to the story, so much more that one hardly knows where to begin. With Captain Wilson, I think, about whom George Keate told us so little, although without his voyage aboard the *Antelope* there would be no story and you would have been unknown beyond your own islands. Perhaps that would have been best. But ships must sail, men must sail them, and some never return. It has always been so. But few are so well remembered. Few have ships named for them as did you—one of them a real ship that sailed to Hawaii within ten years of your death, and one that is real only to the readers of Mr. Kipling's *Captains Courageous.*

Today there are many who sail away in search of the knowledge and experience that you sought, knowing that there is more to the world than island kingdoms, far more than even the most privileged

Englishman could learn in 1784. Now, in the last quarter of the twentieth century, the present Abba Thulle (Ibedul) has traveled to London and back to his islands in a matter of days, not months. He has visited your tomb and he has named a son for you. Yes, Lee Boo, you are remembered. And best of all, the dreaded smallpox that caused your death is now eradicated, scourged from the face of the earth by the efforts of good people everywhere, including the doctors and nurses of your own islands.

DJP

2

ROTHERHITHE'S
CAPTAIN WILSON

SHIPWRECK! The word has been happily exploited in more books than can be counted, books whose authors appeal to the Robinson Crusoe in all of us. But among those who have gone to sea there have been precious few who have welcomed shipwreck or, having survived it, would have described the experience as anything other than unfortunate. It is the fictional Crusoe who is envied, not the real Selkirk. Cast away or marooned, most of us, given the choice, would rather it happened to someone else. We seek to be involved only vicariously and from a distance safe enough in both space and time to make the experience enjoyable.

If the shipwreck occurs on or near a tropical island previously unknown and uninhabited, if the original element of fear is overcome by courage and good judgment, and if there are nearby islands peopled by natives who have the capability of savagery but the wisdom of restraint, the setting for vicarious enjoyment is complete. So much the better if there is the added dimension of rugged beauty: dark ocean waters calmed by barrier reefs forming a varicolored habitat for an awesome multitude of marine creatures and, on the quiet side of the reef, islands with half-hidden sandy beaches protected by mounds of coral rock and shaded by exotic trees. Oroolong, where the English first met Lee Boo, was such an island. The inhabitants of the nearby islands governed by Lee Boo's father, the Abba Thulle, were such a people, and the actual experience of being shipwrecked in the islands he called Pelew became the single most satisfying event in the long and rewarding career of Captain Henry Wilson.

A Rotherhithe man from London, England, Henry Wilson had first gone to sea in 1754 at the age of 14. He rose to the rank of third mate on his fourth voyage, to second mate on his sixth, and to first mate on his seventh. He then qualified for and received a captaincy at the age of forty-two. As captain, his first ship was the *Antelope,* the East India Company ship that was wrecked on the reef near the island of Oroolong on the night of 9 August 1783.

For at least ten years prior to the wreck of the *Antelope,* Henry Wilson had maintained a home on Paradise Row in Rotherhithe. It was one of several brick-faced houses lined tightly in a row, each comfortably spacious enough to permit a good life, but with a collective appearance that fell short of paradise. Where it traced the south bank of the Thames, Rotherhithe was a bustling community busy with the riverfront work that served the sailing ships crowded at anchor below London Bridge. But just inland a few hundred feet it acquired the look of a rural community with gardens, orchards, and even farms. Doubtless Henry Wilson lived here to be close to the ships that gave him his livelihood, but his house was even closer to the rural aspect of Rotherhithe. Perhaps he had the best of both worlds. In any case, it was here, on 24 November 1766, that Henry Wilson married Christiana Suthern; here the Wilsons attended church at St. Mary's Rotherhithe; and here, in the churchyard, they buried their second son, John Kenderdine, who died at the age of four. Their lives were representative of a seafaring society that had sent men to sea for centuries, including some of the men who sailed the *Mayflower.* The men went away on long voyages; the women stayed at home raising the children—until the boys joined their fathers and went to sea at an early age.

Because he made sixteen voyages to the Far East during his career, as many or more than any other East India Company captain, and because each voyage took an average of eighteen months to complete, Henry Wilson was away from home when his only daughter was born, when his wife died, and when all three of his granddaughters were born.

When he was at home, Henry Wilson must have given his full attention to his immediate family and it is doubtful that he had time to cultivate friendships outside his own neighborhood and the parish of Rotherhithe. His acquaintances across the river in the city of London were probably limited to the men who owned the ships he sailed. But after he returned fresh from his adventures in Belau, his range of acquaintances broadened considerably. For example, the London Member of Parliament, Brook Watson, introduced him to George Keate, a London gentleman of leisure. Keate must have warmed to Wilson and his story of adventure from the beginning and he had both the time and the talent to undertake the task of rendering Captain Wilson's saga of shipwreck and survival in a manner suitable for publication. So it happened that Keate's pen described the loss of the *Antelope* and introduced the people of the "Pelews" to the world. But it was Henry Wilson's true story and it had come at the mid-point in a career he could not interrupt for the purpose of writing a book—that would not profit him as much as a single voyage to the Far East, even if he thought himself capable of such an enterprise. Keate was the man of letters, Wilson the man of action. Whereas Henry Wilson might have written a book, it is more than doubtful that George Keate could have captained a ship. But Keate was a skillful and experienced writer of both prose and poetry and it is unfortunate that he did not apply his descriptive talents to the man whose adventures he recorded—Henry Wilson himself. Consequently, we do not know if Wilson was short or tall, lean or stout, puny or burly. Lacking such a description, I see him as taller than his men—many of whom were lads who had not yet reached their full height—in vigorous good health, with a sturdy physique hardened by long years of apprenticeship to the sea, his face and hands tanned and toughened by the open air, the sun, and the salt.

Before Keate's book was published in 1788, Henry Wilson completed another voyage to China for the East India Company. There followed seven more voyages to China, all of which he commanded. He was sixty-seven years old on his last voyage, having spent some twenty-four years of his life aboard ships at sea and, adding time spent in English ports other than his own, a much longer period of time away from home.

When he gave up the sea, Henry Wilson retired with his family to the quiet village of Colyton in Devonshire, some one hundred forty miles southwest of London. Here his home was named Oroolong House in memory of the island in the Pelews that, twenty-three years earlier, had provided a refuge for him and his crew. The people and incidents relating to his experiences in the Pelew Islands were his fondest memories—more precious even than the five hundred guineas he had been awarded in 1804 for defending his ship, the *Warley*, and helping to beat off a French squadron under Admiral Linois in the Strait of Malacca. His memories and achievements were respected by his children—his daughter, Christiana, and his son, Henry Junior, who had sailed with his father on the *Antelope* and on five other voyages, including the one in which the French were engaged in battle. Upon Captain Wilson's death in 1810, his son and daughter had a memorial plaque inscribed with words that gave greatest prominence to his adventures in "Pelew" where, as they put it, he "was wonderfully preserved with the ship's company amongst strangers in a land unfrequented and unknown."

Henry Wilson's experiences in Pelew were unique, not because he lost a ship there but because he was able to look back upon his adventures with nostalgia. The loss of a ship was a common occurrence; survival of a shipwreck in uncharted waters was far less common; and humanitarian treatment of those stranded by shipwreck was such a rare event as to be worthy of commemoration.

3

JOHN COMPANY'S
ANTELOPE

H AD HENRY WILSON been an owner of ships and stayed at
home when his ships went to sea, as most owners did, his
courage would have been tested in quite different ways. The
owners knew that shipwreck was but one of the possible results of
voyages that took their ships across oceans and into poorly charted if
not totally uncharted coastal waters. They knew the fear of losing
family fortunes when their ships went up in flames or were captured
by pirates, privateers, or enemy men-of-war. They also knew the anxiety of waiting endless months without word of a voyage's success or
failure. Theirs, in short, was a more constant fear than the fears experienced by Captain Wilson, who could hold his courage in reserve
until needed and, confident of his skills, command his ship in such a
way as to inspire confidence in others.

During the period just prior to Henry Wilson's time, the owners in
London had consoled each other and drowned their cares with cups of
coffee at Edward Lloyd's coffee house. In time, those among them
willing to risk their money to insure ships against disasters at sea
became known, collectively, as Lloyd's of London. Similarly, those
who developed a specialty in surveying, inspecting, and listing ships
for the purpose of insurance founded Lloyd's Register. The *Antelope*
was one of the ships listed in *Lloyd's Register of Shipping* for 1782, the
year that Henry Wilson sailed it for the first time.

About the same size as Captain Bligh's *Bounty,* the *Antelope* was
approximately 90 feet in length, 25 feet in breadth, and the mainmast
must have reached 90 feet above the deck. But these estimated overall

dimensions are not included in the information recorded in Lloyd's Register, which reads:

Antelope Ss HWilson 280 Nwbry 79 E.Ind.Co 14LoE.Ind. A1
    sC31   SDE   86P

This cryptic data can be deciphered as:

> The *Antelope,* a ship captained by Henry Wilson and owned by the East India Company, was constructed in 1779, had a draft of 14 feet when loaded, had a capacity of 280 tons, had been sheathed in copper, had a single deck (with beams), carried eight cannon (6-pounders), and was in A1 condition when surveyed at London prior to an anticipated voyage to the East Indies (a term applicable to India and all of southeast Asia).

Omitted from this description is the entry Lloyd's provided indicating the place of construction: that is, "Nwbry." Other ships listed in the same *Register* have, for place of construction, such entries as "Philad," meaning Philadelphia, and "N'flnd," meaning Newfoundland. The clerks who made these entries employed contractions of place names in a manner not unlike the present-day practice of airlines that contract Honolulu into HNL and San Francisco into SFO. But today no one knows for sure what "Nwbry" means. The authorities at Lloyd's Register explain that "Nwbry" and some of the other place name contractions appearing in the earlier years of the *Register* have, in a sense, lost their meaning.

Obviously "Nwbry" could mean Newberry or Newbury, but which of the many places so named? There are several on both sides of the Atlantic and although elimination of those without appropriate facilities helps, London-owned ships were built in many unlikely places. Without the further documentation that extensive research has failed to produce, it is impossible to make an absolute determination. Authorities appear content, however, to hold that the *Antelope* was constructed not in England, but in New England at the mouth of the Merrimac River in Newbury or Newburyport, Massachusetts.

The first entry in Captain Wilson's log of the *Antelope* has it "launched" on the Thames at Deptford, "10 A.M., 31 December 1781." This launching at Deptford must have been the result of the owners' determination to have the ship's hull sheathed in copper. This practice had come into vogue and was believed to result, among other things, in a faster sailing vessel of the type the owners wanted.

Be that as it may, there is no doubt as to who the owners were, no matter where and under what circumstances the ship was obtained. They were the "United Company of Merchants Trading to the East Indies," the famed East India Company also widely known as the "John Company" or, more respectfully, "The Honourable Company." Nor is there any doubt as to why the *Antelope* was owned by this old and worthy company, whose origins were not unlike those of Lloyd's of London. It was to be one of the few ships whose sole purpose was to serve as the Company's ocean-going messenger. In 1782 the *Antelope* must have been one of the newest and fastest vessels to fly the Company's flag.

With shipping extending halfway around the globe and back, the Honourable Company had reason to be concerned for the valuable cargoes that had to travel so far to reach England. Communication between the Company's headquarters in London and its representatives in India and China was essential if they were to manage an uninterrupted and controlled flow of commerce.

By Captain Wilson's time, the East India Company had grown to a point where it was said to have the greatest mercantile service in the world, and as it grew, so did the complexities of management. Yet the people of Lee Boo's islands would have understood a company that built a special house—they would have called it a *bai*—for the purpose of discussing the sailing of ships—not the art of sailing, which could be left to experienced sailors, but the time and place of sailing, the routes to be taken, the cargoes to be carried and traded, and the goods to be purchased and delivered home. Lee Boo's father and the other chiefs would also have understood that certain seats in this house of business were assigned only to those qualified to participate in decision making, with directorships often passing from generation to generation within one extended family.

East India House, on Leadenhall Street in the inner city of London, housed the Company's headquarters, with its myriad of meeting rooms to accommodate the directors and their numerous committees. Here also the Company's correspondence was prepared by "writers" some of whom, notably John Stuart Mill, composed far more memorable prose during their free time. However mundane most of the messages they prepared for the Company, some were urgent dispatches with high enough priority to require that, whenever possible, they be carried by the fastest ship available.

The Company's handwritten dispatches were normally placed in a pouch which, like the ships that carried them, were called packets. Because packet ships carried the most urgent messages, they were not subject to delay. They were permitted to fly flags signaling that they were "charged with dispatches" and not to be interfered with. Should enemy vessels overtake them, the dispatch pouches were tied with weights, ready to be thrown overboard.

There were, of course, ships from other nations on the seas, some of them friendly, if competitive, some of them—depending on what wars were being waged—hostile. Although the English East India Company may have been the largest of its kind, it was by no means the only East India company. The Dutch, the French, the Swedes, and others also had such companies and it was only by chance that the first Europeans the people of Belau came to know well were the English. They might just as easily have been the Dutch, who had a strong hold on the spice islands just to the southwest. They might have been the Portuguese, sailing to their colony at Macao, and they might have been the Spanish, who claimed an even closer neighbor to the west— the Philippines.

But England's John Company had a hold on India, and from India its captains sailed their ships to China for trade at Canton. From India, cotton and a variety of other products, including opium, were shipped to China. From China the English obtained chinaware (porcelain), silks, and many other things, including rhubarb, turmeric, and especially tea.

By Lee Boo's time, the English had become addicted to tea. Dr. Johnson, to name but one, described himself as "a hardened and shameless tea drinker who has for many years diluted his meals with only the infusion of this fascinating plant; whose kettle has scarcely time to cool; who with tea amuses the evening, with tea solaces the midnight and with tea welcomes the morning." The East India Company supplied the tea—except for smuggled tea, all of the tea for England. In part, it was because English merchants wanted the American colonies to be dependent on the Company's tea that the most famous of all tea parties was held in Boston Harbor in 1773, just nine years before the *Antelope* sailed under Captain Wilson.

4

THE *ANTELOPE'S* SECRET VOYAGE

WHEN, at the close of 1781, the directors of the East India Company deliberated over the shape of world events, they had to consider the loss of the American colonies and the menace to their shipping as represented by the hostility of the French, the Spanish, and the Dutch. During the previous year, 1780, at least five of the Company's ships failed to complete voyages to the Far East via the customary route around the Cape of Good Hope and through the Indian Ocean.

Prompted by a desire to learn the fate of the missing ships, as well as the need to keep their agents in Canton informed, the Company's Secret Committee decided that the *Antelope* should be sent on a secret voyage to China by a different route. In the hope that their communications would be more certain to arrive safely, they instructed Henry Wilson to take the *Antelope* around Cape Horn rather than around the Cape of Good Hope. Although the route around the Horn and across the Pacific was by no means untried, it was unusual, if not unprecedented, for an East India Company ship to sail for China in a westerly rather than an easterly direction.

There is reason to believe that the *Antelope* was also charged with a mission of exploration. If the voyage succeeded, other Company ships would follow as long as hostile ships infested the established route, especially the approaches to the South China Sea. The long voyage would require safe harbors where wood and water could be obtained. As will be seen, the *Antelope* was to carry three people capable of charting coastal areas that might serve such future needs.

But when Henry Wilson first took command of the *Antelope* it is possible that he did not know what his route was to be. He may have known only that once a sufficient number of officers and crew had been signed on at Gravesend he was to take the *Antelope* on to Falmouth and there await further orders. Among those signing on at Gravesend were the captain's brother Matthias, twenty-seven, his own fifteen-year-old son, Henry, who signed on as a midshipman, Philip Benger and Peter Barker as first and second mates, John Blanch as gunner, John Meale as cooper and steward, James Swift as cook, Albert Pierson as quartermaster, and John Sharp as surgeon.

With two officers, a surgeon, and eleven men, Wilson apparently had enough of a crew to sail down the Thames and, after brief stops en route, the *Antelope* arrived at Falmouth on 9 February 1782. Here Wilson was to have a wait of six months before receiving final instructions to sail. During this time a boatswain, a carpenter, a carpenter's mate, and an additional midshipman were signed on, plus seven more seamen, including a young man named William Cobbledick and a man destined to play a unique role in later events, Madan Blanchard. Additionally, the log of the *Antelope* reveals, "13 Chinese" were put on board by the Company for passage to China.

On 27 July "at 6PM" Captain Wilson left his ship and went to London "by order of the Honourable Court of Directors." Whatever the Company's reasons for summoning the *Antelope*'s captain, they must have included instructions or at least permission for him to visit the school at Christ's Hospital for the purpose of obtaining two students who had received instruction in draftsmanship. The school's records show that Henry Wilson called on 3 August 1782 and signed out two boys: Robert White and John Wedgebrough. These two not only sailed from Falmouth with Captain Wilson, but were to continue to be involved in the various events stemming from the wreck of the *Antelope* well into their adult lives.

A man of even greater artistic skills and training, Arthur William Devis, had already come aboard at Gravesend. The nineteenth child of artist Arthur Devis, Arthur William had studied at the Royal Academy where some of his work had been exhibited and praised when he was nineteen years of age. He was now twenty-one. The Secret Committee had "invited" him to accompany the voyage to make "coastal profiles" and promised him a fee of "one hundred guineas" when he returned to England. Devis apparently fulfilled his commission. At any rate, he collected his fee long before he returned to England. It remains something of a mystery as to why the East India Company and Captain Wilson perceived a need for so much artistic talent. That may forever be a secret of this secret voyage, but it is our good fortune that they did, for some of the artwork produced later graced the pages of George Keate's book. Even Henry Junior, the young Harry, found time to do creditable drawing when not engaged in more urgent duties.

The long period of idleness at Falmouth, a period of boredom and discontent for those without talents to occupy their time, caused some of the men to desert the ship. Although East India Company records reveal that none of those who "ran" were officers, one Samuel Kelly was apparently led to believe that a position of mate was available to him aboard the *Antelope*. Kelly, about whom more later, sailed into Falmouth in July 1782 aboard the *Grenville* and recorded this experience:

> We found the *Antelope*, Captain H. Wilson, an East India Packet, laying in Carrick road, and on going on shore was informed that one of her mates had left her . . . and being applied to for this purpose, I was under the necessity of declining the situation, as I was not only bare of clothes, by being captured, but my father could not now afford to supply me the 100 pounds at least being requisite to equip a mate for the East Indies.

One hundred pounds was a very great deal of money in those days—a captain's wages for ten months, a mate's wages for twenty months or more!

To qualify as a mate aboard the *Antelope,* Kelly would have needed a "Blue coat, with blue lapels, [a] white waist coat, and white breeches with buttons of yellow metal engraved with the Company's crest." (The crest was a lion and a crown.) The blue coat, along with the rest of a dress uniform and accoutrements, would have been worn only on special occasions at sea and when calling on the Company and its agents when ashore. Kelly would have needed an only slightly less colorful nondress uniform as well, plus various other items considered essential for a long voyage.

By contrast, there was no uniform for an ordinary seaman. Although a midshipman might carry a dirk at his belt and wear a round hat with a cockade, there was little of a distinguishing nature in the garb of those of lower rank. An ordinary seaman wore trousers and a "sailors jacket" and came aboard equipped for bad weather. In short, he needed little more than his courage and gained little more than his experience. His pay, in those days, was about two pounds a month and that was often wasted at every opportunity ashore. As the English proverb would have it, "Sailors get their money like horses and spend it like asses." Only the captain and his officers could expect substantial monetary reward and that not from salary but from "private trade," which the Company permitted. But not the *Antelope*'s officers. The practice of carrying private cargo, commonly permitted aboard India-men, was not allowed aboard the Company's packet ships. Captain Wilson and his officers were, in fact, paid "gratuities in lieu of private trade."

Because a sailor's pay was little enough and easily dissipated during a voyage, the Company made it possible for him to have some of his wages paid to a member of his family who remained at home. East India Company records indicate, for example, that Henry Wilson, Jr., arranged "by virtue of a letter of Attorney" that Christiana Wilson, his mother, would be permitted to sign for and receive some of his pay during his absence. Similarly, John Cooper, seaman, requested in writing that "two months pay of my wages yearly, as the same shall grow due unto me during the whole time of my absence" would be paid to his wife, Jane, according to a document witnessed by Captain Wilson.

Captain Henry Wilson himself had the primary responsibility of ensuring that his wife and daughter would be cared for during his absence. The records show that on 15 January 1782 he received an advance payment of twenty pounds "being two months' impress." ("Impress," as used in this context, represents advance pay, which, presumably, Wilson would have shared with his wife.) The same records indicate that "Commander" Wilson also signed for two pounds for two months' pay on behalf of his "servant" Thomas Dalton. Quartermasters Godfrey Minks and Albert Pierson made X marks upon receiving five pounds each, and John Blanch received eight pounds as "Gunner [and] in lieu of a servant."

All of these matters settled, the *Antelope,* manned, fitted, and stored with both "dry provisions" and "wet provisions" and with "two small boxes of treasure" (presumably trinkets for trading), Captain

Wilson sailed from Falmouth on 1 September 1782. The secret voyage had begun, and although Henry Wilson had his instructions, it is doubtful if his crew knew they were embarking for China by a route they had never before taken.

In order to deter attack while sailing in waters still close to the European continent, the *Antelope* sailed out of Falmouth in the company of five other ships: the *Hanover,* Captain Todd; the *Queen Charlotte,* Captain Clerke; the *King George,* Captain Wacup; the *Cartret,* Captain Newman; and the *Swallow,* Captain Greene. Once clear of European waters the *Antelope* parted company with the convoy and sailed on alone to complete her mission.

On 18 September, Captain Wilson sighted Madeira and passed to the west, making a course for South America, which was reached on 28 November. The captain explored the coast of Patagonia, searching for adequate watering places in answer to the *Antelope*'s own needs and, presumably, for the future needs of Company vessels that might follow. He spent the remainder of November and half of December along the long coast of what is now Argentina. On 2 December 1782, artist Arthur Devis sketched a "Plan of Antelope Bay on the East Coast of Patagonia" (Lat. 44°31'S, Long. 64°50'W). Much use was made of the ship's two boats, the pinnace and the jolly boat, in these explorations. On 5 December the log reads: "sent boat on shore again with Mr. Benger, Chief Mate, to search for harbour . . . anchored being now satisfied this is Helena Bay. Unable to find water. Mr. Benger reports country burnt up by dryness of the season . . . saw deer, about 20, followed their trackes about 27 miles up country . . . could find none."

It must have been a cheerless experience, this slow creep down the coast of South America searching parched lands for water and hunting phantom herds of deer. No wonder Barker, the second mate, drank to excess and no wonder the captain would react out of frustration. The log for 9 December reads: "this morning at 7AM ordered the 2nd Officer's cabin down and have it all cleaned and then put up again the same dimensions as when we left the river Thames; ordered his tobacco and liquor to be taken away and given in care of the gunner as he is frequently intoxicated therewith. Ordered also that he should not smoke in future unless the Surgeon thinks it necessary for his health"—his mental health, presumably.

On 16 December, close to the tip of South America and in the area

CHINA

CANTON

Pescadores I.

FORMOSA I.

Boql Tobago

Bashee I.

Pratas

Five I.

Po Taya

S.t Esprit

Habspranes

C. Bexeador

Cape Engano

CHINA

LUZON

vulgo

LUCONIA

Amphitrite I.
Triangles

Lincoln I.

N.th Maroena

Maidesfield

Mindoro

Candunanes

S.th Maroena

Scarborough Shoal

Marivelas Shoal

SEA

Calavit P.t

PHILIPPINE   ISLANDS

Fathom Shoal

SAMAR

C. Espiritu Sant:

Calamianes P.t

Sabut Jung

Gaspar

Pit I.

Douglas I.

Ganges I.

LEYTE

Capiz

Mahaba

Royal Captain lost
1773

Capinan

TALAWAN

Carili

Fuegos

Balabac

Tijinan Pic

MAGINDANAO

Balambangan

Banguey

Caligan Sooloo

Island Bay

Maludee

Hara's Eufo

Basilan

C. S.t Augustin

Sooloo

Rummeck I.

English Rangers

Palmas

S. Canales

Laboan

Siboe

Haras Marat

BORNEO

The Whale

Borneo

Saughin

Chimur

North Cape

Maxinlay

Maranai

JELOLO

BORNEO

CELEBES

Longit:

CHART
of the
PELEW ISLANDS
and
ADJACENT SEAS
By Cap.ᵗ H. Wilson.

LADRONE I.ˢ

Tinian

Guam

Bank of S.ᵗᵃ Rosa

NORTH   PACIFIC

THE CAROLINAS

Egoi

Feys

Palalu

Yap

Ladde

Fahnu

Lamnil

Orocol

Hogolen

vulgo PALAOS

A.ᵗKati

Pulo

Pulep

Olimaroa

Lamurck

Emuugus

Schug

Emiligur

Eurrupuc

Beliat

Coup

Flenis

Arengoit

Pour

Never

Schrug

Paum

Esup

OCEAN

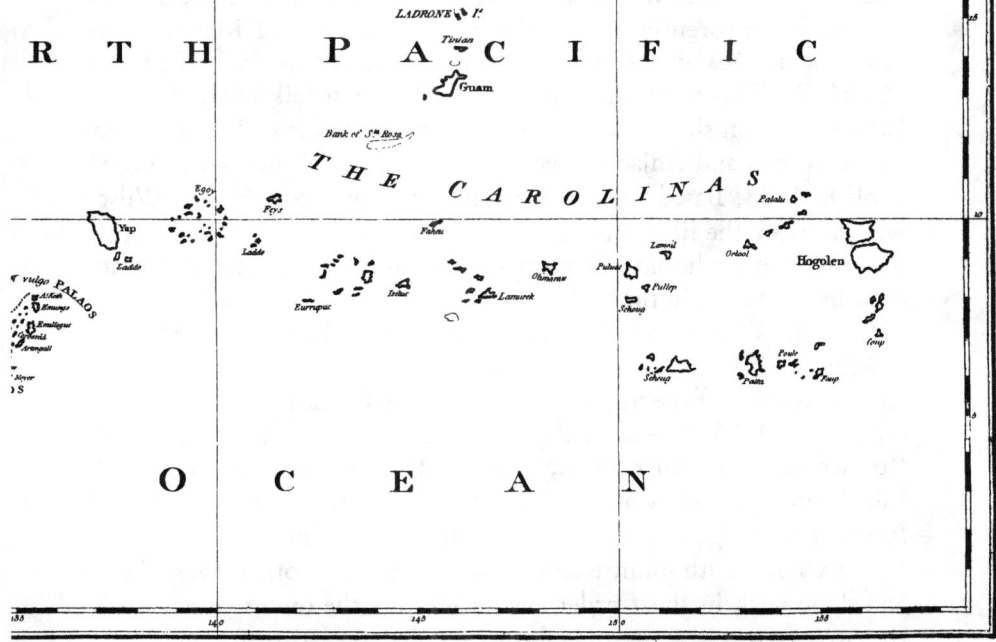

Published May 1.ˢᵗ 1788. by H. Wilson.

of Tierra del Fuego, Henry Wilson himself "went to look for the watering place" and, having seen some natives, wanted to establish contact with them. On this and the following two days attempts were made to trade with the natives. Captain Wilson gave them "some beads and knives and trinkets with which they seemed very much pleased." The natives, in turn, gave Wilson "two arrows, but would not part with the bow." The *Antelope* was now standing off the mouth of an unnamed river, and in this bleak area Christmas day was observed: "kept the remainder of the day as a festival; and in the afternoon several of the people went on shore to wash their clothes which I was very glad to see . . ." Cleanliness was next to godliness on this holiest of holidays.

Without mention of bringing in the New Year, 1783, the *Antelope* "passed the Straits Le Maire" on 2 January and entered the Great South Sea. Captain Wilson then made his way northwestward across the Pacific, apparently without sighting land until 21 March, when two small islands were seen from the masthead at "Lat. 6 31N., Long. 217 41W." This must have been the atoll of Eauripik in the Caroline Islands. Wilson shows this as "Eurrupuc" on his own "Chart of the Pelew Islands and Adjacent Seas," which was published with Keate's book in 1788. Based on all of the available evidence, Henry Wilson was probably the first, among the English at least, to have seen Eauripik, but neither he nor Keate made any note of this and apparently took little interest in the atoll.

Instead, Wilson steered a course southward, taking the *Antelope* out of Micronesia and into Melanesia (as these two areas are known today) and the waters off the northern coast of New Guinea which he reached on 1 April 1783. The next day canoes came out to the *Antelope* and "traded in a very fair manner," but whatever rapport had been established through trade was lost "when suddenly the people in the boats [canoes] discharged a flight of arrows at us . . ." The men of the *Antelope* answered with gunfire and drove the attackers off. It was all over and done with in short order and, ironically, the only man struck by the arrows was the presumably noncombatant artist, Arthur Devis, who suffered two hits: one in his cheek and one in his chest, "but not much in the breast as it went through a double breasted serge waistcoat lined with flannel." The arrow in Devis's cheek, however, caused a wound that did not heal well. Some said the arrow must have been poisoned, but whatever the cause, Devis never fully recovered from what was called "locked jaws" that bothered him for the remainder of his life.

Captain Wilson and his men were now in no mood to linger, but the winds were of no help in getting away. A crew at the oars of the pinnace had to tow the ship farther out to sea before they could be clear of this unhappy place. Arrows of another kind of misfortune soon struck the gunner, the carpenter, and the cook—scurvy! The crew, no doubt, thought it poetic justice that the cook should fall prey to the inadequate diet he provided.

It was not until 19 April 1783 at the island of Bajseelan (Basilan, at the southern end of the Philippines) that Wilson was able to trade for food. Presumably with the cook, the carpenter, and the gunner recovering, the *Antelope* was well into the Sooloo (Sulu) Sea by 23 April and on 15 May anchored in Balambangan Harbor. Underway again, the *Antelope* was off Palawan by 25 May, headed northwest through the South China Sea for Macao and Canton.

Captain Wilson's entry for 3 June was perhaps a portent of things to come. He reported damage to his "main top gallant" during "light squalls"—just the day before the *Antelope* sailed into the waters off Macao, dropped anchor in Macao Roads, and ended her westward voyage nine months and three days out of Falmouth. Here, too, Captain Wilson put a period to the last entry in the only log known to have survived all the years since then. (The Wilson journal used by George Keate to describe the homeward voyage out of Macao has not survived.)

The arrival of the *Antelope* at Macao proved a mixed blessing for the East India Company's agents—the supercargoes. They received the news they needed from England well ahead of the forthcoming trading season, but the Chinese with whom they had to trade were not pleased. The supercargoes recorded the Chinese reaction: A ship that had traveled so great a distance but professed to carry no cargo must be regarded with suspicion.

5

OPIUM AND THE
BLUE-GREEN DRAGON

THE *ANTELOPE* was not the first ship to reach China under a cloud of suspicion. The Chinese had a healthy distrust of arriving foreigners. They called them all "devils" and made them wait at Macao before permitting them to conduct business of any sort, much less sail their ships up the Pearl River and approach Canton, which was the only port from which the English could obtain China's precious goods. But the *Antelope* had not come for teas and silks. In fact, it brought "no cargo or silver," thus confounding the Chinese belief that foreign ships came only to trade or to bring tribute.

Although the *Antelope* was much smaller than most of the cargo-carrying Indiamen, it was large enough to create doubts in the minds of the Chinese that it had come to China for no other purpose than to deliver messages addressed to the council of East India Company supercargoes. Not only were the Chinese slow to accept this explanation, but they showed no sympathy for the agents' statements that the *Antelope* had arrived at Macao "in damaged condition," needed to "refit speedily," and "only wanted provisions to enable her to depart." Nor would they even "permit her water casks to be brought on shore to be repaired."

The Chinese reasoned that a ship claiming to have no cargo could, at a minimum, be carrying contraband opium. Unfortunately, they had reason to be suspicious. Although the East India Company did not permit its own ships to carry opium, the Company controlled the export of opium from India, and from India opium was brought to

China and illicitly sold. Only the year before, in 1782, a British-owned ship similar to the *Antelope,* the *Nonsuch,* had arrived at Canton carrying a large quantity of opium. The East India Company had not been able to keep its hands entirely free of the *Nonsuch*'s transactions, a fact that could not have escaped the Chinese. It follows that the Chinese did not know if they could believe what little they had been told about the secret voyage of the *Antelope,* and although it had not arrived from India and therefore should not have been suspected of carrying opium, it "was not allowed to enter the river" where ships normally anchored —and where the most flagrant traffic in opium had been observed.

It was a frustrating time for the East India Company's agents, who could see the *Antelope* from their houses in Portuguese Macao but were powerless to assist Captain Wilson and his crew. Because the agents were, at this time of year, at home in Macao rather than at their factory (warehouse) in Canton, Captain Wilson had been able to deliver his dispatches on the first day of his arrival, but neither he nor the agents could do anything about taking care of the *Antelope*'s needs until the permission of the Chinese was sent down from Canton, the seat of authority for the area.

Finally, on 27 June, after twenty-two days of waiting, and after "repeated applications to Canton," the Company's agents "received leave to victual the Vessel, and put her in a situation to depart." But by then the council was incensed, not because the *Antelope* had been refused permission to enter the river and use anchorage facilities there, but because of the delay in granting permission "to purchase the necessaries of Life," which delay, they wrote to the Chinese authorities, was "a circumstance unheard of in any Civilized Country upon Earth."

The Company's "Factory Records," prepared by the council of agents, provide no further clues as to what repairs, if any, were made to the *Antelope.* Nor does Keate comment on this; in fact, he makes no mention of the difficulties the *Antelope* encountered prior to its departure from Macao. Keate begins his account with the statement that Captain Wilson "received orders from the Company's supracargoes to refit his ship with all possible speed," and one must assume that this was done. Certainly the ship was restocked, cattle and fowl being specifically mentioned as having been taken on board, while "Chinese hams" and "smoked fish" are referred to once the *Antelope* was again at sea.

Captain Wilson's last act at Macao, according to Keate, was to provide the customary advance pay to the sixteen Chinese he had taken on to complement his regular crew, which had proved insufficient to his needs. Perhaps because it was not unusual for an East India Company to augment its crew in this way, Keate takes little notice of them; nor for that matter, does he tell us anything about the Chinese whom the *Antelope* presumably delivered to Macao from London. Some of them may have chosen to remain on the *Antelope* and work for Captain Wilson, just as they had worked, and been paid for working, on the voyage to China, although this was not customary on outward voyages from England. In any case, the matter of the Chinese aboard the *Antelope* seems to have been of little interest to Keate and it is upon his word that we must rely for the remainder of the *Antelope*'s story.

What is more puzzling, although Keate begins his account with Wilson departing Macao, is that he makes no comment whatsoever about the *Antelope*'s destination. However, it is reasonable to assume that having completed the principal mission of the voyage, the *Antelope* had only to return to England, thus completing a circumnavigation of the globe. The Company's agents gave Captain Wilson dispatches to carry, but there is no indication whether these were all for delivery to London or whether some of them were for one or more ports en route. Whatever his instructions, Captain Wilson departed Macao on 20 July 1783 with a nine-gun salute for his "friends" on shore.

Enter the dragon—the blue-green dragon. In the mythology of the ancient Chinese, the blue-green dragon was the spirit god who ruled the winds that came from the southeast bringing the life-sustaining rains of spring. The rains delivered by the blue-green dragon had been collected by the winds blowing toward China from across the southwest Pacific and the China Sea. These winds blow from late spring until early fall. Ships did not, by choice, sail against them.

The captain, therefore, put the *Antelope* on a course to catch the blue-green dragon's winds and let them take him almost to Formosa (Taiwan) before making the more difficult tack southward to the east of the Philippines. Although the *Antelope* was not the first ship to have done this, it was probably a first for Wilson and his crew. Other English ships had sailed this route, which had already become known as the "Eastern Passage."

For the first few days out of China, Captain Wilson and his men were kept busy holding the ship on course and tending to the livestock on board during "squalls, rains, and bad weather." The *Antelope*, in keeping with common practice among the East India Company ships, carried cooped-up flocks of geese, ducks, and chickens to supply fresh food. There were also two pet dogs on board. It is no wonder, then, that the first fair weather found the men turning their attention to cleaning the ship and even "fumigating" with gunpowder.

As the fair weather continued, Captain Wilson chose to "exercise some of the Chinese men with rowing in the jolly boat . . . to teach them to use an oar if needful." And the following Sunday, "being also fair, divine service was performed upon deck; a ceremony never omitted on Sundays when the weather would allow." As it happened, no further Sunday was to be permitted the men of the *Antelope* aboard their ship.

By the time the *Antelope* reached 8 degrees north latitude on its southern course to the east of the Philippines, it was approaching the islands now known as Belau. The month was August, for which geographers have described an imaginary line north of Belau sometimes called "the heat equator." It is an area of unpredictable weather at this time—calm one day, with squalls and thunderstorms the next. Such weather and such a storm put an end to the *Antelope*'s secret voyage.

As Captain Wilson later explained, he knew of no islands in the area the *Antelope* entered on the night of 9 August. Had he known that he was now sailing along a reef that stretched for nearly a hundred miles at the surface of the water, protecting, like a submerged Hadrian's Wall, a chain of islands just to the east, he would certainly have taken every precaution. As it was, only the bad weather had kept him from retiring at a reasonable hour on that stormy night. It was just after midnight when he "quitted the deck" and left Mr. Benger, his chief mate, in charge. Then, just as Benger thought the weather was clearing, he heard the lookout call out "BREAKERS!" But too late. No sooner had the warning been sounded than the *Antelope* was upon the breakers.

Captain Wilson "sprang upon the deck in an instant" when the ship struck the reef. But it took him more than an instant to collect his wits and issue orders. The scene that confronted him could not have been easy to assess. The questions that must have flashed through his mind had no easy answers: What had they struck? Can the ship be saved? Can the men be saved? Go where? Do what?

As raging waves crash against the reef, swirl, and recede, there is a moment when jagged coral is revealed. What Captain Wilson must have seen in that moment could have offered little hope for his ship. The lurching *Antelope* was impaled upon the reef. If the ship could not be saved, the men must act together to save themselves. With everything in the hold in danger, vital materials must be saved before the ship could be abandoned. Captain Wilson issued his orders:

> Secure gunpowder, ammunition, and small arms.

> Bread and other perishable foods to be brought on deck and covered from the rain and water.

> The three masts to be cut away to prevent the *Antelope* from overturning.

The ship's two boats were hoisted out, filled with provisions and drinking water, provided with a compass, some small arms and ammunition, and manned with two crewmen each. The crewmen were ordered to keep the boats to the lee of the ship and away from the reef.

These things done, Captain Wilson summoned all the men to the quarterdeck. Having sought the highest point above the water, he spoke to their condition. Their situation was critical but not hopeless. There had been no loss of life, no critical injuries, but they would have to abandon ship in unknown waters at an unknown place. They must act with the greatest courage and do nothing that would further endanger themselves or their companions. They must not seek courage in hard liquor but, to soften this blow, the captain ordered that all should have a measured drink of wine and eat "some biscuit."

The storm did not abate through the long hours of the night. Some of the men "imagined" they had seen land ahead of the ship during flashes of lightning, but the closest land that was revealed at dawn lay to the south, about "three or four leagues distant." With the coming of daylight other islands were seen ahead to the east and to the north, but at a greater distance.

The two boats were sent off to the closest land, the island to the south, under the command of Mr. Benger. The chief mate had been instructed to be particularly sagacious as he approached the island and to do everything within his power to ensure that any first encounter with inhabitants be a friendly one.

As soon as the boats were gone, Captain Wilson put the remaining men to work fitting the ship's booms together to make a raft. Not only did the work keep them occupied, but it provided hope that if the *Antelope* totally disintegrated there would at least be a perch upon which to escape drowning in the sea. There was also the possibility, if not the fear, that the two boats would not return, moving off, as they did, to an entirely unknown fate at an uncharted island that would have to be approached in bad weather.

But the boats did return. They reached the scene of the wreck at about four in the afternoon, having left the provisions and five men on shore. And they could not have brought better news. The island appeared uninhabited, it had a secure little cove, and fresh water had been found!

Renewed and more spirited efforts were now made to load the raft so that the remaining men and their personal possessions could be hauled to the newfound haven before dark. The process of rescuing personal belongings had gone on throughout the day. The crew had saved their clothing by the simple act of putting on whatever they owned. For Quartermaster Godfry Minks, however, his wardrobe proved his undoing. He was called upon to help free a mast that had become entangled at the stern of the ship and fell overboard. The men in the boats could not get to him in time to prevent his drowning. Having saved his clothes, he could not save himself.

With the raft loaded and every man appointed to a place in one of the boats or on the raft, a most unusual scene unfolded. The pinnace, the largest of the two boats, with the strongest of the ship's crew at the oars, took the raft in tow. The jolly boat, in turn, assisted by towing the pinnace until it cleared the reef, an effort that took more than half an hour. Those on the raft tied themselves down so as not to be swept overboard. The ship's two dogs, five geese, and uncounted chickens, presumably caged or tied, made up the rest of this Noah's raft. The experienced seamen took all of this calmly enough, but the Chinese were reported to have "shrieked" in fear as the raft crossed the thrashing waters of the reef.

Once the procession was clear of the reef, the jolly boat proceeded alone to the island and reached shore at eight o'clock at night. The men in the pinnace decided to anchor the raft for the night, take the men from the raft into their boat, and, with fresh hands for rowing, speed their way to the island. But the additional men so crowded the pinnace that it was in danger of swamping when a "hallo" was heard from a distance. Captain Wilson, with four men in the jolly boat, had set out from the island in hope of assisting the pinnace, but neither party could see the other in the darkness. The enthusiastic yells the captain and his four men heard in response to their "hallo" were mistaken for the shouts of imagined wild natives, and they at once returned to the island for safety! The pinnace somehow found its way into the cove and all of the *Antelope*'s men were finally reunited on land.

The boats were hauled on shore and a watch assigned to protect them. A fire was started "by means of discharging a pistol, loaded with powder, into some match which they picked loose to serve as tinder." Soaked through from the rain and the ocean spray, the men tried to dry themselves without much success in the continuing rain. They ate a late supper of cheese, biscuit, and water and prepared to endure their first night on land—a night in which, no doubt, their fondest wish was for the small comforts of their home aboard the *Antelope*. Instead they spent a miserable night on the ground, made scarcely more comfortable for those who had improvised a tent of sailcloth over their heads. With muscles aching from the strains of rowing and hauling, their skin already irritated by rashes from heat, sweat, and wetness, they awaited the dawn.

The next day the weather improved and the boats were sent back to the wreck to procure rice and other necessities. Those who remained on shore were busied with drying their clothes and attending to their arms and ammunition in case of need. Although no inhabitants of the islands had yet been seen, evidence of there having been fires and related activities on the island suggested that it would be only a matter of time before they were confronted by their as yet unknown hosts— the people who presumably lived somewhere on the chain of islands that were visible to the east and continued north as far as the eye could see.

The pinnace returned from the wreck with bad news. The *Antelope* was now in such a state of disintegration that any hope of repairing it for a return to China would have to be abandoned. The only remaining possibility was to salvage materials that might be used to construct a new vessel—if that could be considered a realistic hope.

There followed another night of discomfort—the glow of fire and the warmth of dry clothing were the only weapons for fighting off the despair of the marooned. In the dead of the night there could be little else, other than their faith in God, captain, or both, to protect them from fears that they had intruded among islands where they were not wanted, where they did not want to be, and where at any moment a savage people might decide they should not remain.

6

KELLY WAS WRONG

O N THE MORNING of their second day ashore, still weary from the long hours of labor salvaging supplies from the shipwreck and still fearful of the unknown in the islands on the horizon, the men of the *Antelope* faced the future. Having explored enough of their island to know that it offered them no food, and knowing that the provisions now secured inside their camp could hardly feed fifty men indefinitely, they must have wondered how long they could survive as a society of castaways. Could they even think of the other islands as a possible source of help? If Robinson Crusoe had his Friday, could they hope that the inhabitants might be a society of Fridays? Had London Gentleman George Keate been with them, he almost certainly would have answered in the affirmative. Under the influence of French philosopher Jean-Jacques Rousseau, Keate was representative of those who would be most eager to learn of a primitive people living in a "natural" state who were capable of greater benevolence than might be expected of Europeans.

In contrast, Samuel Kelly, the sailor who declined a berth aboard the *Antelope,* would have anticipated the worst. Instead of sailing from Falmouth with the *Antelope* in 1782, Kelly had sailed on other ships among other islands and eleven years later, in 1793, found himself walking the streets of London when

> On passing a booksellers in the Strand, I saw a volume in the window, relative to the loss of the *Antelope,* East India packet, on the Pelew Islands. This brought to my recollection that I had been solicited at Falmouth to take a situa-

tion on this ship, the voyage on which she was lost, and being curious to know how I should have been treated, I purchased the book and still keep it as a momento to the kindness of Providence to one of the unworthiest of its servants.

But Kelly was wrong—at least in assuming that if he had been aboard the *Antelope* he would somehow have been mistreated. By whom? The captain? The people of the islands? Or fate? Perhaps fate, if fate can be blamed for the shipwreck. But there is nothing in Keate's book to warrant the implication that the men of the *Antelope* were at any time mistreated. More likely, in spite of what he read, Kelly could not free himself of the assumption that anyone cast ashore among an unknown and primitive people would be tortured if not eaten. In this he was not alone. It was primarily because of such fears, as well as the need to protect men and property from the pirates of the East Indies, that East India Company ships were well armed. If Kelly had read Keate's book carefully, he might have agreed that the treatment received by the men of the *Antelope,* both before and after the shipwreck, was not something to abhor. Providence might better have been thanked for the fair-handedness of Captain Wilson, who did not discipline his men in any way that they themselves did not approve, and also for the attentions of the people of the islands, who, to use the Biblical phrase later quoted by the Wilsons, "showed us no little kindness."

George Keate, however sentimentally inclined he may have been, enjoyed a reputation for honesty and accuracy that was based on his earlier descriptive writings. There is little reason to doubt that he would have been just as faithful to the task of reporting accurately what had been communicated to him by Captain Wilson. Keate described himself as the "historian" of the *Antelope* affair and held up publishing his account of the shipwreck and the people of Pelew until his manuscript could be verified by the captain, whose integrity has never been questioned. The story presented here of the adventures of Henry Wilson and his men in Belau is, for the most part, abstracted from portions of Keate's *Account* as told to him by the captain and others who were there. All quotations, unless otherwise noted, are from Keate.

Early in the morning of 12 August 1783, two canoes were seen approaching the island that sheltered the men of the *Antelope*. They were sighted by men on high ground who called down to Captain Wilson, close to the shore below. The crewmen wanted to take up arms at once and defend themselves against what they perceived to be hostile invaders. The captain, though sensing the apprehension of his men, prescribed patience and instructed them to remain out of sight. Only Henry Wilson and a man named Tom Rose remained in full view of the approaching canoes. Rose is described as a "native of Bengal calling himself a Portuguese" who had been recommended to Captain Wilson at Macao, where he was signed on as a "linguist" in the event an interpreter would be needed. When the men in the canoes were within hearing distance Wilson told Rose to call out to them. There was at first no reply. Then, in "the Malay tongue," a voice called out from the canoes asking those on the island who they were and whether they were friends or enemies. Wilson told Rose to reply that they were Englishmen who had lost their ship on the reef and that they were friends. After brief words among themselves, the men in the canoes stepped into the shallow waters and Henry Wilson waded out to meet them and by gesture welcomed them ashore. Only two men remained behind, one in each canoe.

Wilson and his men were now able to see for the first time what sort of people inhabited the other islands. As they later reported to Keate,

> The natives were of a deep copper colour, perfectly naked, having no covering whatsoever, their skins very soft and glossy, owing, as was known afterwards, to the external use of cocoa-nut oil. [They were of] middling stature, very straight, and muscular, their limbs well formed. [Their legs,] from a little above their ancles to the middle of their thighs [were tattooed.] Their hair was of a fine black, long, and rolled up behind in a simple manner close to the back of their heads, and appeared both neat and becoming.

Most, if not all, of the "Pelew Island" men, Keate was told, held baskets in their hands for the purpose of carrying betel nut and a tube of polished bamboo, which contained burned coral (powdered lime) that was dispensed onto a leaf as from a saltshaker. Lime, leaf, and nut were taken into the mouth as one morsel and leisurely chewed, causing noticeably discolored teeth.

The man who had called out when the canoes were still offshore was the first to speak, addressing himself to Tom Rose, who translated his words into English. He said his name was Soogle; he was a Malayan who had been cast away on an island to the south some ten months earlier and had since learned to speak the local language. He now served the "King of Pelew," whom he described as a kind man whose people were "courteous."

That both sides in this initial confrontation had someone who could act as interpreter was the greatest of good fortunes. Fortuitous too was the timing of this first encounter, for the English had not yet had their breakfast tea and everything was ready for this morning ritual. The visiting party was invited to join them for tea and "Chinese bis-quits." This friendly gesture was appreciated more than the tea, which the visitors did not care for. The acts of giving and receiving created an atmosphere of sharing that relaxed tensions on both sides and the bis-cuits, at least, were enjoyed. With Captain Wilson, his officers, and Tom Rose seated, the visitors squatting, and each side growing more confident in the presence of the other, it was now possible for them to talk in a more leisurely manner, and for the captain's crewmen to calm their fears, even if remaining prudently vigilant.

Through the two interpreters, the English were able to learn that the wrecked *Antelope* had been seen by fishermen who had carried the news that ultimately reached the highest ranking chief, or *rubak,* a man called Abba Thulle, who, they gathered, was the king, the high-est in authority. Consequently the king, very early in the morning, had sent this group of emissaries headed by his own two brothers, whose names the English recorded as Raa Kook and Arra Kooker. Raa Kook they took to be the "Commander in Chief of the King's forces." Arra Kooker, although lesser in rank, was greater in size and was the only bearded man in the group.

Arra Kooker was to report to the king this same day. One of the canoes was to return to the king's home island, which Wilson under-stood to be called Pelew. Several weeks were to pass before Captain Wilson learned that the island where the king resided was properly called Coorooraa (Koror on modern maps) and that the name of Pelew (Belau on the map) applied to all of the islands. At least the English learned from this first encounter that the island on which they had taken refuge was called Oroolong, as they spelled it. (It is spelled Ulong today.)

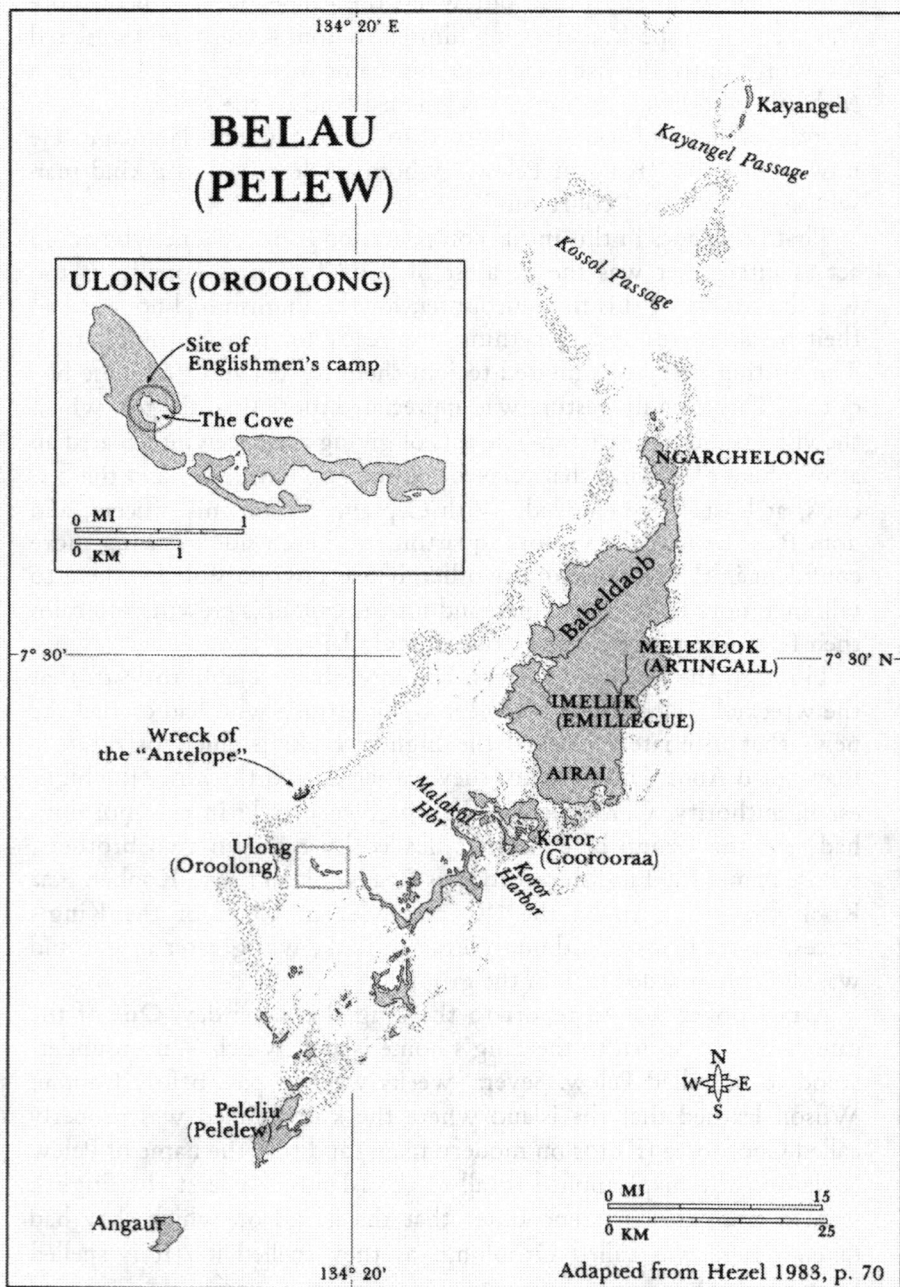

BELAU
(PELEW)

Kayangel

Kayangel Passage

Kossol Passage

ULONG (OROOLONG)

Site of
Englishmen's camp

The Cove

0 MI
0 KM 1

NGARCHELONG

Babeldaob

MELEKEOK
(ARTINGALL)

7° 30'

IMELIIK
(EMILLEGUE)

7° 30' N

AIRAI

Wreck of
the "Antelope"

*Malakal
Hbr*

Koror
(Coorooraa)

Ulong
(Oroolong)

*Koror
Harbor*

N
W—E
S

Peleliu
(Pelelew)

0 MI   15
0 KM   25

Angaur

134° 20'

Adapted from Hezel 1983, p. 70

The king, the English were told, was anxious to know "what sort of people they were" and what better way to satisfy his curiosity than to have an Englishman accompany Arra Kooker on his return to Pelew. Captain Wilson agreed to this suggestion and selected his own brother, Matthias. The king had sent his brothers to Oroolong; Captain Wilson would send his brother to the king. Whether by prearrangement or by happenstance, the king's other brother, Raa Kook, remained on Oroolong after Matthias Wilson had left with Arra Kooker. In any case, this sort of exchange was to characterize the relationship between the English and the people of Pelew through the entire history of events stemming from the wreck of the *Antelope*.

There were a few anxious moments on Oroolong when the men from Pelew became alarmed at the sight of an English boat crew making preparations to leave the island. It was quickly explained that this was to be a routine trip to the scene of the shipwreck for the purpose of obtaining more food and supplies. The Pelew Islanders then suggested that one of their men go with the boat crew to ensure that they would not be hindered in any way by curious islanders who might converge there by canoe.

Captain Wilson now wanted to introduce his officers before the group dispersed. As each man's name was called, the officer stepped forward and, in true English fashion, shook hands all around with the men from Pelew. From the first it became apparent that the white skin of the English, so pale that blue veins could be seen at the wrist, was as intriguing to the islanders as the garments so proudly worn by the officers. Both skin and cloth were touched with intense interest, and the officers were asked to reveal more of their arms and chests to the islanders, who were especially surprised to see that the English grew hair upon their chests. This and several subsequent scenes of a similar nature convinced the men of the *Antelope* that the islanders had never before seen white men at close range. Nothing that ensued, however, led either party to fear the other at this time, not even the discovery of a bullet that one of the islanders found upon the ground. Nor was there any immediate alarm when the use of the bullet was explained by Soogle, the Malay interpreter who had come with the men from Pelew. The conduct of both parties was typified by a cautious curiosity and growing interest in each other.

Introductions and amenities concluded, Captain Wilson now thought it appropriate to show his visitors around his hastily erected camp, but not before issuing orders that firearms inside the tents were to be carefully covered with canvas. The guided tour underway, the English had reason not only to admire the physiques of their visitors but also to note that they had "a particular majestic manner in walking," and that they gracefully trod barefoot over very rough surfaces, an act that none of those shipwrecked could emulate.

The two dogs from the *Antelope* had been placed out of sight in one of the tents. When this tent was visited astonishment reigned! Apparently the English had brought the first dogs to land on these islands. The crew's favorite, a Newfoundlander named Sailor, became an instant favorite of the visitors, who had never before seen a dog, much less heard one bark. Their fascination was unrestrained and they could not resist making whatever gesture would draw a quick response from the dogs. The English, in turn, learned one of the first words they would later provide Keate for his "vocabulary": *weel*, which they heard exclaimed over and over during this first visit. It is an understandable spelling of the word *ungil*, which, as they reported to Keate, means "good."

Satisfied with what they had seen, Arra Kooker and the men of his canoe now had to leave. Before they took Matthias Wilson away with them, the captain took his brother aside and instructed him to solicit the king's friendship and to inform him who they were, how they had had the misfortune to be shipwrecked, and how, with the king's permission, they proposed to construct a vessel for their return to the place they had come from. These instructions were of paramount importance, for the English needed the good will of the Pelew Islanders not only in order to survive but also to make use of the island of Oroolong and some of its trees, which would be needed if they were to construct a vessel successfully. Matthias Wilson was therefore sent off with gifts for the king, including cloth, tea, sugar, and rusks (pieces of twice-baked bread).

The remainder of this eventful day was taken up with campsite chores, including fetching water. The islanders who had remained assisted by taking the English to a better "well" of fresh water, and in getting there, they carried the fifteen-year-old Richard Sharp over the rough terrain.

The next day, 13 August, the pinnace returned from a trip to the wreck with word that the ship had been visited by islanders who had found, among other things, the medicine chest. It had been looted, medicine spilled, and bottles carried off. Because this could (and did) prove harmful to the culprits, Captain Wilson ordered all of the remaining medicine removed from the wreck and destroyed. Mr. Sharp, the ship's surgeon, had already brought ashore such medicines as he felt might be most needed.

After a meeting with his men, and with their agreement, Captain Wilson also ordered all of the alcoholic spirits remaining at the ship destroyed lest these too prove harmful to any of the people of Pelew. For his part, Raa Kook, the king's brother who had stayed with the English at Oroolong, suggested that those who took such property belonging to the English should be severely punished by the English; if not, he would recommend that punishment be ordered by the king. However, the precaution of destroying the casks of hard liquor was taken also to remove temptation from the crew who, in this time of peril, needed to give their undivided attention to survival, which was by no means assured, although the portents were now good.

Raa Kook himself represented the best early portent for a good relationship between the English and the people of Pelew. He was obviously intent upon friendship. He accommodated himself to the English by adopting their manners: he sat with them at table and slept in their tent. He expressed interest in everything of theirs that he saw and insisted on learning the operation and purpose of every tool and piece of equipment in the Englishmen's camp. In turn, he answered freely all questions put to him by the interpreters at the request of the English. (Keate does not explain how Matthias Wilson was to communicate at Koror; we must assume that there was another interpreter in the king's service.) One of the questions put to Raa Kook concerned a bone bracelet he wore, which, it had been noted, was like one worn by his brother. Raa Kook explained that this was "a mark of great distinction" awarded by the king to those of highest rank. The English then took comfort in the thought that one of such high status had not only chosen to cultivate their friendship but seemed bent on emulating them. When, the previous day, Soogle, the interpreter, had requested and received a pair of trousers and a jacket, a similar outfit of trousers and a uniform coat was presented to Raa Kook who delightedly put them on, saying "Raa Kook Englis." (After this first visit was concluded, Raa Kook chose to place these garments with his most treasured possessions at his home, preserved, perhaps, for the most special of occasions.)

But it was Arra Kooker, the bearded brother of Raa Kook, who became the favorite of the English. He not only emulated them, but took great joy in mimicking them, and the English loved it. He would put on a hat and then mimic the man who had worn it. And it was Arra Kooker who, on 14 August, returned to Oroolong from Pelew bringing gifts of boiled "yams" (taro) and coconuts. His first act was to inform his brother, Raa Kook, that three men had died as a consequence of drinking the various medicines they had earlier taken from the wreck of the *Antelope.* Raa Kook expressed satisfaction that these men had "suffered for their bad conduct."

Arra Kooker had brought with him a son of Abba Thulle the king: a fine figure of a young man who had lost his nose in battle, or so the English supposed. (It is much more likely that this unfortunate man had lost his nose to a disease, presumably yaws, which was common in many Pacific islands until Sir Alexander Fleming's penicillin wiped it out entirely some one hundred seventy years later, following World War II.) This eldest son of the king, whose name the English spelled "Qui Bill," brought a message from the king that the interpreters translated for Captain Wilson. In essence, the message stated:

> The King welcomes you to his country and gives permission for you to build a vessel on this island or you may come to the King's island and build your vessel there under his close protection.

Thus, the results of Matthias Wilson's mission were known before Matthias himself returned.

When the captain's brother did return in another canoe a short time later, he gave Henry Wilson his report. Not knowing what had been expected of him upon being introduced to the king, Matthias had knelt and kowtowed at the Abba Thulle's feet but soon realized that this was not necessarily expected of him as a foreigner, although the king's own subjects displayed similar forms of obeisance. He had been treated as an honored guest. He was given a drink from a coconut from which the king drank first. He was served "yams," shell fish, and a "pudding," which he described as being similar to mashed potatoes. After feasting he was taken to another house where a woman provided him with a woven mat upon which to sleep and a block of wood for a pillow. In this same house there were some "40 or 50" other people, all of whom stared at him with great curiosity until they lay down and went to sleep. During the night a fire had been lit nearby and Matthias had prayed for his life, fearing that he was to be roasted over the coals. He later learned that such fires were common practice, designed to ward off the damp night air. The next day he had been taken on a tour, during which he noted "yams" (taro) growing "like rice in India," and that coconut and betel-nut palms grew near every dwelling.

In all, Matthias Wilson's report of kind treatment at the home island of the king was another encouraging portent for the future of the castaways, but his return in the company of still more islanders presented a new problem. Because of the increasing number of visitors, the captain decided that it would be prudent to conceal some of the camp's indispensable materials and remove them from temptation. He put nine men on guard duty at all times and instituted a password among them; he also put his men through small arms exercises, which were witnessed by and explained to the visitors.

Perhaps to nullify any undue apprehensions the Pelew Islanders might have felt at seeing this show of force displayed by the English, Captain Wilson provided the king's son with a "silk coat and a pair of blue trousers" to wear. A similar outfit was provided for Arra Kooker, who proved to be very candid about his preferences in the matter of attire. The English reported to Keate that this robust and bearded brother of the king did not "relish" wearing trousers, but had a "passion" for a white shirt which, when he first put it on, gave him so much joy that he "danced and jumped about."

On 15 August, early in the afternoon of the fifth day the English had been on Oroolong, "King Abba Thulle" paid his first visit. He approached the island with many canoes, some of which stayed well behind his own and nearly out of sight. As Abba Thulle's canoe advanced toward the shore, the lead canoes, two on either side of his own, paused, and their men made an elaborate display of their canoe paddles, exhibiting great dexterity in flashing them from side to side and above their heads in unison. Conch shells were sounded. Captain Wilson was advised to go out to the king's canoe, which he did by having two of his own men carry him out through the shallow water. On reaching the king's canoe, Wilson was invited to join Abba Thulle on a "stage" erected at the center of the canoe. The captain obliged and "embraced" the king who, like his men, was "perfectly naked" and without ornaments of any kind except for the "hatchet" (adze) deftly carried on his shoulder.

Speaking through interpreters, Henry Wilson reviewed the circumstances that had put him on one of the king's islands and repeated his request for permission to build a vessel with which to sail away. Abba Thulle again agreed to this but stated that they would fare better if they came to his own island where they would not have to fear his enemies and would enjoy better health. In response, Captain Wilson thanked the king, and explained his preference to remain where he was because Oroolong was much closer to the wreck of the *Antelope,* from which wood and other materials would be needed in order to build a new vessel. Wilson wisely added that he felt he need fear none of the king's enemies "whilst they enjoyed his protection and friendship."

These preliminary discussions dispensed with, everyone went ashore, where Captain Wilson welcomed Abba Thulle by presenting him with a scarlet coat and inviting him to be seated upon a sail that had been spread for this purpose. The king sat down with his brothers Raa Kook and Arra Kooker beside him. Other high ranking chiefs, *rubaks,* sat nearby and still more men, about three hundred in all, squatted farther back. Tea was served and more gifts presented to the king, including cloth and rolls of colored ribbons, which the king shared with his retinue.

Captain Wilson then introduced his officers and, although the interpreters had some difficulty with titles—First Mate Benger, for example, became "*Kickaray* Captain" (Little Captain)—the king seemed interested to meet them, especially Mr. Sharp whose position as surgeon he understood; he was pleased to hear Captain Wilson offer medical services for the people of Pelew.

During the introductions Raa Kook was observed describing to Abba Thulle by word and gesture the various roles the captain and his men had played during the exercise of firearms he had previously witnessed. Predictably, the king requested a demonstration. Captain Wilson responded at once by ordering his men to take up arms and assemble on the beach where the low tide provided ample space for a routine drill. The men of the *Antelope* marched in front of their large audience and this time actually fired their muskets—three volleys from three different positions. Keate was later told that "the hooting, hallowing, jumping and chattering" of the surprised onlookers "produced a noise almost equal to the report of the musquets." To further demonstrate the use of arms, a chicken from among those rescued from the *Antelope* was driven across the sandy cove where Mr. Benger fired a "fowling piece loaded with shot" that dropped the bird and silenced the crowd. The chicken was then carried to the king for his examination. All eyes were on Abba Thulle as he inspected the wounded bird. When he looked up, the amazement that registered in his face was instantly reflected in the faces of his men.

But Raa Kook knew there was more that could be shown to impress his brother and he proceeded to guide Abba Thulle to the grindstone, which he turned to demonstrate his knowledge of its operation. Captain Wilson ordered a hatchet to be sharpened to further demonstrate its use. The scattering sparks produced renewed murmurings of excitement and the manner in which the "stone, so well wetted, became so soon dry" was an understandable source of bewilderment to the visitors.

The king, with Raa Kook as his guide, was also shown the bald-headed cook at work with his iron pot, tea kettle, frying pan, poker, and fire tongs. Raa Kook was again able to show off his newly acquired skills by operating the bellows that fanned the cook's fire. Before the royal visitors left the scene, a ham was selected and presented as a gift to the king.

The place where the two dogs were being kept was next on Raa Kook's itinerary. Treating the dogs as he had the grindstone and the bellows—as objects with which to impress the king—he caused them to bark with such frequency and constancy that the captain was wondering how he could put a stop to it when the *Antelope*'s flock of geese scampered by, creating a diversion. Now a goose was added to the assortment of gifts that had been presented to the king, and at the same time the dogs were discreetly moved out of sight.

The tent that housed the Chinese was visited last, with the result that Raa Kook felt disposed to explain to Abba Thulle that these short men with their long braided hair hanging behind their backs were only one example of the different peoples of the world—that, for example, there were the French with whom the English were at war. Whether it grew from this bit of knowledge that the English were also engaged in warfare, or whether it was inspired by the show of arms, a plan was apparently evolving in Abba Thulle's mind that should have come as no great surprise when, before the visit was concluded, it was revealed to Captain Wilson.

7

YOUR ENEMIES ARE
OUR ENEMIES

AT ENGLISHMEN'S CAMP on Oroolong's sandy shore, two tents had been prepared for the visit of the king—one for the Abba Thulle himself and one for his attendants. When the king retired to his tent for the night he had with him his son, Qui Bill, his brother, Raa Kook, and several chiefs. Whether by invitation or out of a desire to inspire a general feeling of confidence and camaraderie, Captain Wilson had assigned himself to spend the night in the king's tent. In the quiet of the night, just when it might have been thought that everyone was safe and secure, there arose such a shout from inside the tent that the English thought the worst imaginable fate must have befallen their captain. Two of the sentries, Bender and Sharp, ran into the tent to see if he was all right. At the same time the voices they had heard were taken up in chorus by the various encampments of the Pelew Islanders and it was soon realized that this was a round of songs or chants and nothing more. The captain, apparently, could not have been safer.

The tension eased and fell away when the English were asked to provide a song or two by way of entertainment. Young William Cobbledick, a seaman known for the songs he had sung aboard the *Antelope,* was chosen to oblige. The visitors were very pleased with his rendition of "sea songs and songs of battle." In fact, Abba Thulle was so impressed that he requested a song from Will Cobbledick on every future occasion that their paths crossed. His favorite, according to Keate, was "A Hunting We Will Go."

And a-hunting he would have the English go, to help settle

accounts with his enemies. The next day Abba Thulle made his formal request of Captain Wilson: Would the English help with an expedition against "an island that had done him injury"? It did not take Captain Wilson long to consider his reply. If there was a rival force in the islands equal to Abba Thulle's, what chance would he and his men have against them without the king's friendship and protection? Stating, in effect, "we are friends, therefore your enemies are our enemies," he agreed to help by providing the five men requested.

Captain Wilson did not want for volunteers. Every Englishman from the *Antelope* volunteered to join and, if necessary, do battle for the king. But Henry Wilson was not to go; his men thought that to be too big a risk—better the lesser risk of sending a third mate, Mr. Cummin. With him, the captain's steward, Thomas Dulton, and three seamen, Nicholas Tyacke, James Bluitt, and Madan Blanchard, were chosen to go, along with Tom Rose as interpreter.

For his part, Abba Thulle suggested that Matthias Wilson should visit the king's home island again to procure what food the English might want; he also offered to have his craftsmen help with the construction of a vessel, should the captain wish.

On the afternoon of 17 August 1783, the king and his fleet were ready to sail, as were the Englishmen selected to go off in the canoes with him. Abba Thulle shook hands with everyone on the shore and promised to take good care of those he now took into his charge. The English were well armed and dressed in "blue jackets, cocked hats, and light blue cockades." As they entered separate canoes they were given three cheers by their fellow countrymen, who had assembled to give them a proper send-off. Abba Thulle instructed his men to stand in their canoes and return the salute with cheers of their own. He then confidently assured everyone that the entire affair would be over in four days and departed.

On Oroolong, meetings were now held to consider the size and design of the vessel to be built to carry the castaways back to Macao. Fortunately, Peter Barker, the second mate, had worked in a shipyard; he was therefore given the principal responsibility for the design and construction of the vessel, but by consent overall authority remained with Henry Wilson. In a footnote Keate explains that Henry Wilson's authority as captain technically ended when the *Antelope* was wrecked, but that his men had settled any misunderstanding this might have created by electing their former captain as the "master or manager of the yard" where the vessel was to be built. The construction of a vessel being central to everything they might do while in Pelew, the honor thus bestowed conveyed with it what amounted to control over the lives of everyone on the island. In other words, Henry Wilson was now "Lord of Oroolong"—in fact, if not in title. But Captain-cum-Lord Wilson wanted at least some decisions made in a democratic manner, for he exacted an agreement whereby no man would be punished without the "majority of voices" deciding in favor of such action. Nor did he lose his humility; this being Sunday, he concluded the meetings by reading prayers to the assemblage in the "great tent."

But the English did not leave their protection entirely to God. They deemed it "expedient to form a barricade in front of the tents." This modest fortification was made with a "double row of strong posts, interlaced with branches of trees to form a thick fence" with an opening where a six-pounder could be mounted. They also mounted two swivel guns on the stumps of trees that had been removed from the encampment.

With the English now physically secure, even if their minds may have harbored doubts that would not be put to rest until the safe return of the five comrades now off on a mysterious and uncertain mission, it may not be deemed inappropriate, as Keate would say, to describe a typical day in the lives of the men of Oroolong.

The day would begin at sunrise to the sound of the boatswain's pipe bringing the men out from their tents. Morning ablutions completed, early morning chores would be carried out: bringing fresh water, fueling the fires for cooking, and changing the guard. Then the big event of the morning—breakfast tea along with whatever solid foods the cook could spare. The men would then spread out over the island to conduct the day's business, some of the English felling trees, and the Chinese hauling the trees to the dockyard where the carpenter and his assistants trimmed them into timbers of the sizes needed. The cooper, John Meale, would be at work repairing casks to be used to store food and water for the voyage to Macao. The grindstone would be busy keeping tools sharp enough to work the very hard wood that grew on the island. And sparks would also fly from the blacksmith's anvil, where the bellows would be busy helping to fire the forge. Caring for the sailcloth was the province of the boatswain. Captain Wilson, when not overseeing it all, helped fell trees. He had an observation post cleared on the hill above the camp, from which he could search

out the best passage through the reef for the day that their vessel
would be completed. If men could be spared there would be an
attempt at fishing—usually without much success for the English and
a cause for humility when the men of Pelew would come ashore with
huge quantities of fish for them taken from the same waters! Most
days, weather permitting, there were renewed trips to the wreck of
the *Antelope* to salvage needed wooden planking, copper, and other
materials. On one such trip a new cask of arrack was found and
although the men had pledged themselves to abstinence, it was agreed
that at day's end a "pint" would be a fitting reward for a day's work
well done and a sedative for a good night's sleep. Presumably those on
guard duty during the night abstained. The others took to their tents,
stretched out their bits of canvas and tried to sleep, perchance to dream
of such things as English sailors dreamed of—home and family, a
favorite port away from home, or even of remaining in Pelew.

On Monday, 25 August, Oroolong was visited by four canoes that
approached from the south, presumably from an island not under the
jurisdiction of Abba Thulle. Captain Wilson and his men were without an interpreter and this added to their apprehensiveness at the unexpected visit. But the new visitors came ashore peacefully and were very
civil, indicating by gesture that they wanted only to look around.
Within an hour they were gone, having, it appeared, satisfied their
curiosity. The incident gave the English cause to be grateful for the
precautions they had taken with posted guards and a system for com-
municating among the various tents within the barricade should the
need arise for quick defensive action. These precautions seemed all the
more appropriate considering the "four day" expedition that had gone
off with their comrades and had now stretched to nine days without a
word.

Then, on the afternoon of that same day, four canoes approached
again, this time with the occupants "splashing and flourishing" their
paddles in the unmistakable style of the king's men, and with them
returned the five musketeers. Mr. Cummin, reporting to Captain
Wilson and all of the eager listeners who gathered around, declared
that Abba Thulle had been victorious in the battle with his enemies at
Artingall (Melekeok). At least one hundred fifty canoes and more than
one thousand men had gone forth to do battle with their "darts" and
"throwing spears" but a few shots fired by the English had put the
otherwise brave enemy to rout. A shot from Thomas Dulton's musket

had put the enemy's casualties at one, with no losses to the king's forces. Mr. Cummin explained that their return had been delayed by Abba Thulle's insistence that they visit his island of Coorooraa (Koror) and participate in a victory celebration. There had been feasting and rejoicing, singing and dancing. The songs of the dancers appeared to be impromptu narratives of the battle, which had brought honor to the king and his people. Before returning to Oroolong they had been taken to the king's house, where they were given stewed turtle meat, and when they did depart, the canoes that took them were "laden with yams for the rest of their countrymen." Now on Oroolong, the newly found cask of liquor was tapped again to celebrate the safe homecoming.

Soon after this victory, Raa Kook informed Henry Wilson that Abba Thulle "had given" Oroolong to the English, whereupon a British pennant was hoisted and three volleys were fired in token of "taking possession" of the island. Now Henry Wilson was truly "Lord of Oroolong."

There followed a succession of visits between the "Englishmen's Island" and the island of Coorooraa. First, Captain Wilson decided to send some of his men to compliment the king on his victory. And, in the hope of finding additional fresh food, he sent one of the Chinese along with instructions to look for vegetables. But Wilson was disappointed, for when the party returned, the man from China reported that he was unable to find anything good other than items that had already been given to the English. Where the English had not found beans or onions, the Chinese had not found rice or cabbage.

Then Wilson himself made a visit to Coorooraa. He took Sharp the surgeon, Devis the artist, and his son Harry. The captain was favorably impressed with much that he saw there, especially the finely constructed permanent causeways and walkways. Special foods were served to him during this "state visit" including "Seville Oranges" and "broiled pigeons." Devis sketched several of the women present and attracted the attention of Abba Thulle, who wanted to try his hand at this new art. The necessary materials were provided for him, but the king soon realized that the skills exhibited by Devis, an artist with many years of schooling, could not be easily matched, at least not in the first attempt.

During Captain Wilson's visit to Coorooraa a council meeting of *rubak*s was held at which a further attack on the warriors of Artingall was discussed. This time the king requested that ten Englishmen be permitted to accompany him against his archrivals and, again, the captain was ready to oblige. When the Wilsons, father and son, Devis, and Sharp returned to Oroolong their jolly boat was filled with "every kind of provision" the island of Coorooraa could yield.

It was now Abba Thulle's turn to pay another visit to Oroolong. He toured the dockyard, taking great interest in the work of the blacksmith, the cooper, and the carpenters. He was personally interested in the work of these men, as a man on whose shoulder the adze was no idle symbol but an efficient tool that had gained him a considerable reputation as an artisan. In this capacity he must have greatly admired the tools of the English, but as protector of his people he coveted the weapons he now saw displayed—the canons and the swivel guns, one of which was fired for his edification. It was explained to Abba Thulle that the guns were mounted in such a way as to make it possible to shoot at any of the king's enemies who might approach and thereby discourage any hostile intention they might have before they could land and engage in battle. The king requested that one of the swivel guns be taken along on his forthcoming military expedition, but Captain Wilson was able to deny this request on the grounds that it would be impractical to operate and fire such a gun from a canoe.

Prior to Abba Thulle's visit a list of ten men had been posted on a tree in the dockyard. By agreement, these men were to accompany the king as he and his party embarked for Coorooraa on the first leg of their journey to oppose the forces of Artingall.

After spending the night at Coorooraa, they left the following evening, at the signal of a conch shell that caused over two hundred canoes to rendezvous and proceed to Artingall. They traveled most of the night, stopping for only three hours of rest on friendly ground. Although they arrived at the enemy's shore before light, they waited for the sun to come up, it being their custom, according to Keate, "never to attack at night, or take him by surprise." In fact, the enemy had been warned several days earlier that a battle was being planned should the chiefs of Artingall not adhere to the terms sought by Abba Thulle.

A canoe was sent ashore with men wearing white feathers in their hair as a signal of truce for a party wishing to parley. This canoe soon returned with word that the terms had been refused outright, and soon after the battle was joined. Abba Thulle maneuvered his canoe and feigned a retreat, thus drawing the warriors of Artingall away from the shore in their canoes. Abba Thulle's forces then cut them off and captured six canoes and nine men. The prisoners, all of whom had been wounded in battle, were put to death. The English thought some of the methods used to kill them were abhorrent but were told that Abba Thulle had given up taking prisoners because those who had escaped in the past had revealed valuable information to the enemy. The entire engagement had not lasted more than three hours.

Upon returning to Coorooraa there was, as before, much feasting, singing, and dancing. The songs frequently included the word "Englees" thus acknowledging the help the ten men of the *Antelope* had provided to Abba Thulle and his people.

With the ten men safely returned to Oroolong, the pace of work on the vessel increased and more trips to the *Antelope* were made to obtain planking and spike nails. But food supplies were running low, and the rice recently taken from the wreck had been under water so long that it became an unappetizing gelatinous soup when cooked.

Abba Thulle's gifts of taro at this time were, therefore, most welcome at Oroolong. They were sent with Tom Rose, the interpreter, who had stayed behind on Coorooraa at the request of Abba Thulle, who wanted to learn more about the English. Abba Thulle also demonstrated his understanding of the needs and wishes of the English by taking pains to keep curious people away from the Englishmen's camp so that construction of the vessel could be carried out without the hindrance of avid spectators.

Next to visit Oroolong was Raa Kook, accompanied by two *rubaks* from the neighboring islands bringing more taro, coconuts, and three jars of "molasses." There followed a scene that gave further evidence of the remarkable understanding the Belauan leaders had of the priorities of the English. It was Sunday, 28 September, and Captain Wilson was reading prayers to the crew. A messenger arrived and began to speak to Raa Kook, who immediately ordered him to remain silent until Captain Wilson had completed the reading and prayers had ended.

The message, it was then revealed, was for fifteen men and a swivel gun to go on yet another expedition. Captain Wilson took the opportunity of this request to recite a number of recent grievances, principal among which was the English objection to the cruel execution of prisoners, stating that he would not consent to assist another expedition unless it was agreed that the prisoners would not be put to death. Raa Kook spoke to each point raised in a very conciliatory manner, but as for the prisoners, well the English could have them! After consulting with his men, Wilson agreed to send a swivel gun and ten men but no more.

The account of this third battle, as provided by the captain's brother, Matthias, varied somewhat from that of the second battle. Abba Thulle's forces were even greater in number and this time they suffered two dead, including a son of Raa Kook. Additionally, some thirty or forty of the king's men were wounded, some of them dying as a consequence. This time the people of Artingall did not take to their canoes but fought on land with much bravery. Their dead and wounded were not mentioned, nor was there any mention of the unwanted prisoners. However, the causeway at Artingall was destroyed and a "regal stone" taken away, which Keate compares in relative importance to the Stone of Scone.

A special celebration of this latest victory was held on Coorooraa at a place called Emungs where those who had allied themselves with Abba Thulle were honored. At the request of the king, Captain Wilson attended, along with his son, his servant, Thomas Dulton, and the linguist Tom Rose. It proved to be another round of feasts, inspiring more songs and dances, with the women joining in. As a most honored guest, Captain Wilson was carried into the great house on a board, served food by "two butlers," and presented with a variety of gifts. But the captain wearied of celebrations that lasted throughout the night and after a few days he asked to return to Oroolong. He was not to return, however, until after a visit to the village of Emillegue and then another overnight stay with Abba Thulle on Coorooraa.

Meanwhile, the work of constructing a boat had continued on Oroolong, but not without difficulties. On 8 October, Mr. Barker "fell backward from one of the stages and was much hurt." Then high tides threatened the vessel, necessitating the building of a seawall to protect the dockyard.

There had also been difficulty with the cook, who was punished with a "cobbing" after a majority had voted that this paddling with a flat board was deserved. The cook's assistant and another Chinese were punished in a like manner.

On 15 October, Oroolong was visited by the first women to come to the island. Abba Thulle came, bringing his daughter Erre Bess and some eight or nine other women including one of his wives, Ludee, whom Devis sketched. This was no routine visit. A canvas was spread, and a proper meal served to the guests. It is not recorded but this was doubtless one of the occasions when young Will Cobbledick was called upon to entertain the king with one of his favorite songs.

Perhaps because the meagerness of the Englishmen's larder had been demonstrated by the frugality of the meal served Abba Thulle and the women, or possibly as just one more act of friendship, ten very large fish were presented to Henry Wilson. The captain respectfully declined six of these, saying that four would be all that he and his men could eat at one meal and they did not want to see any of the fish wasted. Abba Thulle then ordered that the remaining fish be cleaned and smoked so that the English could eat them at their leisure. This must have been another humbling experience for the men of the *Antelope* whose efforts at fishing had failed. In addition to the fish, there had been numerous gifts of taro and other vegetables, which represented the work of the women of Pelew who now, for the first time, had the opportunity to see all of the hungry men they had helped to survive and remain strong.

At the dockyard, where the hull was now complete and masts were being fashioned from the *Antelope*'s "small spars," it became apparent that the vessel would soon be ready to enter the water. The work of laying ways for a launching began. (Keate described the new vessel as being one-sixth the size of the *Antelope*.)

There would be only one more interruption to the work at the dockyard, and that a short one. Although the people of Artingall had sued for peace and there was apparently no longer trouble in that quarter, Abba Thulle felt that he still had matters to settle with adversaries to the south at Pelelew (Peleliu). Once again, ten men from the *Antelope* set off, this time with a fleet of at least three hundred canoes, in which the king's men were joined by those of all his allies. Devis reported on this engagement, which, to everyone's relief, was bloodless. The people of Pelelew surrendered to Abba Thulle without a fight and gave up two Malays who had apparently been the source of the friction between the two factions.

On Oroolong, with the ability to depart assured, Captain Wilson told his men that he would like to explore all of the island chain before leaving the Pelews. He thought it would be advantageous to be able to make a full report to the East India Company describing these islands "on which no European had ever been." But his men, fearing unpredictable and prolonged delays caused by the exploration of islands whose size and number they had been unable to determine even after climbing the highest "eminence," asked him to give up the idea. Henry Wilson, who was probably no less anxious to get the new vessel into the water and underway for China, yielded to the wishes of the ship's company. He "stifled" his desire for further exploration and focused his attention entirely on what remained to be done before departing from Oroolong.

8

MADAN BLANCHARD
AND LEE BOO

NO ONE will ever know how many of Captain Wilson's men may have wished to remain in the Pelews rather than return to China and from there to England. We know of the wishes of only one man—Madan Blanchard. Although the first, he was not the last Englishman to decide to try a Crusoe-like life in what he considered a grand style among a people who were seen to be obliging enough to provide more than one Friday for aid and companionship. But Captain Wilson found a way to limit to one the number of his men who would make this decision. Simply put, if anyone were to stay it would have to be with the king's permission, and only the captain would make such a request of the king.

On Thursday, 6 November 1783, the captain wrote a letter to Abba Thulle announcing plans to depart the Pelews in the vessel now in the last stages of construction. The letter was also intended to thank the king for all of his kindnesses to the men of the *Antelope*. More tangibly, gifts of all the iron and tools that could be spared were to be sent with the letter requesting that the king and his *rubak*s visit Oroolong again that thanks might be conveyed personally. The letter and the gifts were to be delivered by Mr. Sharp who would be accompanied by Tom Rose as interpreter.

Upon hearing the captain discuss this letter with Tom Rose, seaman Madan Blanchard requested that the king also be informed of his desire to remain in the Pelews. Although Blanchard's shipmates had heard him speak of such a plan, word of it had not previously reached the captain. Henry Wilson was not pleased with what he now heard. He instructed Tom Rose to say nothing of the sort to Abba Thulle, and then turned his attention to Blanchard. More in the role of counselor than commander, Captain Wilson reminded Blanchard that he had no trade such as carpentry or smithing that might endear him to the people of the Pelews; that his future, therefore, as a stranger in a strange land would be precarious. But Blanchard had made up his mind, and Wilson, who could not have been totally insensitive to the allure of the islands in contrast with the life of a seaman—whether aboard ship or at home—gradually relented. In the end he gave his reluctant consent on the grounds that Blanchard could be charged with the responsiblity of caring for the guns being left for Abba Thulle, thereby at least appearing to render "a favour to the King."

It is doubtful that Henry Wilson would have given Madan Blanchard his consent had it not already been intimated that Abba Thulle would be asking him to take two people from the Pelews with him to England. This "exchange," which was soon to be consummated, made it possible for Blanchard to have his wish. But, in his wisdom, when Henry Wilson later presented the idea to Abba Thulle he made it appear that it was his own idea rather than Blanchard's, thus ensuring a far greater potential for a successful outcome than if Blanchard had spoken for himself. In this way he also served notice to the rest of his men that anyone entertaining thoughts along similar lines would have to negotiate through him and not act without his consent.

On Friday, 7 November, the party of Sharp and Rose departed for Coorooraa to deliver the captain's letter and the gifts. En route, their boat was intercepted by a canoe carrying Raa Kook, who informed Sharp that Abba Thulle was on his way to Oroolong but had taken shelter nearby to escape bad weather. Mr. Sharp therefore diverted the pinnace to the shore, where he came alongside the king's canoe. Without delay he read aloud from the captain's letter as Tom Rose translated into Malayan and Abba Thulle's Malay man interpreted into Belauan. This formality completed, the king suggested that they all spend the night on a nearby island.

Once ashore, they all repaired to a large house, where everyone was assigned a seat according to custom. Torches were lit and stuck between the boards that ran the length of the house. Every variety of island food, a veritable feast, was served on banana leaves and on a variety of plates, some made of tortoiseshell, some of wood, and some of earthenware. When the feast was over the leavings were swept into the cracks of the floor to fall to the ground below. Woven mats, which Abba Thulle's party had carried with them in the canoes, were then brought in by attendants and beds made ready for the night. Mr. Sharp and his party were provided the same accommodations. The night was then spent peacefully and quietly, except for an incident in the very early hours of the morning. A messenger from one of the northern villages arrived. He had come on behalf of the northern chiefs friendly to Abba Thulle who wanted to know when the English would be departing Pelew so that they might bring gifts and say their farewells. The king responded by giving the messenger a cord made of coconut fibers on which he had tied as many knots as there were days remaining before the English would sail away. All then resumed sleeping until daybreak.

After the morning ritual of bathing, Abba Thulle and his party proceeded toward Oroolong by canoe. Raa Kook followed as a guest of the English aboard the pinnace. In the blustery weather, the pinnace made much better progress than the king's canoe, prompting Raa Kook to suggest that Abba Thulle be invited to transfer to it. Once aboard the pinnace the king was most favorably impressed with the performance of the Englishmen's boat. His own canoe, he is said to have declared, was fit "only for smooth water." When he was then told that the English planned to make him a gift of the boat, he instructed Raa Kook to make very careful note of its operation.

Early in the morning of 8 November, the king, now on Oroolong, ordered his men to set to work painting the Englishmen's schooner. The paint, which Abba Thulle had previously brought to Oroolong for this purpose, consisted of red and yellow ocher which, according to Keate, were the two predominant colors used by the people of Pelew, along with black made from charcoal and white from coral. The final touches were adminstered by Raa Kook, who painted a design on either side of the stern: "two circles, one within the other, in black and white, with some little zig-zag ornaments hanging from them." Abba Thulle, who had supervised the painting, suggested that the vessel be named the *Oroolong* in memory of the island the English had lived on these many weeks. The suggestion was gladly accepted and, although we are not told, one supposes that the talents of Devis, White, or Wedgebrough were called upon to paint the letters "OROOLONG" on the vessel's bow.

Captain Wilson chose this time to ask Abba Thulle if Madan Blanchard could stay in Pelew. The king consented readily, stating that he would make Blanchard a *rubak* and give him a house and two wives—Fridays enough, indeed.

Perhaps Abba Thulle had come to know Blanchard during the various expeditions and perhaps he had formed an opinion of him similar to that stated by Keate to the effect that Blanchard was a likable, "good tempered [fellow whose] inoffensive behaviour [had] gained him the regard of all of his shipmates." But it is doubtful that Abba Thulle knew anything at all of Blanchard's background, or, as Keate put it, that "life having denied him any advantage of education, he was unable either to write or read." One wonders whom Abba Thulle would have chosen had he been given a choice: Devis, whose artistic skills he envied; Sharp the surgeon, whose medical knowledge had been demonstrated to the benefit of Abba Thulle's people; or little Will Cobbledick, whose songs he never tired of hearing. We will never know. But in Madan Blanchard he got a man who had knowledge of guns and this, in the last analysis, may be as much as he might have hoped for.

Very early in the morning of 9 November, the work of launching the *Oroolong* began. It proved more complicated than had been anticipated. At one point the king personally tried to lend a hand but was advised to leave it to the English with their hawsers, tackles, wedges, ropes, and equipment designed for this sort of work. Finally, after several hours of effort and thanks to a favorable high tide, the *Oroolong* was launched. As the boat entered the water there was much cheering on all sides, the English giving "three loud huzzas" in which they were joined by the men of Pelew. The breakfast that followed was the most high spirited event ever for the Englishmen of Oroolong.

The following day, 10 November, Abba Thulle organized a ceremony for the purpose of investing Captain Wilson with what Keate describes as "the order of the bone," thereby making him a "Rupack of the first rank." It was a solemn ceremony and not an easy one for the captain. The objective was to provide Henry Wilson with the same sort of large bone bracelet as those worn by the king's brothers, Arra Kooker and Raa Kook. To get the bone bracelet around Wilson's wrist, his left hand was lubricated with coconut oil and a cord attached to each finger. All five cords were then passed through the opening of the bone and as they were pulled by men standing at some distance from Wilson, others forced the bone over his knuckles and into place on his wrist. The men of Pelew crowded around the captain, admired his new emblem of authority, and spoke of the "Englees *Rupack*," while the English cheered this new honor bestowed on their captain. But with the honor went responsibility. Captain Wilson was told to rub the bone bright every day and not suffer its loss from his arm without defending it valiantly. George Keate, speaking as an English gentleman well aware of the various honors that could be bestowed upon his countrymen, has the last word on this tribute to Wilson when he assures us that it was surely as meaningful as a "strip of velvet tied round the knee, a tuft of ribband and cross dangling at the button-hole, a star embroidered on the coat."

Returning to the more urgent business at hand, the *Oroolong* was moved to deeper water while remaining just within the cove. Raa Kook, who was on board observing, later explained to his peers the English method of "heaving lead" to determine the depth of water and their method of anchoring. In keeping with the king's orders, he was learning all he could of English boatmanship.

On shore Henry Wilson and Abba Thulle were huddled with the two interpreters. The king reminded the captain that he had previously indicated he might want to have two of his people travel to England with the English when they returned to their homeland. He now explained why. He told the captain that although he was respected both for his high rank and for his knowledge, he had been humbled by observing the lowliest of Wilson's men performing tasks that he himself could not. This, he said, had inspired him to ask Henry Wilson to take with him to England his second son, Lee Boo. He wanted to place his son in the captain's care and give him the opportunity of learning all that he could from the experience of being with the English. He hoped that the things his son would learn could be applied to the "benefit of his own country" when Lee Boo returned. He described Lee Boo as "an amiable and gentle" person who was "sensible and mild-tempered." He told Wilson that he had sent for his son, who had been at a "distant place" where he had been tutored by "an old man." He was now on Coorooraa saying his farewells.

The poignancy of this scene, of this powerful leader voluntarily humbling himself before a man he could have destroyed, would not have been lost on Henry Wilson. The captain could have given no reply other than to unhesitatingly agree to do for the king's son what the king would have him do. The stilted prose George Keate used to record the response Henry Wilson gave to the king can hardly represent the words actually spoken and translated, but it does describe what must have been the captain's sentiments:

> He was exceedingly obliged and honoured by this singular mark of confidence and esteem; that he would have thought himself bound to take care of any person belonging to Pelew whom the King might send; but in this case, he wished to assure him, that he would endeavour to merit the high trust reposed in him by treating the young prince with the same tenderness and affection as his own son.

Raa Kook, who had enjoyed his relationship with the English from the very beginning, had, it was now revealed, also harbored hopes of going to England. But this was not to be, for he could not win the consent of the king. He would have to content himself with command of the pinnace and with the gifts that were being left for him. Abba Thulle, like Captain Wilson, was not permitting the exchange of people to get out of hand. He denied all such requests; anyone going with Wilson would be of the king's own choosing. The second person he did select to go away with the English was to serve as an attendant for Lee Boo. This man, named Boyam, was not a Belauan but one of the Malays recently released from Peleliu.

The king, pleased with all that had been said this day, had another favor to ask—that the *Oroolong* pass by Coorooraa before departing so that everyone on his island could see it. But Captain Wilson succeeded in dissuading him from this proposal, knowing that the men were impatient to get away now that their vessel was ready to sail. In fact, Captain Wilson informed Abba Thulle that he would leave the next day, a day earlier than previously announced. Abba Thulle was unhappy with this news for it meant that the *rubaks* coming from the north would not arrive in time for the farewell. (The reason for Captain Wilson's leaving earlier than expected, according to Keate, was to avoid the crush of canoes carrying well-wishers who the English feared would impede safe passage through the reef.)

The king's disappointment with Wilson's decision to depart earlier than expected was assuaged somewhat by the gift-giving that now began in earnest. Arra Kooker was given Sailor, the Newfoundland dog he had coveted from the first. Raa Kook, already promised command of the pinnace, was given a plan whereby he could construct more boats, plus some of the building materials. He was also presented "a brace of pistols, and a cartouch-box loaded with the proper cartridges." Not to be slighted, Abba Thulle was given five muskets, five cutlasses, "near a barrel of gunpowder with gun flints and ball in proportion," and Captain Wilson also made him a present of "his own fowling piece." The people of Pelew, for their part, were arriving with every variety of food and other gifts to be loaded onto the *Oroolong*.

And on 11 November, Lee Boo arrived, brought by his brother, Qui Bill. He was introduced first to the captain and then to each of the officers. He made a remarkably good first impression. All of the English warmed to him from the time of their first handshake. He was described by them as having "so much good-humour and sensibility in his countenance, that every one was immediately impressed in his favour." Obviously Lee Boo was off to a good start.

Most of the English spent their last night in Pelew by sleeping aboard the *Oroolong,* but Wilson stayed ashore for a last discourse with Abba Thulle and with Blanchard. The king spoke to Wilson as one leader to another, stating, in effect, that he knew the perils of sending his son away but that he trusted the captain completely and that he would be welcome to return to Pelew no matter what happened in the unforeseeable future. Wilson was implored to let Lee Boo be with him and to "make him an Englishman." The captain, choosing to speak to Abba Thulle more in the manner of one father to another, stated again that he would care for Lee Boo as he cared for his own son. (The sincerity of both men is hardly to be doubted; were it not so, Keate would have given more than passing reference to the fact that a son born to Abba Thulle was named Captain in honor of Henry Wilson. It is as though, given the evidence of their mutual trust and regard, it was to be taken for granted.)

Now it was Blanchard's turn. As the captain took Blanchard aside and sought a place where they could speak in private, the irony of the situation must have weighed heavily on his mind. He had just entered into a solemn agreement with a man whom he had known for hardly three months but a man he respected as at least his equal. He had agreed to take this man's son, an island boy he had only just met, and make an Englishman of him. And here was Blanchard—a man who had been under his command for more than fourteen months, a man he had come to know well, well enough to know that his prospects at sea or on land were not good whether he remained in Pelew or returned to England. Yet, every time Abba Thulle would look at this man in the future, as months stretched into years, he would think of his son. What could he do for this man other than exhort him to be the best man he knew how to be; to remember his Christian duties; to keep the Sabbath; to try to help others; to instruct them; to be beneficent to them "particularly in working such iron as had been given to them, and what more they might hereafter obtain from the wreck, and also in taking care of the arms and ammunition they had left them." Finally, he advised Blanchard that if he preserved "the form of dress his countrymen had appeared in, he would always support a superiority of character." To make this possible the captain saw to it that Blanchard was "furnished with all the clothes they could spare," and when these were worn out, as would inevitably happen, he should "make himself trowsers with a mat which he could procure from the natives." Blanchard, in short, was to look the part of an Englishman even if his humble past had ill prepared him to act the part to Abba Thulle's satisfaction.

Captain Wilson remained on the island for the entire night along with his son Harry and Abba Thulle's men, whose ranks had now been joined by Blanchard. In the morning the men of the *Oroolong* hoisted the "English Jack" and fired a swivel gun as a signal that all was ready for sailing.

Before departing, the English "cut upon a plate of copper" an inscription which was fixed to a tree where they had camped informing the world that:

> The Honourable
> English East India Company's Ship
> The *Antelope,*
> Henry Wilson, Commander,
> Was lost upon the reef north of this island
> In the night between the 9th and 10th of
> August;
> Who here built a vessel,
> And sailed from hence
> The 12th day of November, 1783.

When a boat crew of five men came ashore to fetch the Wilsons, the captain asked the crewmen to join him, his son, and Blanchard in prayer. The people of Pelew who stood by respected the moment as the English went into a *bai* that Abba Thulle's men had erected for the *rubak*s who had been expected from the north. The captain read them their prayers. It was the last time that Madan Blanchard would ever kneel in prayer with his fellow countrymen.

Not only would the illiterate Blanchard be unable to read his prayers in the future, but he would never read Keate's book; and he would never learn from such readings that there were people in England who envied him. The reviewer of Keate's *Account* for *Gentleman's Magazine*, for example, must have thought he was speaking for such people when he wrote: "This is such a shipwreck as would almost make one wish to have been of the party, to have passed three months among the honest friendly-hearted Pelewians."

Whether they envied him or not, the English who read Keate's book when it first appeared in 1788 and wondered what happened to Blanchard would have to wait another fifteen years to learn the end of his story. Meanwhile, on the *Oroolong*, Lee Boo's story was just beginning.

The wreck of the *Antelope*. From *Loss of the Antelope Packet*, by an unknown artist. (Courtesy of the Trustees of the National Maritime Museum, London)

The *Oroolong* passing the reef. Convoyed by Palauan canoes, the boat built in Palau is ensured safe passage through the reef that destroyed the *Antelope*. (Drawn by Henry Wilson, Jr., and engraved by W. Taylor; Keate's *Account*, 5th ed.)

Abba Thulle at Oroolong. In this first meeting between the two leaders, Captain Wilson is carried out to the canoe of the "King of Pelew" as unarmed English and Chinese crewmen of the *Antelope* watch from the shore. (Sketched by Henry Wilson, Jr., engraved by J. Landseer; Keate's *Account*, 5th ed.)

Arra Kooker, brother of Abba Thulle, and a favorite friend of the English, sketched in Palau by A. W. Devis, 1783. (By permission of the British Museum)

Lee Boo wearing a sailor's pullover, as sketched by Devis either aboard the *Oroolong* or at Macao or Canton before he was dressed in English finery. The original caption is probably not an autograph. (By permission of the British Museum)

Abba Thulle. Portrait by Arthur William Devis, 1783. The "King of Pelew" is shown in a characteristic pose with his adze on his shoulder, but the men of the *Antelope* came to know him more as a crafty and able statesman than as the skillful artisan he was reputed to be. (Engraved by H. Kingsbury for Keate's *Account*)

Ludee. Devis did this portrait of "one of the wives of Abba Thulle" on the island of Oroolong when Abba Thulle brought her to see Englishmen's Camp and the shipwrecked men whom the women of Palau had provided with food. (Engraved by Kingsbury for Keate's *Account*)

John Wedgebrough, the student draftsman, sketched this "View of the Causeway" while in Palau. Piers of the type he saw are still in use today. One of the *Antelope*'s boats is in the foreground. (Engraved by Landseer for Keate's *Account*)

Robert White, the other student from the Drawing and Mathematical School at Christ's Hospital, London, drew this view "of a part of the Town of Pelew" which the English later recognized as the town of Koror. (Engraved by W. & J. Walker for Keate's *Account*)

View of the cove. Henry Wilson, Jr.'s "on the spot" sketch of Englishmen's Camp at Oroolong shows the men at work cutting timbers and manning the forge (far right) to build the boat that would return them to China. (Engraved by T. Medland for Keate's *Account*)

The *Oroolong* under construction. A. W. Devis labeled his pen and colored wash drawing "*Oroolong* on the Stocks." Never embellished by engravers, it is a closer representation of the island terrain where he and his fellow castaways lived, worked, and exercised the resourcefulness that ensured survival. (Courtesy of the National Galleries of Scotland, Edinburgh)

9

FAREWELLS AND
FIRST KNOTS

WHEN LEE BOO boarded the *Oroolong* he brought very little with him, less even than those who had been shipwrecked. He had only a woven mat and a length of cord made of coconut fibers. The mat was to be used as a mattress aboard the *Oroolong* or for as long as he would need it; the cord was to be used to mark the progress of his travels with Captain Wilson. By tying knots in the cord—a knot for each major event—he would keep a record of his journey into the world beyond Belau. But he would not need to tie his first knot to preserve the memory of the tearful farewell of 12 November 1783.

Captain Wilson had been correct in anticipating that a large number of canoes would converge on the *Oroolong* just before it was to make its way through the reef into the open ocean. There was no turning away well-wishers who brought gifts for the departing Englishmen and their royal passenger. The *Oroolong* had soon received all of the food and other gifts that could be carried and had to decline more than had been accepted. Finally, taking only token gifts from those who cried out, "Take only this from me—only this from me," the *Oroolong* sailed toward the reef.

But the swarming canoes did not impede the *Oroolong*'s progress. Abba Thulle had also anticipated this scene and was on board to ensure that it did not happen; his canoes maintained order and safely guided the newly launched schooner to the best opening in the reef.

Before leaving the *Oroolong* for his own canoe, Abba Thulle, who had already said his last farewell to Lee Boo, shook hands with all the officers and then embraced Captain Wilson for the last time. His last words, as translated, were: "You are happy because you are going home;—I am happy to find you are happy; but still very unhappy myself to see you going away."

Raa Kook stayed with Captain Wilson until the *Oroolong* had made her way safely out to the sea. Then, putting off the painful farewell, he lingered for a considerable distance beyond the reef before finally transferring to his beloved pinnace. Keate recorded that Raa Kook departed the English by taking them "cordially by the hand, and pointing with the other to his heart, said 'it was there he felt the pain' of bidding them farewell." On board the *Oroolong* there was not a dry eye as the Englishmen watched the pinnace turn back for the islands of Pelew.

Wilson's journal for the voyage to Macao, if it could be found, would probably contain an entry for the *Oroolong*'s first day at sea that might read: "Having taken leave of our humane friends of Pelew we headed a course N by NW: winds variable from the E SE." Henry Wilson was more than 134 degrees east of Greenwich and his Rotherhithe home and some 1,400 statute miles from his destination on the coast of China.

For Lee Boo, the degrees of latitude and longitude meant nothing. No instrument could measure his feelings as his home islands faded to the southeast and the *Oroolong* took him into the unknown. He spent the first night on deck. Boyam, his interpreter and servant, spread his mat for him and Captain Wilson produced a blanket to protect him from the cold night air. When he awoke in the morning he was out of sight of land and would not see more for nearly two weeks.

It was November. Soon the *Oroolong* would reach much cooler climes than were ever known in Belau. Captain Wilson found clothing for Lee Boo: a shirt, a waistcoat, and trousers. Lee Boo did not want to be encumbered with shirt or coat but wore the trousers constantly. Eventually colder weather forced him to put on the upper garments as well.

Lee Boo was seasick during the first four days at sea. He ate only rare and special apples that Abba Thulle had given to Captain Wilson. From their description, "not unlike the Dutch Paradise Apple" or the "Jamboo Apple," Keate decided they must have been "*Eugenia Malaccensis* of Linnaeus," that is, mountain apples, a fruit that is still found in Belau today. Even if Lee Boo felt too sick to eat ordinary fare he may have found it difficult to refuse these apples that, according to Keate, only a very privileged few were entitled to have. They must also have brought his father vividly to mind and may have prompted his comment to Boyam that his father would be unhappy "knowing he had been sick," as if by some extrasensory perception his father did, in fact, know. Perhaps it was Lee Boo's way of saying that he was homesick.

On 16 November, the fifth day at sea, a flying fish was caught when it landed on the deck of the *Oroolong*. With some taro, it was served up as a meal for Lee Boo, who then felt much better. This was Sunday; afternoon prayers were conducted with all "hearts full of gratitude" for the good weather and the favorable winds. Only a small leak in the boat had caused any concern and this was kept under control by vigilant manning of the pumps. Even the nine days of unsettled weather that followed created no greater problem than discomfort in the crowded quarters of the *Oroolong*.

On 25 November the weather cleared and the Bashee Islands were sighted as the *Oroolong* passed to the north of the Philippines. Lee Boo repeated the name of these islands until he had the pronunciation correct. He then tied his first knot so that he would not forget the first land he had seen since leaving Belau.

Captain Wilson took the *Oroolong* between two of the Bashees and into the China Sea. The next day there was another island and another knot for Lee Boo. This was Formosa (Taiwan), and now Captain Wilson set a westerly course that would take the *Oroolong*, its motley shipwrecked crew, and its young passenger on to Macao.

On 28 November several Chinese fishing boats were seen, then a "China Junk," which Wilson explained to Lee Boo was the "European" word for the Chinese vessels that sailed the coast of China and sometimes went off to Batavia and Malacca to trade. Another knot for Lee Boo.

"The Asses Ears," landmarks pointing the way to Macao, were sighted the next day. Wilson maneuvered the *Oroolong* westward, working his way through islands off the coast of China. In the evening he anchored among "small Chinese vessels. . . . Lee Boo appeared quite delighted at the sight of land, and the number of boats in the water."

On 30 November a pilot was hired to complete the run into Macao. Captain Wilson hoisted the "English Jack" taken from the *Antelope* on the mast of the *Oroolong*. When the flag, which was much too large for the *Oroolong*, was seen by the Portuguese of Macao, they sent boats with food and men to help, for they perceived that the men in the approaching boat must be a crew that had been shipwrecked.

The men who came to assist the English to shore were, for Lee Boo, yet another strange people speaking yet another strange language—an occasion for yet another knot in his cord.

Then a man speaking a tongue more familiar to Lee Boo appeared in the person of one John McIntyre, a permanent resident of Macao who sometimes acted on behalf of the East India Company when, as now, all of the Company's agents were at Canton. McIntyre had provisions sent to the *Oroolong*, and with his help Captain Wilson sent his first report to the authorities at Canton, informing them of the fate of the *Antelope*. And McIntyre brought the good news that there were several large ships at Canton, some of them ready to sail home to England. Lee Boo and the shipwreck survivors would not have long to wait before they would be given passage to England. Unlike their experience aboard the *Antelope* six months earlier, Captain Wilson and the men of the *Oroolong* would suffer no difficulties or delays in settling their affairs at both Macao and Canton. The Chinese authorities had nothing to fear from a ragtag crew of shipwrecked Englishmen and certainly had no reason to be suspicious of Lee Boo.

But for now, Lee Boo was engrossed in the sights of the coastal waters surrounding the island of Macao. He was seeing *clow* ships; some of them, in his words *kmal clow*, very big, compared with the boat that had brought him to China. Close to the *Oroolong*, the Chinese came alongside in houseboats or sampans housing entire families and begged the English to give them food. From among the items at his command, Lee Boo gave what he liked best—oranges, for example—and not the mere "fragments of victuals" that, according to Keate, sailors usually gave. Whether or not Lee Boo tied this scene into his cord of memories, it was his introduction to the world he had left home to see.

At the gates of China, Lee Boo had seen only the poor of China. Unfortunately, he would not be permitted to pass through the gates and see any other Chinese way of life. Although they were free to move about on Portuguese Macao, even the East India Company's agents could enter and leave their compound at Canton only by water. They rarely, if ever, saw any more of China than was visible from the verandah of their factory-warehouse, which overlooked the area where, along a very confined stretch of the riverfront, Europeans could mingle with Chinese merchants and their servants. For foreigners, it was a transitory if luxurious life at the narrow end of the huge funnel through which the teas of China flowed into the ships of Europe and, later, America. Most Englishmen soon saw all that they would ever be permitted to see and became bored unless lost, for a time, in their work of extracting from the unseen mainland of China all that their ships could carry and that the merchants of London could sell. But for Lee Boo, everything he saw, whether Chinese or European, was new and strange. Because he too was new and strange, he now became the "New Man."

10

THE NEW MAN

THE FIRST American ship to reach China was, appropriately, *The Empress of China*. When it arrived in 1784, the Chinese so admired the star-spangled banner it flew that they called the captain and his men the "Flowery Flag Devils." But Lee Boo had arrived a few months earlier, and the emblem of his country, as perceived by those who saw his tattooed hands, had also been admired. The Americans who came after Lee Boo would become known as the "New People," but Lee Boo was the "New Man"—singular not only because he was the first of his kind, but because his appearance and demeanor were singularly different from those of other visitors.

On 1 December 1783, Henry Wilson, along with the Honourable Company's representative John McIntyre and an unnamed "Portuguese Gentleman," accompanied Lee Boo ashore at Macao. The Portuguese gentleman had requested that the "New Man" be permitted to visit his home. It was the first European-style house that Lee Boo entered. The elaborate decorations and furniture inside it fascinated him, but he gave his most searching attention to its interior construction. The box-like rooms puzzled him; he could not comprehend how their walls could be so smooth and their ceilings so flat.

Lee Boo's wide-eyed curiosity charmed his hosts. The Portuguese ladies in their delicate finery welcomed him warmly. Because he reportedly showed no sign of embarrassment when these ladies touched and admired his tattooed hands, Keate was prompted to observe that even in his first exposure to European society Lee Boo had displayed "amiable manners and native polish."

Later in the evening of that first day at Macao, Lee Boo and some of the men from the *Oroolong* were taken to another house, the home of Mr. McIntyre. Here Lee Boo encountered a larger room than any he had yet seen—a hall, lighted to reveal a table laden with everything required for a sumptuous supper. He was especially struck by the glasses, "the vessels of glass," on the handsomely decorated sideboard. But something at the end of the hall caught and held his attention as never before—the first mirror he had ever seen. What he saw in this object was no undulating visage as seen over the side of a canoe or in streams and tide pools, but the perfect and complete reflection of himself standing just ahead. The English sailors stared at the mirror inordinately, for they had not seen themselves since the shipwreck. But Lee Boo's fascination was something special, enhanced, no doubt, by the sight of himself in English clothes. As he posed, moved backward, and stepped forward again in disbelief, his puzzled expression was not lost on his host, who sent for a handmirror, thus providing Lee Boo with no less an object of mystery but one he could handle at will and come to grips with. By the end of this eventful evening Lee Boo must have wondered how many knots he should tie in remembrance of so many marvelous things.

After spending the night in the McIntyre home, Lee Boo resumed his examination of rooms with the solid walls and ceilings that revealed no clues as to how they had been constructed. Whom could he ask for an explanation? Boyam? Boyam would doubtless have been at a loss for words that Lee Boo could understand—if indeed he understood the puzzle himself. For the time being, at least, it would have to remain a knotted mystery.

When Captain Wilson arranged for the use of a house, everyone left the *Oroolong* except those taking turns standing watch over the vessel. Those coming ashore for the first time made a foray into the town, but Lee Boo did not accompany them. Captain Wilson must have felt here, as later in London, that he did not want Lee Boo exposed to the illnesses that often thrive in the crowded places and enclosed quarters frequented by sailors. When the men returned they brought gifts for Lee Boo, including a "string of large glass beads." Lee Boo was elated! He ran to show them to Captain Wilson, exclaiming that he wished they could be sent to his father, who would distribute them in such a way as to let the people of Belau see for themselves what splendid things came from the place Lee Boo had traveled to.

When Lee Boo did go along on an excursion it was not into the town but the countryside of Macao. Here he saw goats, sheep, cows, and, most captivating of all, horses! The only similar animal of any size that he had seen before was the Newfoundland dog named Sailor. His first horse, therefore, became an even larger Sailor or, in his words, a "*clow* Sailor." It doubtless inspired the largest of several knots to be added to his cord that day.

The next morning, from the window of the house where they were all staying, Lee Boo saw not only a horse, but a horse being ridden by a man! He called at once to his English friends to come and see this astonishing sight! He was then taken to the stables where more horses could be seen and, upon discovering they did not care for the oranges he offered, wanted to know what they did eat. This explained, the climax of the day's adventure came when he, too, was mounted on the back of one of these largest creatures he had ever seen. Now it was a horse that he wished could be sent back to Belau.

By this time letters had been received from the East India Company's representatives at Canton expressing concern for the men of the *Antelope* and requesting that Mr. McIntyre arrange for Wilson and his men to be provided with money "and everything else they might be in want of." Letters were also received from various commanders of John Company ships offering accommodations and passage to England. Captain Wilson was also informed that the *Oroolong* should be disposed of at Macao in order to avoid payment of "duty and port charges" at Canton. The *Oroolong* was put up for sale at auction and brought the handsome sum of seven hundred Spanish dollars—a tribute to the men who built it. Nothing is known of the new owner, but one hopes that he kept the boat's name and insignia and thereby helped to perpetuate the memory of Lee Boo over a period of years.

Henry Wilson, Lee Boo, and most of the men from the *Oroolong* now made their way up the Pearl River as guests aboard the Honourable East India Company's ship the *Walpole*, Captain Churchill. None of the houses Lee Boo had seen at Macao were more amazing to him than the accommodations he found himself enjoying aboard the *Walpole*. The furnishings of tables, chairs, and lamps, all comfortably appointed in a great cabin, made, in his own words to Henry Wilson, "*Clow* ship a house." Ironically, many of the Chinese vessels the *Walpole* would have passed as it made its way toward Canton would have been houseboats with so little space that children played on the roofs, some with buoys tied to their backs to prevent drowning. Looking beyond the shores of the river, Lee Boo would have seen houses of ample size and far different design from those he had seen in Macao.

The slow journey upriver would have taken an entire day or longer. The Chinese pilot would have to take the *Walpole* through the estuary and into the Bocca Tigris (the "tiger's mouth"—the first rocky narrows of the river), where fortifications guarded the approach to Canton; there would then be another twenty-five miles to navigate before they reached Whampoa, the anchorage for all foreign ships trading at Canton; and at Whampoa they would still be twelve miles from the city. A riverboat would have to take Lee Boo and the others the rest of the way.

If Lee Boo had been awestruck by the houses of Macao and the commodious ship that transported him to Whampoa, what would he think of the Company's "factory," which had been criticized as being more of a palace than a warehouse in which to conduct business? His first view of that three-storied building would have been from the river. Then, as he stepped ashore at the busy waterfront and found himself in the midst of bales of silk, crates and baskets of chinaware, and chests of tea awaiting delivery to the anchored Indiamen, he commented that "China must have a *Tackalby* [artisan] for everything."

Lee Boo was taken inside the Company's Great Hall, where he was seated at a banquet table that displayed more glass vessels than he had seen at Macao. Even the chandeliers that hung above his head were made of glass! He sat with Captain Wilson and others from the *Oroolong,* waited on by a "number of attendants" who always supplied a "different plate" for each serving, and different "sorts of vessels" to drink from. Although he had liked tea from the first, Lee Boo now discovered that he did not care for coffee, not even the smell of it, but he told Captain Wilson that "he would drink it if he ordered him to." As to liquors or strong drink of any sort, Lee Boo would have none of them. He had seen one of the English sailors drunk from celebrating the safe arrival at Macao and, not understanding why the sailor was sick, had reported him to Mr. Sharp, the surgeon, who had then explained the cause of the problem so effectively as to convince Lee Boo that "it was not drink fit for a gentleman."

After Lee Boo had been in Canton for a few days, Mr. Benger and others who had stayed behind in Macao to settle the sale of the

Oroolong arrived by boat. Lee Boo, who was having breakfast where he could look out at the river, saw his friends approaching. He sprang up and ran to greet them at the riverside, shaking their hands and greeting them affectionately. He was, as they later related to Keate, "impatient till he could get them into the house, fearing that by staying behind they had not fared so well as himself." By these signs of sincere regard Lee Boo must have been well on his way toward winning the friendship of his English companions.

Friendship was not all that Lee Boo won at Canton. Some men "who had been at Madagascar" were seen practicing the art of spear throwing in the Honourable Company's "hall of the factory," using a painted bird in a "gauze cage" for a target. Lee Boo, on being invited to participate, took a spear, balanced it in his hands, "shook and poised it," and declared himself ready to throw. He aimed the spear "with apparent indifference," threw, and hit the bird in the head! The best the others could do, "at the great distance" from which they threw, was to hit the cage!

While at Canton, Lee Boo had further opportunities to resume his examination of house construction. He compared the flat ceilings with the sloped roofs of Belau and vowed he would learn how it was done before returning to his home islands. Keate relates that most of Lee Boo's attention was directed at objects and activities that offered new knowledge that might be of benefit to his father's people.

The last and probably the most treasured gift that Lee Boo received during his stay in Canton resulted from a visit to the home of a Mr. Freeman, one of John Company's supercargoes there. He was invited for tea and when his host noted the pleasure Lee Boo took in viewing the sugar bowl made of blue glass, he was taken to another room where he was shown "two barrels of the same kind of blue glass (which held about two quarts each) placed in brackets." Lee Boo was so enthralled with these splendid containers that his host gave them to him! No knots would be needed to remind him of Mr. Freeman.

The time had now come for Henry Wilson to make decisions concerning the voyage to England. He had already turned down two offers to command country ships trading between China and India in favor of returning home as soon as possible. He wanted to make his own personal report to the East India Company, and there was the matter of his obligation to take Lee Boo to England in keeping with Abba Thulle's wishes. He therefore assembled the officers and men of the *Antelope* and advised them of the various financial settlements that had been made, including the proceeds from the sale of the *Oroolong,* which were divided among them. He told them they were now free to take up whatever positions they wished, but recommended that all, especially the officers, return to England.

Mr. Sharp, who had been taking care of Lee Boo, was the first to leave. He turned his ward over to Captain Wilson and sailed for home on the *Lascelles,* Captain Wakefield. Wilson, with Lee Boo in hand, sailed with Captain Joseph Elliott on the *Morse.* Most of the others followed aboard various John Company ships, including the *Walpole.* Only Devis is known to have remained in Canton from where, after several months, he went to India and established himself for a time as a portrait painter of some importance before returning to England in 1795.

The *Morse* was the largest of the Honourable Company's thirteen merchant ships that had called at Canton during 1783. It was listed as a ship of 864 tons burthen, a true Indiaman, about three times the size of the *Antelope.* Among other things, it carried 885 chests of tea consigned to London merchants of the East India Company.

Although Lee Boo was treated well by the captain and officers of the *Morse,* he missed his friends from the *Oroolong,* particularly the captain's young son Harry, who had taken passage on another ship. He spent most of his time with the two Wilsons who were on board—the captain and Matthias. He had not gone far on the *Morse* when he asked for a book that he might learn to read. Henry Wilson not only obliged but worked "with his young pupil" and discovered in him "great readiness in comprehending every information given him."

Nor was Lee Boo's education on board the *Morse* limited to what, with Wilson's help, he could gain from books. The log of the *Morse* reveals that Captain Elliott "confined Thomas Smittan in Irons for abusive language." And, a few days later the apparently unrepentant Smittan was given "a dozen lashes." Although Lee Boo may not have witnessed such punishments, he could not have escaped the scuttlebutt that would have spread the word and he would have had time to reflect on the strict code of conduct enforced on the Honourable Company's ships.

Other ships were seen at sea. Lee Boo wanted to know their names and the names of the countries they were from. He repeated the names over and over until he had learned them, then added them as knots to his cord. But his strand of memories now included so many knots that he sometimes had to review them with Captain Wilson lest he forget. When the officers of the *Morse* saw Lee Boo "busied with his line" they said among themselves that he was "reading his journal." He was soon to add another knot to this unique journal, for the *Morse* was approaching St. Helena, the island yet to be made famous as the last island on which the Corsican Napoleon Bonaparte would live.

The log of the *Morse* records that on entering the harbor at St. Helena it "saluted the fort with nine guns which was returned." For Lee Boo, these salutes may have signaled what were to be some of the best experiences of his entire journey. Here he not only saw and mounted a horse, but he rode a horse: "He sat well, galloped, shewed no fear of falling and appeared highly pleased." Here he not only saw a *clow* ship with many guns, but was taken on board one of His Majesty's ships of war, *The Chaser,* and given a demonstration of the mighty ship's weaponry.

On St. Helena, Lee Boo was rejoined for a time with Surgeon John Sharp, who arrived aboard the *Lascelles*. After several months of separation, Lee Boo was delighted to see his friend, the man who had been closest to him from the day they left Belau on the *Oroolong* until their departure from Canton on separate ships. The two ships now in the same harbor, the two friends were reunited. As at Canton, it was Lee Boo who took the initiative and ran to meet his arriving friend. And Lee Boo was the first to extend his hand in the Englishman's form of greeting. Well in advance of his arrival at London, he firmly established his reputation as an outgoing personality anxious to make abiding friendships and learn the ways of the English.

At St. Helena, however, Lee Boo learned that not all of those who knew the English could call them friends. The greater part of the island was in the hands of the East India Company, which here had a plantation tended by slaves. There was also "the Company's garden," where Lee Boo saw bowers made of bamboo forming shaded walkways that impressed him so favorably that he resolved to recommend them to Abba Thulle. In this instance, perhaps, a knot in his journal was not needed, for it was a vision he could easily transpose to Belau and would therefore stay with him.

For the stay at St. Helena the log of the *Morse* records only that the ship "received three Bullocks," took on water, and sailed "in company with the *Francis.*" (Another Indiaman, the *Francis* had sailed from

Canton at the same time as the *Morse* and was under orders to accompany it to England.)

The *Morse* now made for its destination—Portsmouth, in the south of England. Before Portsmouth is reached, the Isle of Wight comes into view, with "the Needles" at its southern tip. These pointed rocks may have appeared more needle-like when Lee Boo saw them than they do today. Nonetheless, they are famous landmarks—the first sight of British soil for many a homecoming sailor and the first that Lee Boo saw of England.

At the Isle of Wight, Lee Boo packed his barrels of blue glass, pocketed his string of precious glass beads and his even more precious string of knotted memories, and left the *Morse* with Henry and Matthias Wilson. Captain Wilson wanted to get to London by the speediest route and had the opportunity to travel with the officer of the *Morse* who, because he was charged with dispatches, was sure to be first ashore, first to Portsmouth, and first to London. Lee Boo and Matthias Wilson had to wait for the next coach to London, leaving that evening.

Lee Boo arrived at Portsmouth on 14 July 1784. "The number and size of the men-of-war in the harbor, the variety of houses, and the ramparts were all objects of attraction" for him. But now, if not before reaching Portsmouth, the number and variety of ships, houses, and things worth remembering had proliferated in such a way that, according to Keate, Lee Boo had given up trying to match each new sight or experience with a knot in his journal. The still greater sights that he was destined to see in London had already challenged the most discriminating observers, many of whom had found their journalistic skills wanting. Lee Boo would be forced to trust to memory. London, Rotherhithe, and all he was to see of England would have to be tied into one grand knot.

11

A HOUSE "RAN AWAY WITH BY HORSES"

DESCRIBING the trip from Portsmouth to London, George Keate quotes Lee Boo as having said "he had been put into a little house, which was ran away with by horses—that he slept, but still was going on; and whilst he went one way, the fields, houses, and trees, all went another!"

Would that all of Lee Boo's experiences in England were so well described. However, Keate recorded scarcely more of Lee Boo in England than of Lee Boo in China. Presumably he believed his British readers would be less interested in the familiar than the exotic, even though Lee Boo was some five months longer in London than in China. With so much of the England that Lee Boo saw in 1784 remaining to be seen today, one wishes that Lee Boo's friends had been more mindful of posterity and provided us with a more detailed chronicle of his activities and observations. As it is, except for this one priceless cameo of the trip to London and a very few similar observations, we have been left little more than vague clues to help us retrace Lee Boo's movements from the time he reached England.

The "little house" he rode in from Portsmouth to London was, of course, a coach—presumably a coach-and-four. However comfortable a "house" it may have been, it traveled a rough road, so rough that one coach earned the sobriquet of Land Frigate. Captain Wilson had taken the same route a half-day earlier in a hired coach—a post chaise —that provided a faster and smoother ride. By contrast, Lee Boo traveled in the "purgatory" wherein passengers were "sealed up on the jolting and rambling machine." At least Lee Boo was put inside and spared the outside ride on top of the coach that some endured at the risk of falling off and at the cost of acquiring bruised bodies. But even inside, such sleep as could be had came in the late hours of the night as the sleep of exhaustion.

In his innocence, Lee Boo was spared the fears experienced by passengers who knew that highwaymen sometimes stalked these roads and that all too recently the bodies of murderers had been displayed along the very road he traveled. But with Matthias Wilson, veteran of the battles of Belau by his side, he had little to fear.

Traveling at six or seven miles an hour, the coach took some twelve hours to cover the seventy-three miles to London, with stops at Petersfield and Mousehill before reaching Godalming. There, while the horses were changed, there was time to visit an inn—The King's Arms—where passengers could partake of cold meat, bread, and a cup of tea, plus stronger drink for those who, unlike Lee Boo, needed to fortify their courage. Those who abandoned the journey at this point and put up at the inn often had to share a bed or sleep on the floor. But whether they continued that night or the next day, there were still stops to be made at Guildford, Escher, and Kingston before they reached London.

During the stops, the village dwellings Lee Boo saw, with their sloping thatched roofs and exposed beams, held fewer architectural mysteries for him than those he had seen in Macao and Canton. Even as he traveled he obtained fleeting glimpses of roadside houses, as well as of sheep and cows at summer pasture, cultivated fields between rambling hedgerows, and the trees that passed him by.

But in the torpor of Lee Boo's night ride to London he could not have learned much from the shadowy scenery outside his coach, or for that matter, from the scene within. Whoever the passengers huddled there with him and with Matthias, they were nonentities to Keate. However, Lee Boo presumably learned their names because it was customary, Besant tells us, "for passengers to introduce themselves by name and to say something of their calling, and their reasons for travelling . . . by way of precaution; otherwise one might be taken for a highwayman." Names and credentials of fellow passengers aside, Lee Boo could not help but learn without introductions, if with epithets, the names of the horses as they were repeatedly called out by the driver during this, his first and longest journey by coach.

After the command for the horses to halt at the last stop in London,

Lee Boo and Matthias had still farther to go to reach the Wilsons' home on Paradise Row in Rotherhithe. Too weary to walk, not to mention carry their kit, they had only to hail a hackney coach and travel the remaining distance in relative comfort.

Reaching Rotherhithe ahead of Lee Boo, Captain Wilson had time to inform his wife and young daughter that Matthias was following and would soon arrive with a special guest. But there was little time for Mrs. Wilson to prepare for someone who had traveled so far and to whom her family owed so much. After all, it was not just the likable Lee Boo they were taking into their home, but the son of the man who had ensured the survival of three Wilsons in Pelew. It is hardly surprising, then, that all of the Wilsons prepared to treat Lee Boo as a member of the family and that Mrs. Wilson would be "Mother" to Lee Boo from the first.

When he did arrive at 28 Paradise Row, after the usual pleasantries of conversation relating to a journey just completed, Lee Boo was taken to his "chamber" and shown what was to be his bed—a four-poster with curtains that provided total privacy. Lee Boo pulled aside the curtains, got inside, then got out again to admire this wonderfully constructed object that had been provided for his comfort. He is said to have remarked before going to sleep that "in England there was a house for everything!"

Friday, 16 July, was Lee Boo's first morning in Rotherhithe. How strange to awaken that first morning not knowing, within his enclosed bed, whether it was night or day. Pushing aside the curtains and stepping out into the bedroom, his first sight may well have been of a wall-papered interior that would hardly have assured him that he was not still dreaming. Rubbing his eyes and walking to the window, he had only to look out over the rooftops and see the masts of ships in the nearby river to be reminded of the long voyage he had just completed and of the Wilsons who had brought him to this many-chambered house he had yet to explore.

The Wilson home, he would discover, was a three-storied brick-faced house within a row of houses hugging the street named Paradise Row. There were three large windows at the street level, four windows on the second floor facing the street, and two double windows on the third floor. There were fireplaces with mantels on the various floors, but the kitchen was in the basement. A backyard or garden to the back of the house was similar to those at the backs of all the houses along the row and across the street. A housemaid helped with the kitchen chores, but the Wilsons, including the captain now that he was home, doubtless saw to the garden themselves and would soon introduce Lee Boo to this favorite summer activity.

Lee Boo would soon be absorbed in all that the Wilson household had to offer. It was a warm home in a wholesome neighborhood, this house on Paradise Row, and beyond Paradise Row the rest of Rotherhithe waited.

12

LEE BOO'S ROTHERHITHE

LEE BOO was fortunate to arrive in England in the summer. Whereas a July in London would never be too hot for someone from tropical climes, a winter month would almost certainly be too cold. The normally mild English climate has known winters so cold that the Thames has frozen solid even in London. On such occasions the communities that bordered the river at London were more understandably one metropolis bound together by the Thames. But in the summer, when the river's swift currents and extreme tides divided the metropolitan area into two unequal parts, Lee Boo could scarcely have comprehended London—the Greater London that is a complex of many communities, including the original London on the more populous north bank, and Rotherhithe on the less prosperous south. Yet it may not have been as difficult as we might suppose, for Lee Boo's homeland was also a complex of communities.

Had he written a letter to his young friends in Belau, Lee Boo might have compared Rotherhithe to Arakabesang, an island that is separate from Abba Thulle's home island of Koror but is also part of Koror, just as Rotherhithe is separate from, but part of London. The river that physically separates the two created them both and is indispensable to both. Legend has it that an English king threatened to remove his throne from London. He was told that although he could do this, he could not remove the Thames. By the same token, the inner city of London is dependent on the satellite communities that provide specialized services for its many needs. The speciality of Rotherhithe has traditionally been to supply the needs of commercial shipping.

ROTHERHITHE, c. 1784

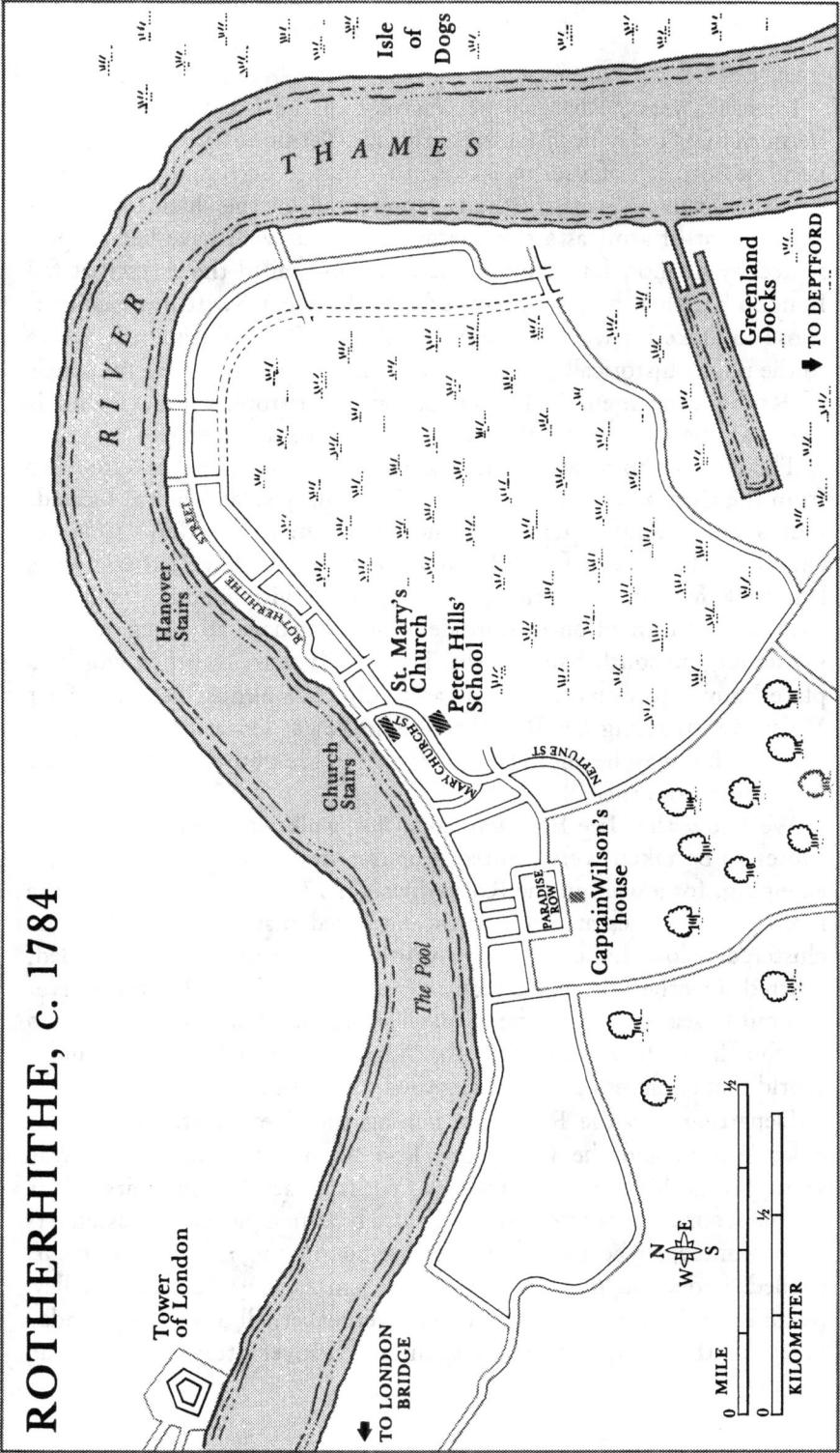

THAMES

Isle of Dogs

RIVER

Greenland Docks

TO DEPTFORD

Hanover Stairs

ROTHERHITHE STREET

Church Stairs

St. Mary's Church

MARY CHURCH ST

Peter Hills' School

NEPTUNE ST

The Pool

PARADISE ROW

Captain Wilson's house

Tower of London

TO LONDON BRIDGE

N
W E
S

MILE
0   ½

KILOMETER
0   ½

In earlier years, Rotherhithe was part of the London Borough of Bermondsey. Today both Rotherhithe and Bermondsey are part of the London Borough of Southwark. As that part of Bermondsey that borders the Thames, Rotherhithe is represented on the shield of Southwark's coat of arms as a ship. It might just as well have been represented by a sailor, for many of the men who sailed the ships that fed London had their homes in Rotherhithe. Jonathan Swift, for example, chose to make his world-traveling Gulliver a Rotherhithe man. More to the point, historically, the voyage of the *Mayflower* was in the hands of Rotherhithe men, including Captain Christopher Jones, who is buried in the churchyard of St. Mary's Rotherhithe.

The Wilson home at 28 Paradise Row was but a few hundred feet from the river and from the church of St. Mary's, which was located, then as now, almost literally on the riverbank. In Lee Boo's time the church could be seen for miles along the river and was, therefore, a landmark for sailors. Although not quite as visible today as it was then, it is still mentioned in guide books that have anything at all to say about the south bank of the Thames. It was, in other words, a place known to everyone in the area. One can almost hear the elder Wilsons instructing Lee Boo that should he get separated from others and lose his way he should "just look for the church and find your way home from there."

We know that Lee Boo was taken for walks in Rotherhithe. The routes to be taken were limited, but the views to be seen were ever changing, for a walk in the Rotherhithe of 1784 was a walk along the river. The Thames at Rotherhithe harbored many of the ships that clustered below London Bridge waiting to be loaded or unloaded, refitted, or otherwise made ready for another journey down the river and out to sea. It was a scene of ceaseless activity, both on the river and on the shore. It was a world that Henry Wilson knew well and a world that could not but have appealed to Lee Boo.

Departing Paradise Row and joining the river at St. Mary's, the elder Wilson and the young Lee Boo would have made their way along Rotherhithe Street, stopping, perhaps, at Church Stairs where people scooped water from the river and boatmen picked up passengers who wanted to be rowed or, depending on the tides and current, sculled across the river. We can see them passing Packstone Alley, Swan Lane, Clarence Street, and Hanover Street, all of which provided access to the river, with stairs again at Hanover Street. Just beyond

Hanover Street was a mastmaker's establishment. Here we can see them examining the pile of long poles while staying out of the way of carpenters, sailmakers, and rope-yard workers who roved the area, along with the lightermen who relieved the big ships of their cargoes and the carters and porters who carried goods to and from the warehouses. There would be not just men at work, but horses too, more horses than Lee Boo had seen in any of his travels.

Continuing on downriver, opposite the Isle of Dogs, we can see the captain and Lee Boo in sight of the famous Greenland "wet docks," where ships floated not on the river but in an inland pool, their masts standing straight as the poplar trees that lined the dockyard. This may well have been the noblest sight that Captain Wilson could show a prince from an island kingdom proud of its own causeways and docks. The ships they saw here were whalers home from the Greenland fisheries, resting now where not even the tremendous tides of the Thames could disturb them.

Leaving the docks and turning their backs to the river, Captain Wilson and Lee Boo would face the open fields that lay between them and Rotherhithe town. Skirting marshes and following the footpaths of hunters and farmers, they would see game birds taking flight and, somewhere in the distance to the south, a windmill turning—to whatever purpose Captain Wilson could have explained.

Approaching the town from the south they would pass many a carefully tended garden, with here and there an orchard; these gardens and orchards provided many of the seeds Lee Boo was to collect and save to take home to Belau. Returning to Paradise Row, the captain and the prince would no doubt end their long walk with enough of "Mother" Christiana Wilson's tea and sweet biscuits to assuage their healthy appetites.

Lee Boo's first Sunday in England, 17 July 1784, was Henry Wilson's first Sunday at home since returning from the Pelews. The captain, who kept the Sabbath at sea and as a castaway on an alien shore, would now go to his own church for the first time in over two years. Lee Boo would go for the first time ever. He had seen St. Mary's from the outside, of course, with its tower and spire rising above all to command the attention of every sailor who came up the Thames, but he had not yet entered this holy place where the Wilson family faithfully joined the parishioners of Rotherhithe in worship.

What were Lee Boo's reactions? Keate tells us that he "seemed particularly pleased at going to church" and although he "could not comprehend the service [he] perfectly understood the intent." What did he think of the artistry displayed in the interior of the church, the stained-glass windows, the memorial plaques and tablets? The son of a master carver would have admired these works of art as well as the church organ with its all-embracing sounds and mysterious appearance. If not the service, could Lee Boo comprehend the reverence that the people of Rotherhithe had for their place of worship, where women prayed for their men at sea and where, in the surrounding churchyard, they buried their dead? Later, Henry Wilson told him that "saying prayers at church was to make men good, that when they died and were buried, they might live again above" and he pointed to the sky. Lee Boo replied that it was much the same in Belau, where "bad men stay in earth—good men go into sky—become very beautiful" and, as Keate described the scene, Lee Boo also raised his hands to the sky and "gave a fluttering motion to his fingers."

Lee Boo met George Keate within the first week of his arrival in England. They met at the home of Keate's friend, one Robert Rashleigh, where the Wilsons and Lee Boo had been invited for dinner. Keate was unprepared for the "ease and gentleness of his manners, [which] perfectly astonished" him. His description of Lee Boo upon the occasion of this first meeting is the most complete one we have:

> He was dresst as an Englishman, excepting that he wore his hair in the fashion of his country; appeared to be between nineteen and twenty years of age, was of a middling stature, and had a countenance so strongly marked with sensibility and good-humour, that it instantly prejudiced every one in his favour; and this countenance was enlivened by eyes so quick and intelligent, that they might really be said to announce his thoughts and conceptions without the aid of language.

Had Keate himself been among those shipwrecked in Pelew he would have noted that Lee Boo was not alone in possessing the skills of speaking with the eyes. Whereas at this early period of his stay in London, Lee Boo may have expressed more with his eyes than with his voice, he "seemed to comprehend the greater part of what was said to him, especially, having the Captain by him to explain whatever he did not clearly comprehend." Keate's description of Lee Boo's conduct at dinner continues:

> he was lively and pleasant, and had a politeness without form or restraint, which appeared to be the result of natural good-breeding. As I chanced to sit near him at table, I paid him a great deal of attention, which he seemed to be very sensible of.

Keate goes on to explain that many questions were put to Captain Wilson concerning the Pelew Islands and Lee Boo's people. When, in the course of his descriptions, the captain referred to the manner in which the Pelew Islanders tied up their hair before going into battle, "Lee Boo, who fully understood what his friend was explaining, very obligingly, and unasked, untied his own, and threw it into the form Captain Wilson had been describing."

Concluding his remarks concerning this first meeting, Keate wrote of Lee Boo:

> there was in all his deportment, such affability, and propriety of behaviour, that when he took leave of the company, there was hardly any one present who did not feel a satisfaction in having had an interview with him.

A few days later Keate visited the Wilsons at Rotherhithe, where he found Lee Boo reading at the window. Lee Boo greeted him warmly as a true friend and the two engaged in a

> good deal of conversation [in which] we mutually managed to be pretty well understood by each other; he seemed to be pleased with everything about him, and said, "All fine country, fine street, fine coach, and house upon house up to sky," putting alternately one hand above another, by which I found (their own habitations being all on the ground) that every separate story of our buildings he at that time considered as a distinct house.

If Lee Boo could speak so eloquently of what he had seen in Rotherhithe, what would he think of that greater London on the other side of the river? Exposure to that far more metropolitan mass of humanity had, in the interest of his health, been withheld until now. But the time was at hand for Lee Boo to meet the directors of the East India Company and to do this he had to be taken across the Thames into the heart of London. Whatever the hazards, the rewards were too tempting to withhold any longer from someone so curious and so appreciative of all that he saw and learned.

13

LEE BOO'S LONDON

A T "ELEVEN IN THE FORENOON" on Tuesday, 20 July 1784, the directors of the East India Company met at East India House on Leadenhall Street. London newspapers of mid-July announced the meeting but did not report, as Keate does, that Lee Boo "was introduced to several of the Directors of the India Company."

Whether summoned to provide a personal accounting for the loss of the *Antelope,* or voluntarily visiting some of the directors, it behooved Captain Wilson to put in an appearance. With Lee Boo by his side, the captain had the opportunity to present living evidence of the people who had befriended the men of the *Antelope* after it struck the reefs of Pelew. Lee Boo's presence may well have softened the blow.

Company protocol prescribed that Captain Wilson call at India House dressed in his best uniform: coat of blue cloth with white velvet cuffs and lapels laced with gold embroidery, white waistcoat, and white breeches, "with buttons of yellow metal, engraved with the Company's crest." He was also required to carry his sword.

Lacking similar rules setting forth what a visiting island prince should wear, we can only picture Lee Boo as Miss Keate remembered him, wearing a pink coat with green collar and brown lapels, breeches, striped waistcoat, and black necktie neatly knotted in a small bow.

Two so splendidly attired gentlemen would, of course, ride rather than walk the considerable distance to India House. Although a coach could be ferried across the Thames it was less bother to cross by

LEE BOO'S LONDON

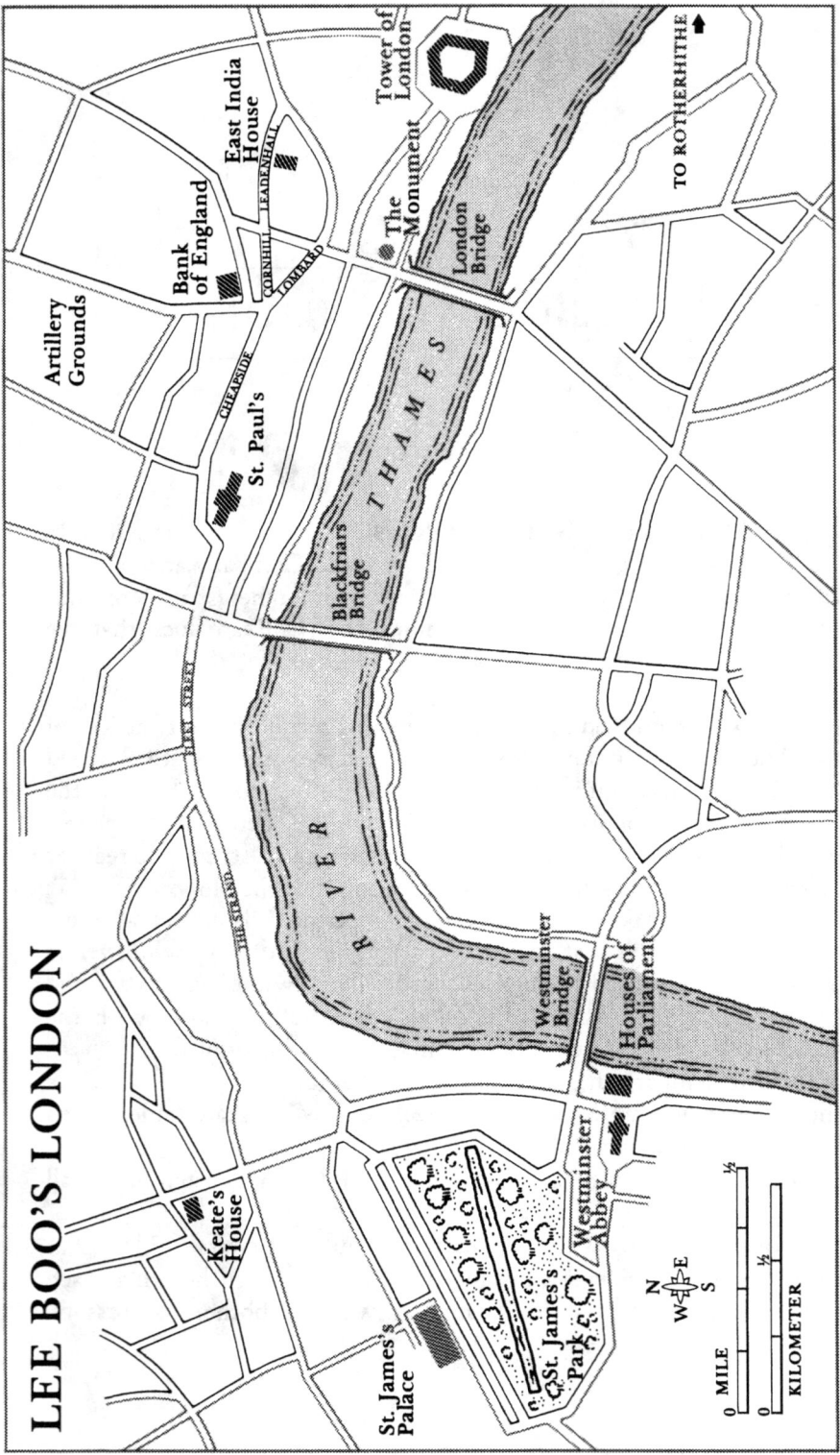

TO ROTHERHITHE

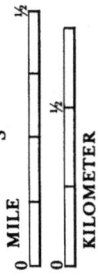

Tower of London

The Monument

London Bridge

East India House

LEADENHALL

Bank of England

CORNHILL

LOMBARD

Artillery Grounds

CHEAPSIDE

St. Paul's

Blackfriars Bridge

R I V E R   T H A M E S

FLEET STREET

THE STRAND

Keate's House

Westminster Bridge

Houses of Parliament

St. James's Palace

St. James's Park

Westminster Abbey

N
W   E
S

MILE
0   ½
KILOMETER
0   ½

bridge, and the closest bridge to Rotherhithe was London Bridge. So Lee Boo crossed the bridge made famous by the nursery rhyme. If the bridge showed no signs of falling down, neither did it show him any of the houses that had once clung to its sides as if there were not space enough in the city. Once across, on entering the "real" London, Lee Boo saw, first of all, the Monument—the 202-foot-high column—commemorating the Great Fire that left most of the city in ashes in 1666. But that was the more fragile, rat-infested city in which Dick Whittington made his fortune. What greeted Lee Boo was a newer, more solid city, but still the historic inner city, the commercial city of banks and merchant establishments, the home of Lloyd's of London, Lloyd's *Register,* and the East India Company.

Fronting on the south side of Leadenhall Street, the Honourable Company's building was well located. Surprisingly, though, it was no more than seventy feet wide, commanding hardly enough space to accommodate the coaches of the twenty-four directors or even the thirteen required for a quorum. On the days the directors met, their private carriages, guarded by their nattily dressed footmen and butlers, left little space for any of the one hundred fifty "officers" or for Captain Wilson, who would dismiss his hired coach here and usher Lee Boo into the building.

The East India House of 1784 was a four-storied building without outward pretensions, but it extended some three hundred feet back from the street and contained more rooms than Lee Boo could have dreamed of—meeting rooms, committee rooms, numerous offices, a "Sale Room," a large hall, even a courtyard and a garden. There were also warehouses to the rear. Inside this labyrinth of rooms Lee Boo saw clerks working by candlelight, messengers and errand boys scurrying from room to room, and the dispatch writers who wrote the messages carried by the *Antelope.* Here, too, he met the directors, some of them titled, some of them doubling as Members of Parliament, including the Honourable Paul Lemesurier who had been elected a director in June 1784 and was also M.P. for Wilson's home district of Southwark.

Having met the East India Company directors, Lee Boo was now to be "gradually shewn most of the public buildings in the different quarters of the town," one of which was dominated by the Tower of London. Just a short walk from India House, the tower loomed in sight most of the way for anyone walking down to the river. Once a royal residence, it had stood fortress-like for some seven hundred years, guarding the southeastern entrance to the city. Between India House and the tower, the remnants of the much older Roman Wall would be passed and doubtless commented on, but not for long. The Tower of London—the White Tower with its four high turrets—commanded total attention. An architectural gem in itself, it housed not only the Crown Jewels but also the Royal Mint. Lee Boo would now learn where the coins that jingled in his pockets came from.

Yet neither the coin of the realm nor the jewels of royalty would have held Lee Boo's attention if, once inside, he saw the Armouries with their resplendent displays of swords, staffs, small arms, and weapons of every description, not to mention the armor designed to cover and protect man and horse alike. Within the walls huge black ravens, then as now, lived their protected lives in keeping with the legend that in their absence the tower would fall. It was no legend that this had been, until quite recently, a prison where even the most illustrious prisoners lost their heads on the executioner's block; graffiti were there to testify to time spent in thick-walled cells waiting for the axe to fall.

On the north bank of the Thames, at the Tower of London, one is within sight of Rotherhithe. It may have been the last sight that many a prisoner had before being taken, by boat, into the tower at Traitors' Gate. But freemen, like Captain Wilson and Lee Boo, could make the short trip across the river and downstream to Rotherhithe at any time. In the manner of taxi drivers, watermen were always on hand to row passengers across the Thames from river stairs to river stairs, at no particular risk to boat or passengers. The risks were greater farther upstream at London Bridge, where the river, rushing with the outgoing tide, plunged between the bridge supports like water over a dam. The force of falling water had carved a deep pool downriver from the bridge, where the largest ships could berth and smaller vessels swarmed in attendance. A waterman had to be expert in navigating through this floating morass and, as Lee Boo was to learn, some of the boatmen who made their living ferrying people across the Thames were more expert on the river than in the water.

Lee Boo saw a waterman being carried away from the river where it was presumed he had drowned. The incident is related in *The History of Prince Lee Boo,* an anonymous chapbook that is largely based on Keate's *Account.* Henry Wilson is said to have taken the occasion to lecture Lee Boo on the proper ways to revive people taken from the water at the point of drowning—like the hapless boatman. Wilson, according to this account, told Lee Boo of the Humane Society that maintained "a house on the banks of the river Thames where drowned persons may be taken, and where people are constantly ready to assist in their recovery." The captain's lecture included things that must not be done—bleeding, for example, "unless by the direction of a Physician," and "the body is never to be held up by the heels"; nor should one "despair of success, even though the patient give no signs of returning life for four hours after you have begun." Lee Boo, according to the anonymous author, was so concerned for the fate of the unconscious waterman he had seen carried away that Captain Wilson "went himself to the house where the body had been carried, and found that after some hours care, the man had shewed signs of returning life, and was then fast recovering." Upon being given this information, Lee Boo was delighted "and told the good news to every person in the house successively, that they might share in his satisfaction."

Such incidental observations of life in London, however satisfying, or even salutary, would not suffice to make of Lee Boo the Englishman his father hoped for. Nor would guided tours of the city. In other words, it was time for Lee Boo to be enrolled in a school. And he was. Without telling us where, Keate merely assures us that Lee Boo went "every day to an academy at Rotherhithe, to be instructed in reading and writing, which he was himself eager to attain, and most assiduous in learning."

Many academies of that time were operated by one or two people who took a small group of children of various ages into their home. Lee Boo may have been enrolled in such a school. Whatever the arrangements, they would have been made by the Wilsons, probably through their contacts at St. Mary's Rotherhithe. There was, in fact, a school building just across the street from the church. According to a memorial plate in St. Mary's, it was established by Peter Hills, "who . . . with Robert Bell, gave the Free School and £3 per annum to the master to teach eight children, sons of seafaring men." Lee Boo might well have qualified to enter the portals of this school, which still stands on St. Mary Church Street, with statues of a schoolboy and a schoolgirl charmingly adorning the front at the second-floor level, just as they were when Lee Boo saw them.

What Lee Boo studied is less a mystery than where. Most schools offered little more than the instruction in reading and writing he

received. Spelling and grammar were learned by rote as part of reading. Writing was the art of penmanship, which Lee Boo must have
mastered early for people were soon collecting his autograph. He may
have learned some arithmetic and he may even have picked up a Latin
phrase or two while listening to his mates at recitation. The curricu-
lum varied somewhat from school to school and from place to place as
doubtless did the quality of the teaching. Most schools could afford to
provide only the three Rs with the emphasis on reading, else what was
a Bible for. There is also evidence that reading was not just the province of the elite. Visitors from France and Germany noted newspapers,
pamphlets, and even books could be purchased on the streets of London, that there were libraries, and that many people were seen to be
reading.

In all, Lee Boo attended school for no more than five months, during which time, according to Keate,

> his whole deportment, whilst there, was so engaging, that
> it not only gained him the esteem of the gentleman under
> whose tuition he was placed, but also the affection of his
> young companions; [and] in the hours of recess, when he
> returned to the Captain's house, he amused the whole fam-
> ily by his vivacity, noticing every particularity he saw in
> any of his school-fellows, with great good-humour mim-
> icking their different manners . . .

Lee Boo's skills at mimicry must have reminded Henry Wilson of
Raa Kook and Arra Kooker, and perhaps Lee Boo had these two
uncles in mind when he told Keate that he was thinking of establishing his own school "when he returned to Pelew, and should be
thought very wise when he taught the great people their letters."

For now, Lee Boo was content to be a member of the Wilson family. As the novelty of his visit wore thin there were doubtless familial
adjustments to be made. Whereas it was not inappropriate for him to
refer to Henry Wilson as "Captain," Lee Boo's practice of referring to
Christiana Wilson as "Mother" was questioned. But Lee Boo would
not be dissuaded by those who thought he should address the captain's
wife as "Mrs. Wilson." To this suggestion, Keate observed, Lee Boo
always replied, "No, no—Mother, Mother." Yet he "adapted himself
very readily to whatever he saw were the customs of the country."

The first of these, rising at daybreak with the rest of the family, would have been no problem for Lee Boo, for whom early risings had been a lifetime practice. But the practice of relieving oneself and depositing waste in a portable chamber pot inside the house may well have been a much more difficult adjustment for Lee Boo, as well as the practice of conducting morning ablutions with a pitcher of water and a basin. Although he would already have adjusted to regular meals at stipulated times aboard ship, the timing of the principal "evening" meal in the late afternoon may have seemed as early to Lee Boo as it does to us of the present day. But since it was the most important family activity of the day, it was conducted at a leisurely pace, beginning with grace and extending well into the evening, with much talk. The typical meal would have consisted of bread, butter, meat, fruit in season, probably a vegetable, and possibly some wine. On occasion there would also have been a special high tea during which, so long as Lee Boo was considered a guest rather than a member of the family, he would have been seated closest to the host and served first, as was the custom of that time and remains the custom today. Lee Boo would also have retired to his bed by nine o'clock, in keeping with the custom of the family, and in London in July it would hardly have been dark. No precious daylight hours would have been wasted, and no precious candles needlessly burned.

At home with the Wilsons and in the company of others, Lee Boo demonstrated "an ardent desire of information and thankfully received it," as Keate illustrates with the following anecdote:

> I was one day in company with him, where a young lady sat down to the harpsichord, to see how he was affected with music; he appeared greatly surprized that the instrument could throw out so much sound; it was opened, to let him see its interior construction, he pored over it with great attention, watching how the jacks were moved, and seemed far more disposed to puzzle out the means which produced the sounds, than to attend to the music that was playing.

That same evening Lee Boo was asked if he would sing a song for this intimate audience. When he obliged, the guests, including Keate, found his notes too "harsh." However, when he later learned some two or three English songs, "his voice," according to Keate, "appeared by no means inharmonious." Shades of little Will Cobbledick! How pleased Abba Thulle would have been.

And how pleased Abba Thulle and the older *rubak*s of Belau would have been to learn of Lee Boo's reaction to the numerous beggars he saw on the streets of London. To quote Keate:

> If he saw the *young* asking for relief, he would rebuke them with what little *English* he was master of, telling them, it was a shame to beg when they were able to work; but the intreaties of *old age* he could never withstand, saying "must give poor old man—old man no able to work."

Lee Boo had great fondness for young Harry Wilson, and although Harry was a few years younger, they became good friends. In Keate's words, "the young Prince looked on him as a brother, and, in his leisure hours from the Academy, was happy to find him a companion to converse with, to exercise the throwing of the spear, or partake in any innocent recreation."

So close had Lee Boo become to both Wilsons, father and son, that when the least friction arose between them he was distraught. On the one such occasion mentioned by Keate, young Harry had failed to deliver a message for his father because he was so engrossed in throwing spears with Lee Boo that he forgot. When the captain returned at the end of the day and learned that the message had not been delivered, he upbraided his son in front of Lee Boo, who left the room in despair. Later, when Harry found Lee Boo and returned with him, the following scene ensued, as recorded by Keate's possibly overly sentimental pen:

> Lee Boo took his young friend by the hand, and on entering into the parlour went up to the father, and laying hold of his hand joined it with that of his son, and pressing them together, dropped over both those tears of sensibility, which his affectionate heart could not on the occasion suppress.

On another occasion when Henry Wilson was ill with severe headaches, Lee Boo sat by the side of his bed as a nurse might, pulling aside the curtain from time to time to see if the captain was resting comfortably. Such acts of compassion and sincere regard are mentioned frequently by Keate, who not only observed Lee Boo with the family in Rotherhithe and in the homes of mutual friends, but in his own home at No. 8 Charlotte Street.

Mr. and Mrs. George Keate, with their daughter Georgiana Jane, lived in a fashionable section of London to which Keate had moved after his marriage to Jane Catherine Hudson at the rather advanced age of thirty-nine. As a bachelor, from the age of twenty-one he had lived in the Inner Temple, where he had embarked upon the study of law so that as a man of property he might be better able to handle his own affairs. But in those days, as throughout his life, he was more interested in literature, drama, and all of the arts than he was in law. His poem *The Temple-Student* conveys his feelings:

> A breakfast first of *Law* I stuff in,
> Then swallow quick my tea and muffin,
> With ink-horn trim'd and quill cut taper,
> And note-book rul'd, and blotting paper,
> Looking as solemn as a Judge,
> Thus arm'd, to WESTMINSTER, I
> trudge.

But he would rather have been going to nearby Nando's Coffee House, where law students sought refuge and refreshment:

> Quite jaded out, I march to Nando's
> And look as grave as any man does,
> Shake hands with friends I wish to see,
> And take my sober pot of tea;
> Touch the light topics of the day,
> Ask for my letters?—What's the play?

Keate had reason to ask for his letters, for he would give Nando's Coffee House as his address. In fact, he gave that address to no less a personage than Voltaire, with whom he had established a long friendship during his visit to Geneva while taking the "Grand Tour" of Europe. His tour must have been a leisurely one, for he lingered in the company of Voltaire, who was at that time in Switzerland, long enough to write a serious work entitled *A Short Account of the Ancient History,*

Present Government and Laws of the Republic of Geneva. The book was much more modest in size and scope than its title might indicate, but it was well received and approved by Voltaire himself who had it translated into French, although that translation was never published.

Keate's circle of friends in London reflected his varied interests. Both before and after his marriage he was popular with a group of ladies of polite society including the Duchess of Portland, Lady Hervey, Mrs. Elizabeth Montagu, and a Mrs. Delany. (Fanny Burney, friend to the most prominent figures of her day, also knew Keate but said she found him dull and egocentric.) Among men, Keate was a close friend of Edward Young, another writer, and was well known to two luminaries in the field of drama: George Coleman the elder, and David Garrick, who had already established himself as the greatest actor of his day. His friends in high political places included Brook Watson who was to become Lord Mayor of London. His friendships with sea captains in addition to Henry Wilson included, at a later date, Captain William Bligh, in whose honor he wrote a poem; he even included Bligh in his will.

Another friend of Keate, Robert Adam, was among London's leading architects at the time. It was Adam whom Keate called upon to improve his house on Charlotte Street. Adam designed a ceiling for Keate's dining room and redid the interiors of two other rooms. This was the house that Lee Boo saw when he was taken to visit the Keates on at least one occasion during the summer and fall of 1784.

The most advantageous route to the Keates' home required Lee Boo and the Wilsons to cross the Thames by way of Blackfriars Bridge. The newest of London's three bridges, it provided an unparalleled view of St. Paul's with its huge dome. On the north side of the Thames their route followed Fleet Street, past Keate's favorite coffee house and the Royal Courts of Justice before entering the Strand. Approaching Charing Cross, they would pass the Adam brothers' imposing Adelphi building before turning north along St. Martin's Lane to Tottenham Court Road, Great Russell Street, and finally Charlotte Street.

This route exposed Lee Boo to some of London's most colorful streets—stone-paved streets congested with all sorts of vehicles, coaches of every description, carts, and wagons, their iron-rimmed wheels clanging out a warning to pedestrians, who moved just out of the way along elevated footpaths. And here and there was a sedan chair, the box-like compartment for a single passenger borne by two men.

It was also a route populated by a slow-moving parade of London's street people, including vendors and hawkers ringing their bells, blowing their trumpets, or calling out to advertise their wares: clothing, oranges, apples, lavender, newspapers, and even printed "street ballads." In places along the route buskers provided entertainment in the form of songs, dances, and puppetry. One wonders if Lee Boo might have thought some of the characters he saw in the streets more intriguing than the polite company he encountered when, with the Wilsons, he reached the home of George Keate and was admitted by one of the servants.

In addition to Lee Boo and the Wilsons, the Keates had invited Dr. and Mrs. Carmichael Smyth. Once the guests had been made comfortable, conversation turned to the arts as befitted a London dilettante who had his own private collections of things fine, rare, and exotic. Not wishing to leave Lee Boo out of the discussion, Keate recognized that his island guest might never have seen a painted portrait, although he must have known that Lee Boo had seen Arthur Devis busy sketching aboard the *Oroolong* and in China. Perhaps he felt that a black-and-white sketch could not compare to a painting in vivid colors. In any case, Keate produced a miniature of himself, handed it to Lee Boo, and noted his reaction:

> he took it in his hand and instantly darting his eyes toward me, called out "*Misser* Keate—very nice, very good." The Captain then asking him if he understood what it signified? he replied, "Lee Boo understand well—that *Misser* Keate die, this *Misser* Keate live!"

Keate was prompted to observe, "A treatise on the utility and intent of portrait painting could not have better defined the art than this little sentence."

Keate also recorded an incident when Lee Boo came very close to committing what would have been a faux pas for a well-mannered Englishman. Christiana Wilson, sitting across the table from Lee Boo, asked him for some cherries that he was in the best position to pass to her. Suspecting that he was about to do this with his fingers, she gestured to him, whereupon, as Keate reports, "He instantly resorted to a spoon; but, sensible he had discovered a little unpoliteness, his countenance was in a moment suffused with a blush that visibly forced itself through his dark complexion." Lee Boo apparently redeemed himself later, when another guest excused herself from the room feeling faint "from the heat of the day." Lee Boo was "distressed" by the incident, "and seeing her appear again when we were summoned to tea, his enquiries, and particular attention to her, as strongly marked his tenderness, as it did his good-breeding." All in all it was a successful outing; the Wilsons must have been proud of Lee Boo's progress in English propriety, and George Keate must have been further inspired to undertake putting into print what he was learning of Lee Boo, the people of Pelew, and the wreck of the *Antelope.*

How different a book it would have been had Lee Boo himself written it! Whereas Keate was enamored of the islands he never saw and of the Belauan people as seen in the person of their young ambassador, Lee Boo saw London as no Englishman could see it. What a Londoner took for granted, Lee Boo found every bit as exotic and intriguing as his islands must have seemed to Keate.

> The river, the shipping, and the bridges he was forcibly struck with; and he was several times taken to see the guards exercised and march in St. James's park, a sight which gratified him much, everything that was military greatly engaging his attention.

The river, the shipping, and the bridges, so lightly passed over by Keate, whose eyes had long since been sated by sights seen throughout a London lifetime, were visual feasts to the visiting Lee Boo. His book might have taken a place in the literature already enriched by visitors to London. His impressions, could he have put them on canvas, might have found a space in some distant gallery, thereby calling Englishmen home to "Father Thames," the river that attracted so many artists to its banks. No wonder Lee Boo was "forcibly struck" with what visitors saw then and may still see today, although the Thames at London is no longer the crowded conduit of commerce it once was.

One might wonder how Lee Boo reacted to the river people who abounded on the Thames, some rarely seen away from their boats, others hidden in shadowy places along the shores. Some pursued honorable lives of toil on the river; others, less honorable, were imprisoned in hulks awaiting "transportation" to labor on foreign soil. There were river pirates and their collaborators—the "light horse-men"; there were mudlarks who worked at the sides of the river at low tide, picking up items that had been thrown from ships by their accomplices. From the riverside at Rotherhithe, from the bridges, or when crossing the Thames by boat, Lee Boo might have seen some of these furtive characters at work—perhaps on one of his trips to St. James's Park.

Crossing Westminster Bridge en route to the park, Lee Boo saw the stately Houses of Parliament and just beyond the bridge, Westminster Abbey. Perhaps St. James's seemed all the more serene, nestled so near such mighty buildings. Although its contours have changed somewhat over the years, St. James's remains much the same green sanctuary that Lee Boo saw. Only the customs of the people have changed. The ladies and gentlemen that Lee Boo saw promenading on the Mall were dressed in the finest garments that money could buy. The ladies some-times wore masks as they mingled with the less fortunate who walked up and down the Mall and in and out of the park. The royal palace adjacent to the park added glamor to the scene. The park was techni-cally the property of the king, and although the most pompous of the parading aristocrats may have preferred it to themselves, it was open to the public—and the public came in droves. This was a most demo-cratic gathering place, a place where Captain Wilson could take his own royal visitor to see a cross section of Londoners at leisure.

Within St. James's Park, Lee Boo saw the swans, pelicans, and ducks that abounded in and around the pond. But the "sport" of turn-ing dogs loose on the ducks had been outlawed, as had such earlier "amusements" as pitting dog against dog or dogs against chained bulls and bears. Pet dogs like Sailor of the *Antelope* were treated with more dignity in this almost pastoral setting, where milk from grazing cows was sold by the cup.

But St. James's was hardly a country pasture. Another visitor, a few years after Lee Boo, described grass there "of incomparable beauty [with grass walks] smoothed and made resplendent by means of a large stone rolled over the ground [where one] can play at bowls upon them as on a billiard table." Lee Boo's appreciation of such delicate smooth-ness underfoot was surely just as keen; he was, after all, in shoes, which could hardly have been comfortable for him.

On these same walkways and greenswards, Lee Boo saw the marching guards who "gratified him much." His fascination can best be appreciated if the scene is brought forward two hundred years and transferred to Buckingham Palace where crowds of spectators gather to see the changing of the guard. In Lee Boo's time this colorful exercise was viewed at the Palace of St. James, where King George III was in residence. Some of His Majesty's troops also "exercised and marched" in the park. Observers of the time mention that flogging was administered in the park when required by military discipline. Perhaps Lee Boo saw nothing of that more sobering side of military life, without which the bright uniforms and crisp precision drill would have captured his fancy as much as that of any young man who has marched off to the beat of fife and drum.

But Lee Boo's reaction to the single most spectacular event during his stay in London showed that he marched to the beat of a different drummer. On 15 September 1784, having himself advertised the occasion in the London newspapers, Vincenzo Lunardi rose above the city in an air balloon—the first such ascent from English soil. Keate records that Lee Boo saw the balloon rising in the air, but had not been taken to join the Prince of Wales and thousands of others who thronged to the Artillery Grounds at Moorefields to see the takeoff.

A native of Lucca, Italy, Lunardi was in London as secretary to the Neapolitan ambassador to the Court of St. James. He must have been a showman for he had all of London anticipating the event and charged admission to the multitude of people who entered the Artillery Grounds to witness the launching, reportedly the largest gathering of spectators in London's history to that time. It was exactly the sort of thing that Captain Wilson would have kept Lee Boo away from. But the balloon had been on exhibit prior to the flight, and it is possible that the captain had arranged for Lee Boo to see it. According to *The London Post and Advertiser,* it measured 33 feet in diameter and 102 feet in circumference. The gondola hanging beneath the balloon, described by Lunardi as the "gallery," contained four paddles that he intended to use in "rowing" through the air. Lunardi was originally to have ascended with another "pilot," but last minute delays and a crowd unwilling to wait forced him to take off alone. Alone, that is, except for a menagerie of small animals including a cat, a dog, and a pigeon. When the balloon rose above the crowd Lunardi rowed his oars so vigorously that one of them broke. In another mishap, Lunardi stepped on and broke open the birdcage, thus releasing the pigeon, which promptly flew back to the starting point where the crowd plucked its feathers for souvenirs. Meanwhile, as he drifted over London, Lunardi waved a flag to assure the people below that there was indeed a human aboard. His flight ended north of London, among astonished farmers in the Hertfordshire countryside at Standon, where a sixteen-year-old girl named Elizabeth Brett was the first to have the courage to help him with his ropes. Although he had gone just a mere twenty-five miles from London, he had risen to such heights that the poor cat and dog nearly froze to death. The flight was a success, and for a time Lunardi was "London's darling." Besant describes his flight as one of the three most important events of 1784 as far as Londoners were concerned.

Lee Boo, however, was unimpressed. When Keate visited him in Rotherhithe on the day of the great event and asked for his reaction, he may have been disappointed to find that Lee Boo "thought it a very foolish thing to ride in the air like a bird, when a man could travel so much more pleasantly on horseback or in a coach." Keate attempts to explain Lee Boo's apparent indifference by saying "He was either not aware of the difficulty or hazard of the enterprize, or it is not improbable that a man flying up through the clouds suspended at a balloon might have been ranked by him as a common occurrence in a country which was perpetually spreading before him so many subjects of surprize." Yet Lee Boo was not the only one who was unimpressed. Sir Joseph Banks, more interested in the scientific than the spectacular, was disppointed in the results and wrote to Sir Charles Blagden that he thought Lunardi had not made "one observation worth a groat." Horace Walpole, whose letters historians are fond of quoting, wrote, "I smile at the adoration paid to these aerial Quixotes; and reflect, that as formerly men were admired for their courage in risking their lives in order to destroy others; now they are worshipped for venturing their necks . . . I smile too at the stupidity that pays a guinea for being allowed to see what any man may see by holding up his head at the sky."

Presumably Walpole would have admired Lee Boo for keeping his feet on the ground, as it were, and not letting himself be carried away by events that were not germane to his mission in England. And Keate was probably right: Lee Boo may have already had a surfeit of surprising events that he had either seen, had described to him by the Wilsons, or read about in the newspapers. For example, the king was on view in the area of Lee Boo's favorite park when, on 20 August, his splendidly gilded coach pulled by eight equally splendid horses carried His Majesty to Parliament. The newspapers of that date explained that a message was "sent to the House of Commons commanding their attendance in the House of Peers [where the King in] his royal robes . . . sat on the throne with the usual solemnity [and gave the] Royal assent" to various acts with respect to the killing of game, raising rates of postage, and an act repealing the duties on raw silk.

Again, on 22 September a grand procession of coaches passed St. James's Park carrying "the Nobility, Foreign Ministers, and other persons of Distinction" on their way to the palace to "compliment Their Majesties on the Occasion" of the anniversary of their coronation. Even if Lee Boo were not at St. James's Park that day, he must have been aware that "At one O'clock the Guns in the Park and at the Tower [of London] were fired; and in the Evening there were illuminations [fireworks], and other public Demonstrations of Joy." Had he missed any of this excitement, the Wilsons need only have counseled patience, for the same events were to be repeated on 10 October in observance of the "Anniversary of the King's Accession to the Throne."

Events that were the talk of the town on both sides of the Thames would not have escaped mention in the Wilson household. What Lee Boo could not witness he could hear discussed at home or at school. Special occasions and historical holidays would be explained. One wonders, in this context, what impressions he gained from Guy Fawkes Day when, on 5 November, the anniversary of the Gunpowder Plot was observed. How confusing to immortalize a man who carried gunpowder into the Houses of Parliament with intent to commit arson. A testing day, perhaps, for Captain Wilson's powers of explanation.

By contrast, 9 November, Lord Mayor's Day, was a more propitious day for Captain Wilson's tutelage of Lee Boo. Crystal clear in its intent, it was, to quote Besant, "one of the principal civic festivals." The new Lord Mayor of London, having taken his oath of office, was feted by the city with lavish pageantry. Had Lee Boo lived on in London he would have seen his friend Brook Watson at the center of the festival as Lord Mayor. Watson was quite a character, the subject of caricaturists and political cartoonists who could not resist such an obvious target as his wooden leg.

Born in England and orphaned at the age of ten, Watson was sent across the Atlantic to live with relatives in Boston. Five years later he obtained work aboard a vessel trading to the West Indies. Stopping at Havana, Watson took a swim in the harbor where he was attacked by a shark and lost a leg before being rescued. Once restored to health and equipped with a crutch, he found his way back to Boston only to learn that his one relative had disappeared without a trace. He somehow found his way to Nova Scotia and won a reputation as a trustworthy and ambitious young man before returning to London where he entered business, prospered, and was elected a Member of Parliament in April 1784, just three months before Lee Boo arrived in England. How the biographers and novelists of the period resisted Watson's life story is a mystery, but at least one serious artist gave it his attention: the American John Singleton Copley. Copley completed his painting, *Watson and the Shark,* in 1775 while visiting London. It was placed on exhibit in 1778 and may well have been seen by Lee Boo.

Galleries were numerous enough to be seen not only in the city but in suburban Bermondsey. In fact, such a large room "hung around with paintings" was in Bermondsey Spa, near Rotherhithe, and at the peak of its popularity when Lee Boo was there. An anonymous visitor of the time "found the entrance presents a vista between trees hung with lamps—blue, red, green, and white." The room hung with paintings opened off the end of the walk. Elsewhere in the park-like area, music was provided, sometimes emanating from hidden places to reach the ear as if by magic. But sounds of a very different sort came from the nearby "fortress or castle," where on "public nights" fireworks simulated a very picturesque "siege."

How much or how little Lee Boo saw of the pleasure gardens Keate does not record. Doubtless the Wilsons thought most of them, including the two largest, Vauxhall and Ranelagh, too crowded for the comfort and safety of their ward. But we do know that he had his fill of the quieter gardens and orchards of Rotherhithe. These could be magic places too, with arbors, bowers, and gazebos. There were hothouses, glass-roofed conservatories, and backyard "fruit walls." From these special places and from the orchards came the fruit that Lee Boo ate and saved the seeds of—apples, peaches, pears, grapes, plums, apricots, nectarines, even oranges, and, of course, cherries. (There is still a Cherry Garden Street and a Cherry Garden Stairs in the area.) Whatever Lee Boo may have thought of England's flowers compared to those of his islands, he would have noted how much they were appreciated by Londoners. Even the more prosaic vegetable gardens of Paradise Row provided the Wilson home with wholesome greens and herbs, as well as ample quantities of beans and peas, some of which, in the fall, would be saved for the next year's planting.

In the end the seeds that Lee Boo saved became symbols of his attainments. He had sought items that he could carry home almost as if his return would be in as small a vessel as the one he had left in. Keate often assures us that he was serious about it, that he was "an attentive observer of the plants and fruit-trees [and] appeared, in viewing objects, to consider how far they might be rendered useful in his own country." He "talked frequently [to Keate and the Wilsons] of the things he should then persuade the King to alter or adopt." But he did not covet material things that would be impractical to import to his distant homeland. Seeds would suffice, but those he had ready for his return, along with the ideas he hoped to plant among his people, were never to reach his islands.

The *Warley*. Captain Henry Wilson's ship, the Indiaman *Warley*, sailing on the Thames near Rotherhithe after returning from the voyage to China in which the French fleet was encountered at Pulo Auro, 1804. Artist unknown, but the painting may well have been commissioned by Wilson himself. (Courtesy of the Trustees of the National Maritime Museum, London)

(Inset) Memorial tablet inside the church, honoring Lee Boo, Abba Thulle, and the people of "Pelew. (Photo by Aaron Photographic, London)

St. Mary's, Rotherhithe, c. 1818 and as Lee Boo saw it, with ship masts clearly visible on the Thames. (Courtesy of Southwark Local Studies Library, London)

Rupack Street, Rotherhithe. The street sign appears on the side of the corner pub—The Neptune—with St. Mary's Church in the background. (Author's photo)

Lunardi's "Grand English Air Balloon" as seen by Lee Boo and all of London on the first such flight in England, 15 September 1784. (Courtesy of the Trustees of the Science Museum, London)

Miss Keate's portrait of Lee Boo, reportedly drawn from memory some fifteen months after his death and showing him as he dressed in London. (Original in Southwark Local Studies Library, Harvard Library, London)

Lee Boo

Lee Boo's signature, above, as found pasted to his portrait in a copy of Keate's *Account* once owned by Captain A. W. F. Fuller. (Courtesy of Bishop Museum, Honolulu)

Lee Boo's tomb in St. Mary's Churchyard, Rotherhithe, London. The weeping elm that served as sentinel for so many years is no more, but a new tree has been planted by a caring parish and Brook Watson's epitaph for Lee Boo, as inscribed on the top of the tomb, has been restored. (Author's photo, 1961)

AN
ACCOUNT
OF THE
PELEW ISLANDS,
SITUATED IN THE
WESTERN PART OF THE PACIFIC OCEAN.

COMPOSED FROM
THE JOURNALS AND COMMUNICATIONS
OF
CAPTAIN HENRY WILSON,
AND SOME OF HIS OFFICERS,
WHO, IN AUGUST 1783, WERE THERE SHIPWRECKED,
IN
THE ANTELOPE,
A PACKET BELONGING TO THE HONOURABLE EAST INDIA COMPANY.

BY
GEORGE KEATE, Esq. F.R.S. and S.A.

———————————

LONDON:
PRINTED FOR G. NICOL, BOOKSELLER TO HIS MAJESTY, PALL-MALL.
M.DCC.LXXXVIII.

Title page from Keate's *Account,*
first edition, published 1788.

Title page from *The History of Prince Lee Boo*—one of many editions widely published and consisting largely of excerpts from Keate's *Account.* In this "new" edition, the artist has given Lee Boo an English face, but gone are his English clothes. (Courtesy of the Pacific Collection, Hamilton Library, University of Hawaii)

Henry Wilson's tomb at St. Andrew's Church, Colyton. The captain had wanted to be buried next to Lee Boo at Rotherhithe; instead, both tombs stand apart in their respective churchyards. (Photo by S. Peacock)

Captain Henry Wilson. Portrait by John Russell. (Engraved by I. Heath for Keate's *Account*

Memorial Tablet for Captain Wilson in St. Andrew's Church. (Photo by S. Peacock)

Oroolong House in the village of Colyton where, during his short retirement, Captain Wilson remembered "Englishmen's Island" in Palau. At the time this photo was taken in 1983, the owners were Teacher-Artist Ann and Teacher-Magician Alan Jones. (Photo by S. Peacock)

14

THE LAST KNOT

LEE BOO'S line of memories stretched all the way back to Belau even though he had long since given up tying knots of remembrance for things seen and learned. His beloved Belau was never far from his mind, as evidenced by many of his London observations and comments. He had now been away from home for more than a year and yet, aside from his first days at sea aboard the *Oroolong,* he was never considered to be homesick, nor, as time went on in London, did he need a personal assistant. Boyam, the Malay who was taken from the Pelews to be his aide and interpreter, proved totally unsuited to this role, and Lee Boo requested that he be returned to his own country. He was replaced by the more companionable Tom Rose. The fact that Keate never mentions either of these men as being at Lee Boo's side in London must mean that the prince had become capable of handling his own affairs, including conversing with those around him in the Wilson household, at school, and at the various social functions to which he was taken.

When George Keate visited Rotherhithe in early December 1784, some five months after Lee Boo's arrival in England, he found that his young friend "was now proceeding with hasty strides in gaining the English language, and advancing so rapidly with his pen, that he would probably in a short time have written a very fine hand." In other words, Lee Boo had reached a point where he was ready to communicate as an Englishman and attempt to be the Englishman his father had hoped for. The time was surely not far distant when consideration would be given to his return to Belau.

But on 16 December Lee Boo "felt indisposed" and two days later Captain Wilson informed Keate that he was going to ask Dr. Smyth to have a look at him. The captain told Keate he feared the "eruption" that had broken out all over Lee Boo's body was the smallpox, "that very disease, which with so much caution had been guarded against."

In turning to James Carmichael Smyth, M.D., Henry Wilson was undoubtedly seeking the best medical help available to him. Dr. Smyth had taken his degree at Edinburgh in 1764 and was entered in the Royal College of Physicians the same year. In 1775 he was associated with Middlesex Hospital after study in France, Italy, and Holland. His hospital work and his work during epidemics aboard prison ships later won for him a remuneration of £5,000 voted by Parliament as a grant, and he was soon after appointed "Physician Extraordinary to the King."

George Keate accompanied Dr. Smyth to the Wilson home in Rotherhithe on the eighteenth. The doctor went in alone to Lee Boo's bedchamber and when he rejoined Keate and the Wilsons he reported to them that there was not the slightest doubt that it was indeed the smallpox, and there was very little hope for poor Lee Boo. The most that could be done was to make him comfortable and provide the appropriate medication, which the doctor was sending for. Henry Wilson wanted to be with Lee Boo, but the doctor forbade this because the captain had not had smallpox and the risk was too great.

When Keate returned the next day he found Mr. Sharp, the surgeon who had been with the *Antelope,* at the Wilsons' ministering to Lee Boo's needs. But, like Henry Wilson, Keate was not permitted to see the prince and had to join the vigil outside his room. Captain Wilson, Keate reports, never left the house.

How fortunate, in this time of ultimate misfortune, that Lee Boo had his old friend Mr. Sharp by his side. Sharp was apparently able to explain to Lee Boo why no one who had not previously had smallpox could be allowed to come in and see him, including the captain. Lee Boo, understanding that his affliction was contagious, would, from time to time, ask if the captain was all right. As it happened, Christiana Wilson was ill at this time too, though not with smallpox. Lee Boo, upon hearing this, exclaimed "What, Mother ill!" and got up from his bed and went to the door of her "apartment" to learn for himself that she was all right. Later, Lee Boo would call out to her from his bed, saying, "Lee Boo do well, Mother." But when he looked at himself in the mirror, "he shook his head, and turned away, as if disgusted at his own appearance, and told Mr. Sharp, that his father and mother much grieve, for they knew he was very sick."

On Thursday, 23 December, when, under happier circumstances the Wilson household would have been the scene of Christmas season activity, Lee Boo

> took Mr. Sharp by the hand, and, fixing his eyes steadfastly on him, with earnestness said: "Good friend, when you go to Pelew, tell Abba Thulle that Lee Boo take much drink to make small-pox go away, but he die;—that the Captain and Mother . . . very kind—all English very good men;—was much sorry that he could not speak to the King the number of fine things the English had got."

Then, as reported by Keate, he told Mr. Sharp that the presents he had been given should be distributed "among the Chiefs; and requested that very particular care might be taken of the blue glass barrels on pedestals, which he directed should be given to the King." Tom Rose, who heard these words, burst into tears. At this apparent sign of weakness, Lee Boo rebuked him, saying, "Why should he be crying so because Lee Boo die?"

On 27 December Lee Boo felt himself sinking and told Sharp he "was going away." These may have been the last words he ever spoke, although his mind remained "perfectly clear and calm to the last."

George Keate was not present at the Wilson home when Lee Boo died. He had kept a previous engagement to spend a week at the home of his friend Brook Watson. The sad, but hardly unexpected, news came to him in a letter from Dr. Smyth, who had called on Lee Boo every day.

> Monday, Dec. 27, 1784.
>
> My dear Sir,
>   It is an unpleasant task for me to be the herald of bad news, yet, according to my promise, I must inform you of the fate of poor Lee Boo, who died this morning without a groan, the vigour of his mind and body resisting to the very last.—Yesterday, the secondary fever coming on, he

was seized with a shivering fit, succeeded by head-ach, violent palpitation of the heart, anxiety, and difficult breathing; he again used the warm bath, which, as formerly, afforded him a temporary relief; he had a blister put on his back, which was as ineffectual as those applied to his legs. He expressed all his feelings to me, in the most forcible and pathetic manner, put my hand upon his heart, leant his head on my arm, and explained his uneasiness in breathing; but when I was gone he complained no more, shewing that he complained with a view to be relieved, not to be pitied. —In short, living or dying he has given me a lesson which I shall never forget; and surely, for patience and fortitude, he was an example worthy the imitation of a *Stoic!*—I did not see Captain WILSON when I called this morning, but the maid-servant was in tears, and every person in the family wore the face of grief; poor LEE BOO's affectionate temper made everyone look upon him as a brother or a child.— Compliments to the ladies, and to Mr. WATSON; who, I make no doubt, will all join in regretting the untimely end of our poor Prince.—From you, my friend, something more will be expected; and, though you cannot bring him back to life, you are called upon (particularly considering his great attachment to you) not to let the memory of so much virtue pass away unrecorded.—But I am interrupted in these melancholy reflections, and have only time to assure you of (what will never pass away but with myself) the sincere friendship of your affectionate, &c.

JA^s CARMICHAEL SMYTH.

By the time George Keate read this letter, Lee Boo had already been buried. The entry in the St. Mary's Parish Register for 29 December 1784 reads: "Prince Lee Boo buried from Captain Wilson's Paradise Row 20." (The "20" refers to Lee Boo's age.)

E. M. Forster would have us visualize a funeral that "all Rotherhithe attended [including] officials from London," but historians will be more comfortable with the Reverend Edward Beck's description:

Captain Wilson notified his death to the India House, and received orders to conduct his funeral with all proper decency. He was interred in Rotherhithe churchyard, the Captain and his brother attending. The young people of the academy were present, and a great concourse of parishioners thronged the church.

Although not specifically mentioned, one assumes that Mrs. Wilson must have been there, and young Harry too, unless "Mother" had not yet recovered from her own illness. Without George Keate in attendance, there was no one to record who was there from the *Antelope*. Sharp, for certain. Others? We do not know. Some would have been at sea, some at distant ports, and some may have found graves of their own.

Later, at the direction of the East India Company, Lee Boo's grave was covered by a tomb of quarried stone that in shape resembles a very large sea chest. It may be seen to the left of the entrance to St. Mary's Church.

Brook Watson composed the epitaph that was inscribed across the top of Lee Boo's tomb. This prominent Londoner, who figured in the beginning by introducing George Keate to Henry Wilson, had the last word for the prince from Pelew, as if Lee Boo's last knot of remembrance had been tied in stone:

To the Memory
of Prince Lee Boo,
A native of the Pelew, or Palos Islands;
and Son to Abba Thulle, Rupack or King
of the Island Coorooraa;
who departed this Life on the 27th of December 1784,
aged 20 Years;
This Stone is inscribed,
by the Honourable United East India Company,
as a Testimony of Esteem for the humane and kind Treatment
afforded by his Father to the Crew of their Ship
the *Antelope,* Captain Wilson,
which was wrecked off that Island
in the Night of the 9th of August 1783.

Stop, Reader, stop!—let Nature claim a Tear—
A Prince of Mine, Lee Boo, lies bury'd here.

15

McCLUER'S JOURNAL

IF BROOK WATSON wrote the epitaph for Lee Boo, George Keate wrote the eulogy. Heeding Dr. Smyth's admonition "not to let the memory of so much virtue pass unrecorded," Keate found ample words of praise for the lamented Lee Boo and completed his *Account of the Pelew Islands* by mid-1786.

Meanwhile, Henry Wilson had sailed again for China, this time as first mate on the *Earl Talbot*. Henry Junior was along as fifth mate—father and son together at least, even if the father was not the captain. We are not told whether Henry Wilson was demoted because of the loss of the *Antelope*, whether his status did not yet entitle him to captain one of the large Indiamen, or, still more likely, whether he took what he could get in order to be back at sea. In any case, George Keate waited another year for the return of the *Earl Talbot*, on 18 July 1787, in order to have Henry Wilson review his completed manuscript, enter corrections, and approve it for publication.

With Henry Wilson's imprimatur, Keate's book was published in 1788. Later, the editors of Rees's *Cyclopaedia* wrote that it was "written with great elegance, and compiled with much care [and that] it had a considerable sale, but the author drew it up from the most disinterested motives, and received no advantage from it whatever." It would seem that Keate neither wanted nor accepted any profit from the book. Aside from its popularity, this may explain why it was printed by several different publishers as well as the profusion of "little histories" of Prince Lee Boo, plus the translations of most if not all of the original work into at least seven languages. The book review in

London's *Gentleman's Magazine* for July 1788, praised the book and contained the following paragraph:

> We could not dismiss this affecting story without repeating a wish that it may stimulate either the Court of Directors of the East India Company, the Board of Control, or the Senate of Great Britain, to give orders for a vessel to be dispatched to the island of Pelew, with a proper cargo of seeds and useful animals, to repay that debt which, as a nation, we certainly owe to the father of Lee Boo; and we are happy to learn, since this article was written, that the *Ariel* sloop is fitting out at Portsmouth for that benevolent purpose.

But the sloop *Ariel* did not sail for Pelew, and whatever action the Honourable Company took was not decisive until almost another two years had gone by. Well before then, the Wilsons were again voyaging to China, this time with Henry as captain of a new ship, the *Warley*, 1,200 tons—four times the size of the *Antelope*—and Harry again as fifth mate. They departed England on 18 March 1790. There is no indication that this ship, owned by Henry Boulton, was authorized to carry a message to Pelew. On the contrary, it is unlikely that a new ship would be permitted to risk such a diversion during its maiden voyage. But it is probable that Henry Wilson had lobbied on behalf of such a voyage, for only seven days later a letter was signed in London by East India Company authorities and dispatched to Bombay directing the Company's representatives there to take action.

Although there was a great deal more involved than simply putting business before compassion, it is not easy to account for the fact that it took John Company over five years to get the word of Lee Boo's death on its way to the father who waited at home in Pelew. And when the Company's directors did take action, they had other things on their minds as well. Their directive ordered the Bombay authorities to select and equip two ships for the purpose of surveying the northwest coast of New Guinea as well as going to "the Peeloo Islands . . . to convey intelligence of the death of Lee Bo, the Prince whom Captain Wilson of the *Antelope* brought from thence, by a disease, to which the inhabitants of this country are very subject." This lengthy directive contains thirty paragraphs of instructions relating to the voyage, its purposes and objectives. For example, the paragraph concerning the vessels to be used reads, in part: "There being many Pirates in the Eastern Seas a small vessel is improper for this voyage. You will therefore equip for this purpose one of our Bombay built vessels on your establishment of not less than 150 tons burthen." The vessel was to be "in good condition, and a prime sailor [and one which] can be got soonest ready, and you will also appoint a small vessel to accompany her."

Similarly, as to personnel: "We direct that Lt. Archibald Blair, or Lt. John McCluer be appointed to Command the Principal Vessel and of the Expedition." Further, as to the Company's reasons for insisting on one of these men: "In our choice of Lt. Blair [or] Lt. McCluer we do not mean to throw any imputation on other officers who are their Seniors; but we direct that one or other of these two be appointed to execute this important service because we have in their *Hydrographic Works* before us full testimony that they have competent abilities to execute the *Survey* completely to the Public Advantage, and consequently to our satisfaction and their own honour." Other officers were to be selected who could work under the commander with "due Subordination and Harmony."

The directive named places where the vessels were to "touch" including Bencoolen (Bengkulu, a British settlement in Sumatra), "to take on board a Linguist" (preferably a "European") and Bally or Lombock (Bali or Lombok, islands to the east of Java) for "provisions and water."

A journal in two copies was to be kept and an "Extra Clerk" was to be sent along to assist with this. One copy of the journal was to be sent to London by any company ship they met that was homeward bound, and the other copy to be sent from Macao, which they were to reach by the spring of 1791 "before the departure of our ships for England."

To command the expedition the authorities chose Lt. John McCluer and in so doing made three titles available to him, all of which were used: Commander (or commodore) of the expedition, captain of his ship, and his military rank in the Bombay Marines which remained that of lieutenant. McCluer's previous work had resulted in at least two documents known to those who selected him: an *Account of the Navigation between India and the Gulph of Persia* and a *Description of the Coast of India (Malabar).*

Although McCluer had established himself by his "Hydrographic Works," he was apparently something of a rebel. When informed of his appointment to command the expedition to Pelew and points between India and Pelew, one of his first actions was to write a formal request for additional pay for the officers who would serve under him, "for I cannot expect much *Vigilance* and *Harmony* upon 30 Rupees per month." And further, "I do not expect anyone in our Service to go with me upon these terms *through choice,* and to be forced by *Order* upon such work will never answer the Grand Point." And, in defiance of his employers, "if such is the case the Company's Orders will not strictly be complied with." For these "disrespectful expressions [which were] so subversive of subordination" the Bombay authorities ordered "Mr. McCluer to attend the Board on Friday when the President will be requested to reprimand him for his improper freedom." The Company's records for Bombay show that on 23 July 1790, "Pursuant to our Resolution on Tuesday Lt. McCluer attends the Board, and the President having reproved him for his late unbecoming Conduct, he is ordered to withdraw."

Apparently John McCluer was not cut from the same mold as the more cautious Henry Wilson. But the officers for whom he went too far out on a limb included two of Wilson's men from the *Antelope*— the former Christ's Hospital schoolboys, John Wedgebrough and Robert White, both of whom were now twenty-three years of age, second lieutenants in the Bombay Marine, and both of whom had been putting their draftsmanship to work as hydrographers. Hydrography was a major occupation of the Bombay Marine at this time, in contrast with earlier days when this veritable navy belonging to the East India Company had been more concerned with protecting Indian coastal waters from pirates.

In this context it should also be noted that Alexander Dalrymple, the man who had believed so strongly in the existence of a Terra Australis Incognita, and who, more than anyone else, had inspired the voyages of Captain Cook, was now associated with the East India Company. Dalrymple was almost certainly responsible for instigating the coastal survey assignments given to McCluer's voyage and for which hydrographers were needed. In addition to McCluer himself, Wedgebrough, and White, the Company's directive appointed one William Henry as an additional draftsman to accompany the voyage. By this means, Dalrymple must have hoped to obtain better charts of the areas to be surveyed than those he had thus far collected and studied, including those he had made himself on a much earlier voyage in the East Indies. In any case, as will be seen, McCluer later dispatched his journal to the esteemed Alexander Dalrymple in London.

The *Panther*, 181 tons, a kind of two-masted, square-rigged vessel known as a "snow," was chosen for McCluer. It carried 14 guns and had been built in Bombay in 1778. Another smaller snow, the *Endeavour*, was chosen as the second vessel, with William Drummond, a second lieutenant, in command. In addition to the 48 Englishmen aboard the *Panther* and 17 aboard the *Endeavour*, there were approximately 40 "Indian Suberdah and Sepoys" distributed between the two vessels. On the *Panther* there were also two boys, one of whom was listed as "Young boy of 8, son of Sergeant King's Regiment, Bombay." (For "son" of the regiment, it might be supposed the word *mascot* applies.) Both boys sailed away from Bombay as wards of Commander McCluer.

The first page of McCluer's journal is entitled simply, "Voyage to the Pelew Islands in the H.C. Snow *Panther* by John McCluer." The first entry begins:

Sunday 23 of August 1790.

> In the afternoon slipt the Moorings but the wind and the tide being unfavourable we came too at the middle ground, where we settle all our private worldly affairs, and I really believe there was no one on board that owed money to anyone when he left the Port, so that we stood away boldly without the least remorse of conscience.

McCluer was only thirty-one years of age when the voyage began, yet he was the oldest of all the officers. Drummond was just twenty-four, the only married man on either ship, and married but fifteen days! "None of us was wore out with age," wrote McCluer, which was just as well if they were to survive what within seven months he was to describe as "a dangerous voyage of discovery."

In keeping with his London directive, McCluer sailed first for Madras on the eastern coast of India where he was to receive "further information." En route, McCluer issued new canvas hammocks and "examined every man's clothing and saw he had not less than six changes, those who were difference were supplied from a slop chest at prime cost." His journal indicates only a slightly more benign interest in the health of his men:

We also regulated their diet, as rice was boiled twice every day for the natives it was thought proper to let the Europeans have the same diet exclusive of their salt meat, on Pork days (twice a week) they were ordered pease soup, and instead of drinking a raw dram in the morning, which is doubtless prejudicial to health, they had a pint of grog at Dinner time.

McCluer reached Madras on 13 September, delivered letters, received two sextants and a "bundle of books with sundry remarks concerning the coast of New Guinea" as sent by the Company from London. He proceeded at once to his next scheduled port of call, Bencoolen, which he reached 9 October. If this first stop in his eastward voyage was a portent of things to come, McCluer could not have been pleased. Not only was "Mr. Drummond laid up with a relapse of his liver complaint," but no European linguist was to be found to fulfill the Company's directive; McCluer had to settle for local linguists. Then, several of his seamen took one of the ship's boats and, instead of returning promptly, took an unauthorized leave of several days during which they were seen plying the waters in the manner of children "gone a pirating." This McCluer could not tolerate. He states that some of his men had the good fortune to be on shore not far from where the truant seamen landed their boat when they had exhausted their food. Their words upon landing were overheard and reported to McCluer, who entered them in his journal verbatim:

1st Man—	"Well, Dam my eyes, we're once on the sod again."
2nd Man—	"Better disposed, Thank God we're all safe. I wish I had some grubb for I'm bloody hungery!"
3rd Man—	"Dam such a Cruise, say I!"
4th Man—	"What, dam the vessel—ain't she gone yet?" (answered another, "no")
5th Man—	"Is the Captain ashore?" (answered "no" by one of the shore men) "That's well."
6th Man—	"Well dam her, there she is—lets go and look for something to eat and drink."

When apprehended on their way to the ship, these men would say only: "Well, give us something to eat and then you may do what you like with us." Only a few days earlier McCluer had written, "Seamen, our English seamen in particular, must be ruled with a rod of severity the smallest relaxation and they begin to be turbulent." The rod in this case was a stint in the local lock-up which may well have housed enough real pirates to make these English youngsters wish they were safe at "home" in their canvas hammocks.

After some twenty days in the area of Bencoolen, the two ships sailed for Java, making Java Head on 10 November 1790. Then, more trouble:

> 25 November 1790 This day Lt. Drummond was cut for
> an abscess in the liver.

Drummond's liver had erupted into something far more serious than a "complaint." The operation performed on him at sea by the ship's doctor proved futile. Passing south of Bali, McCluer reported:

> 1 December 1790
>
> About 2 o'clock in the morning departed this life Lieut. William Drummond, Commander of the *Endeavour,* much lamented by us all, he was an active and enterprising Officer . . . We committed the corps to the deep with three volies of musquetry and his vessel fired 24 minute guns for him, he being at that age when he died.

McCluer had wanted to appoint his second in command, John Proctor, as captain of the *Endeavour* to replace Drummond, but Proctor preferred to remain on the *Panther*. McCluer therefore appointed the twenty-two-year-old Thomas Haswell, also a second lieutenant, to the temporary command of the *Endeavour*.

Furthering his course eastward, McCluer put in for wood and water wherever necessary, yet was mindful that the islands he now negotiated were controlled by the Dutch, making it necessary to "conduct ourselves with due deference to their authority."

"10 December 1790 At the Town called Bally." Here "the Bundermaster and his father" came on board the *Panther* for a visit.

McCluer "gave him a tune upon our Drum and Fife, which he did not altogether admire, he would rather [have] seen a few chests of opium or something for Trade."

On 17 December, McCluer reported that "my two boys"—William Ross and James Mellick, ages 8 and 10—had left the ship without permission with possibly the naive intention of deserting to a life in the islands. When, a short time later, a trader came along with two slaves to sell, McCluer bought them "for a cake of opium each and ten dollars if he would bring the 2 [boys] back." Several days later the trader returned with the two boys whom he had tricked into his boat. McCluer paid the trader as promised, and took it out of the boys' wages plus "a whipping for their thoughtlessness."

This sort of thing created delays, and after consultations with his officers, McCluer decided to prepare for a direct sailing to Pelew. He felt he could not do anything useful at New Guinea, then complete his mission to Pelew, and still "be in China time enough to send our accounts home by the returning ships of this season." He therefore "took in stock for the Pelew Islands." From Laboijee he obtained "6 cows, 2 bulls, and 20 goats with paddy and straw for 3 months." As the voyage progressed, he later bought "several goats, kidds, and fowls."

"26 December 1790 We approached the coast of the Celebes." Christmas came and went without any mention from McCluer and without mention of whether any of the animals or fowls were eaten to observe the holiday season. However, a humorous yet almost tragic event that did occur illustrates the value the men placed on their live cargo. At sea on 2 January 1791, one of the fowls, a duck, fell overboard from the *Endeavour,* which was sailing a short distance ahead of the *Panther.* Young Captain Haswell of the *Endeavour,* determined not to lose the duck, had a "canoe" lowered into the water and took off paddling in pursuit. But the crafty duck dove and swam about, very effectively evading the captain. Although the water was calm, the captain soon tired of this game and took up his musket to shoot the duck. In his haste, however, he forgot about the forceful recoil, and when he fired and hit the duck he was thrown out of the canoe. A large shark appeared and made straight for Haswell, who defended himself with his paddle. McCluer, observing all of this, ordered a small boat into the water. Meanwhile, the wounded duck flayed about in the water, thus attracting the shark away from Haswell. While the shark was busy devouring the duck, McCluer's men were able to rescue Haswell from the water and return him to his ship.

Many days of routine sailing, unrelieved by mock heroics or comedy of any sort, followed before the two ships reached the Pelews. Unaccountably, McCluer does not give the date, but a careful reading of his journal suggests that the southernmost island, Angaur, was sighted on 21 January 1791, a closer approach made on the twenty-second, and both ships inside the reef on the twenty-third. McCluer describes the scene:

> Now for our reception at Pelew. Being now I may say in Abram's bosom sheltered from all winds and seas, we proceeded to putting our large boat in the water. In the afternoon saw 2 small canoes undersail, we waved to them but they would not come near us, we imagined they were going with the account of our arrival, and our conjectures were right so far, for in less than two hours we saw above 20 canoes standing toward us. . . .

Meanwhile, McCluer had sent Wedgebrough off in the longboat to "examine the channel." The longboat met Abba Thulle and his "whole retinue" coming through the channel toward the ships. Lee Boo's father recognized Wedgebrough, whom he had not seen for over seven years. His long wait for news of his son had finally come to an end. Wedgebrough described Abba Thulle's reaction to the word of Lee Boo's death in a letter quoted by Hockin. The chief is reported to have said, *"Weel, weel, weel a trecoy"* (good, good, very good). Meaning, perhaps, it is good that I finally know. And, when McCluer met Abba Thulle a short time later and spoke of Lee Boo's fate, the king reacted stoically, saying, according to McCluer, "It was much the same whether he died in England or Pelew, he was sure the Englies would be kind to him." It made it easier, perhaps, for Abba Thulle to tell McCluer that Blanchard, too, was dead. Blanchard, to quote McCluer, "had not been dead, one moon, he died of this country disorder, breaking out in sores owing to the poverty of their food." This account of Blanchard's death does not agree with two other published accounts, those of Hockin and Delano, both of which describe a violent death. But McCluer's account was the only one written on the scene soon after the event, and McCluer repeated his version at a later point in his journal. Whatever the cause of Blanchard's death, there is more than a little mystery here or at the very least a great deal of confused communication. The first Belauans Lt. White encountered embraced him fondly but did not want to speak of Blanchard, saying only that "He was at Cooroora." Perhaps he had been buried at Koror.

McCluer concludes his description of his first meeting with Abba Thulle by saying that the king "was quite happy to see the English again thinking that they [Henry Wilson and his party] had not reached China in their small vessel, and could not otherwise account for their long absence." Knowing now that all of the English had safely reached Macao, he asked about his old friends, especially young Will Cobbledick, of whom he had been so fond.

After waiting for favorable winds, the two ships made their way up to Koror, with the canoes of Pelew and the *Panther*'s launch showing the way. Since there were more canoes than were needed to act as pilots, some of them shot "past us like so many porpoises." When they passed what McCluer called "Wedgebrough's old residence" at Oroolong, Wedgebrough paid a visit and found the island campsite all overgrown and the inscription that Captain Wilson had left removed from the tree where it had been posted. The coconuts that had been planted when they were there had flourished, although the trees were not yet mature enough to bear fruit.

"27 January 1791   At Arrakappasang." At this island that adjoins Koror, McCluer now landed the stock he had brought for Abba Thulle and the people of Pelew as a gift from the East India Company. By McCluer's count there were "4 cows, 2 bulls, 10 Bengal Ewes, and a ram, 7 she goats, and 3 He, 4 sows with young and a boar pig, 1 pair of geese, 2 pair of ducks, all in good order." The men of the *Panther* and the *Endeavour* made quite a ceremony of this return of the English to the home of Lee Boo's father, coming ashore in uniform, with the drum and fife playing "the Grenadier's March." All in all, McCluer records, it "made no small shew"—a "shew" not unlike some of those Lee Boo had seen at St. James's Park. There were other reminders of Lee Boo. McCluer learned during this time of reunion and feasting that one of those present, a son of Arra Kooker, now went by the name of Harry "from having been the friend of Henry Wilson's son." He was also told that small children were taught to sing and dance in praise of the English.

McCluer now began a personal exploration of Abba Thulle's island of Koror. He found, among other things, a new "canoe house" under construction, with a gable lined out for carving—the work of an old man who "had already delineated the cow, with a sailor in his dress with a round hat and trousers, not badly imitated." He was told that this new building had been completed in three months, without a nail. McCluer found this to be "hardly credible," but he admired the building and the fact that the only metal in the entire structure consisted of two ring bolts "from the *Antelope.*"

McCluer observed the people of Pelew in their daily pursuits and noted that the women did most of the agricultural work, "the men looking upon working the ground to be a disgrace." But McCluer was no tourist. He had work of his own to do, and instructions to lay the foundations for a fort, which he did. In keeping with his instructions, he named the area "Fort Abercromby in compliment of our Governor of Bombay" (Colonel Robert Abercromby). The dedication ceremony "was highly seconded by the King calling all the islands Englees."

"2 February 1791   First thing born at the Pelews." This was a female goat given the name of Peggy. Perhaps taking the birth as a signal that his initial mission to the Pelews had been accomplished, McCluer now prepared to undertake his next assignment, which was to contact a homeward-bound ship that could deliver a report of his accomplishments to date. To do this he would take the *Panther* to Macao, leaving the *Endeavour* behind, with Mr. Proctor in charge of those remaining at Koror. Arrangements were made for a *bai* to be placed at their disposal. The building was divided into three sections— one for the "gentlemen," "one for the crew," and the third for a storeroom. A flag was hoisted and some seeds planted to be cared for by Midshipman and "Acting Second Lt." Samuel Snook, who, according to McCluer, had "a botanical turn of mind." Snook was to "instruct the natives in the use of tools and implements of husbandry [and in the] cultivation of rice-ground, and gardens."

When McCluer's departure in the *Panther* was delayed at the request of Abba Thulle, he occupied his time by beginning a hydrographic survey of the Pelew Islands. Then, with the time for sailing at hand, McCluer wrote, "I was surprised by a visit from the King, all alone, this was only to know if a Bone he had then in his basket could go upon my hand as I must be invested with that order before I went away." This bone proved to be "too small by a great deal," and when a second bone was produced that was also too small for McCluer's wrist, it was cut in such a way as to make it fit.

The newly anointed commander could now depart for China, but first Abba Thulle selected two people to board the *Panther* and join the voyage: a young woman, and a young man whose name McCluer recorded as "Kockywack"—"and a merry cock he is." McCluer goes on to say of this young man, "he is an adopted son the same as Lee Boo was and they are considered by the people of Pelew the same as their own children." McCluer was also asked to choose someone and he chose a companion for the young woman—a young lady whose father had been killed "in the conquest of Pillilew."

"17 February 1791   We now left the Palou Islands"

"2 March 1791 . . . arrived in the Typa" (Macao). At Macao, McCluer rented a house for the three people from Palou and employed people to take care of them. He also obtained the services of a doctor to have the three inoculated against smallpox, not wanting the fate of Lee Boo to befall those in his charge. He also restricted their movements until it was safe for them to be about in this place where smallpox had been observed. In this way, McCluer adds, they "were taught the disorder that Leeboo died of."

Once it was deemed safe for his three charges to go out, McCluer took them to visit several churches; he showed them a prison and told them that it was a place for thieves; and he took them "to the concert but found the music too strong for their organs, they were sent to sleep at every act." But they liked the lights and the chandeliers, and feasted on the cakes and sweet drinks, but not the liquors.

At this time McCluer also arranged for "the famous painter Spoilem" to come down to Macao "at my request, his terms, was to be ensured fifty dollars for his trip, this sum I gave him for a picture of myself and the three Palou people in a group." McCluer goes on to say that this painting, which was envied by many people who would have liked a "copy," was left with Mr. Freeman "to be sent home by the ships of the next season." (The Museum of Mankind in London believes that a painting they have may be the one described by Mc-Cluer. However, Captain McCluer does not appear with the three Islanders.)

Meeting with his friends one afternoon, McCluer was surprised by a messenger who burst in on his group and reported that Kockywack was "dead"! McCluer rushed to the scene, a considerable distance through the streets of Macao, and found Kockywack recovering from a state of unconsciousness. Kockywack, wearing McCluer's "second best uniform coat," had been robbed by a pickpocket. He had chased the thief into his lair where, outnumbered, he had been knocked unconscious. Now rescued by McCluer, he at least came away with an adventure story he could tell his friends when he returned to Belau.

"28 April 1791   The *Panther* departed Macao." McCluer reported a voyage that took "all too long." With time on his hands, he observed his passengers: "Our Palouan girls are making up songs regarding all that they have seen. It is my belief that they do this to ensure that they will not forget anything of their experiences in Macao and the sights that they have seen." During "watering and wooding" operations en route, "our Palou passengers . . . found bettlenut which was a great treat to them being a long time without it." And, "caught a large boobee which was a noble feast for our Palou friends, they preferring it to fine China Capons."

"9 June 1791   Sighted Palou." (McCluer is now using "Palou" for "Pelew"—an improvement indicating a better command of the language than Wilson had.)

"10 June 1791   Made our way into sheltered water." Abba Thulle and his entourage came aboard and were delighted to see and admire "the two girls . . . dressed in blue silk petticoats, yellow jackets adorned with blue and green beads." Answering questions, "the two girls sat down at the King's feet all the time he was on board." For his part, Kockywack "was running all over the vessel . . . he changes his dress (clothes) every half hour, the whole day." McCluer noticed that Kockywack answered questions only from those "of consequence" and that he often "stretched the truth beyond recognition." People would come to McCluer to seek confirmation of some wild story that Kockywack had told. But not the chiefs—to them he took care to tell the truth.

McCluer learned that during his absence those he had left behind had fought three battles for Abba Thulle and as a consequence they had all been made "Rupacks of the first order!" He was not surprised, therefore, when Abba Thulle asked him to assist in yet another expedition against his enemies to show his foes "that the might of the English was behind him." McCluer reluctantly consented in order "to put a period to those disputes and quarrels. . . . The whole [expedition] was committed to the care of Mr. Wedgebrough accompanied by

Mr. Delano, Volunteer, and the Doctor." (This is the first mention of the American, Amasa Delano, who was among "stragglers"— McCluer's term—who were in Macao and given positions as volunteers" aboard the *Panther*. Delano wrote of these events at a later date, as will be seen, particularly in the next chapter.)

McCluer seems loath to say much about the expedition to Artingall other than that it was successfully and peacefully resolved in favor of Abba Thulle who was carried ashore in triumph by his subjugated foes "and all of the Rupacks gave him a bead of submission." In celebration of this painless victory, the English "fired several China rockets and fireworks which greatly astonished the Artingalls." (Delano's description of this expedition is similar to some of those described by Keate. Delano, too, was much impressed with what he saw and heard of the bravery and skill of the men on both sides. He reports that the negotiations to prevent battle went on for three days, during which Abba Thulle encouraged his men to mingle with the enemy and get acquainted in the interest of a peaceful settlement. Perhaps to emphasize the fullness of this bloodless victory, Delano also writes that sixty Artingall women were made available as "hostages" to the victors; and of the women's reaction: "I discovered in their countenances only cheerfulness and pleasure.")

McCluer, who had absented himself from both the confrontation at Artingall and the celebrations, chose instead the more peaceful pursuit of planting several "China orangeseeds on Ameloaked [near Koror], also some peach trees . . . from China." By 22 June 1791 his journal entries note the need to leave Belau and get on with the survey work at New Guinea. When he said as much to Abba Thulle he was again asked to delay for four days—time enough to prepare going away feasts and festivities. McCluer used the additional time for further surveying in the now relatively peaceful Belaus.

At the final feasting before his departure, McCluer surprised Abba Thulle with some presents he had saved for the occasion. While at Macao, he had designed and commissioned imitation "bones" for the wrists of the highest-ranking chiefs. They were made of ivory and had a clever clasp that could be used to fit most any wrist. He reserved to Abba Thulle the right of distribution of these rare gifts. In turn, Abba Thulle asked McCluer to choose who among the Belauans he would like to have accompany him on his voyage to New Guinea. McCluer chose a lad whom he had seen perform with great skill as "first paddle'' on the king's canoe. He also chose three women. Because Abba Thulle wanted someone left behind, McCluer chose William Ross— one of the boys who had tried to run away at Bali—and the doctor then proposed to let his "apprentice," James Mellick, the other boy, stay so that the two could be company for each other. Abba Thulle "instantly took them under his care, and called them his children."

McCluer then describes the scene as they began to leave.

> [Abba Thulle] shed tears like a child as if he was possessed with a second sight of a view of futurity, told us he was going to die, and he would not see us again, however, he said, come back when you please, these islands are yours (pointing to them) calling them Englees. He then unwill- ingly descended into his boat, and gave the sorrowful order to quit their hold. We now filled the sails and dropt from them, who all gathered into a cluster, and gave vent to their grief, continuing in that situation as long as we could descern them. The lad's father [father of the boy going off with McCluer] had still kept by the vessel with a small canoe and we frequently obliged to remind him of the great distance we were from the land, and it was with much ado we got him away by sunset when we were about 6 leagues from the shore—nor did we perceive him making for the shore so long as we could see him.''
>
> 27 June 1791   We now left these islands and a deep com- passionate people, who felt our departure from them with great affliction, and I have reason to believe it was not feigned but real, having in general felt the value of our friendship and acquaintence.

Two weeks later, en route to New Guinea, McCluer wrote in his journal what might well be accepted as evidence of the affection with which his men had been held in Belau: "Since we left the Palou Islands our sick list has increased to the number of 32, from both vessels, entirely occasioned by our amours at that place." Earlier, in February 1791, he had written, "The ladies also never make any bargain for their commodity, but trust entirely to our liberality," and now added, "Our first leaving of those islands gave us sufficient warning to be cautious in our dealings, but the ladies are so complying and loving that it is beyond the power of nature to resist temptations." He also noted that "Blanchard died with the same disorder, and was broken out into one continued sore, and what increased the distemper, was his diet, as they say he soon came into their custom of eating putrid and raw fish, for want of better." Whatever the circumstances of island "amours" and the diseases related to them, there was surely no need to add insult to injury and accuse the islanders of being poor providers. If Blanchard starved, it was almost certainly from failure to avail himself of the ample Belauan diet.

"7 August 1791 Thank God, we are all in perfect health, and recovered from our past distempers." By 22 August, McCluer had started his New Guinea survey work and while so engaged, on more than one occasion, noted that "our Palou girls would paddle about in their canoes by themselves perfectly at ease, which gave the natives a confidence in us." But they did not care for the sago of New Guinea, preferring rice, as, apparently, did the English, not to mention the Asians on board. By the end of August, McCluer decided "to leave off my assignments for New Guinea and go to the Moluccas where we might take in a full supply of provisions then return to our work."

"21 September 1791 At Bouro" (Buru, Moluccas). The Dutch governor here took a liking "to Phymoo, our Palou Prince." (This is the first time we are given the name of the Belauan lad whom McCluer selected for this voyage, but there is no evidence that he was a prince.) Apparently Phymoo was "delighted" at seeing his first European house—a "decent house" to quote McCluer—and even more delighted with the governor, who "shewed him several tricks of slight of hand that so perfectly astonished the innocent fellow that he took the Resident for a God and was afraid to come near him, the deception of swallowing a knife was done with a deal of dexterity, so much that the poor Pelew savage really imagined the knife went through him." Phymoo was so impressed that "he begged of me to leave him the canoe as a mark of his attachment."

"28 September 1791 At Amboyna" (Ambon, Moluccas). Here again McCluer and his men were treated with hospitality by the Dutch. McCluer drilled his troops on board the *Panther* in honor of "our Dutch guests" and laid a table "in the true English taste with good roast beef and beef stakes that made the Dutch gentlemen smack their chops and call for another bit." However, "our liquors were none of the best but as we bought them here they could not find fault with them." At the conclusion of this dinner, McCluer gave orders to his men "on no account whatever to deal in Spice of any kind, whoever was caught to buy the smallest quantity should be severely punished." This was to reassure the Dutch that their English visitors intended to respect their monopoly, a monopoly the Dutch preserved by periodically destroying spice-bearing plants and trees in all regions of the area except those they closely supervised.

On 9 October 1791, to further placate the Dutch, McCluer gave a ball in their honor. "It being Saturday night we could not get one of the godly men to come although there were four in the place, not withstanding a grace was said and we all fell to English fashion helping your friends and yourselves to what is most desirable." Later, "the table was drawn, and recovered with pastry and every fruit the place afforded also Europe preserves, Jellies and every nicety they could invent." The dancing followed. "The first Minuet was led off by Mr. Proctor and Mrs. Bourgellis [the paymaster's wife], we then began country dances. . . ."

"11 October 1791   Departed Amboyna." By 22 October, the two ships were off the coast of New Guinea taking soundings to the southeast of Mysol (Misool). A week or so later they were approached by canoes coming from the New Guinea shore and making as if to trade. The doctor, who was eager for trade, responded by passing out some bright-colored cloth and turned to McCluer to ask for more. When McCluer returned with more items for trading, the doctor was in one of the canoes and the Papuans were paddling away with him. McCluer saw one of them place a hand on the doctor's head and dance around him "like a madman." McCluer instantly ordered the men to arms but not to fire until commanded. The "savages" then shot their arrows at the *Panther,* and the men of the *Panther,* at McCluer's order, returned the fire. But it was too late. The canoes were soon out of effective range. Mr. Proctor then reported to McCluer that he had seen the doctor bloody from a hatchet blow and it appeared that he had also been shot with arrows. Neither of the ships could pursue into shallow water and the doctor had to be given up. McCluer and his men could take satisfaction only in knowing that some of their bullets had found their mark.

"6 November 1791   We have been now 8 days employed at this channel." The channel became known as McCluer's Inlet after a survey that continued into December. When Christmas came, McCluer wanted to entertain everyone from both ships with a "fatted calve" but bad weather prevented this. However, New Year's dinner featured "some good Amboina pork, and we drank to a speedy sight of Timor." This was at eleven degrees south latitude, where McCluer says he named an island "New Year's Isle." But everyone had had enough of exploring, and the ships sailed west for Timor.

On 29 January 1792, according to Delano, the ships anchored between Rotta (Roti) and Timor. McCluer makes no mention of it, but Delano reports that he "found the same generous hospitality which Lieutenant Bligh and Captain Edwards did. The latter had not been gone long, when we arrived." Delano observes that "all the boats but one, in which these different parties of distressed persons came to Timor, were left there as a curiosity, and we saw them."

McCluer reports work of repairing sails and reprovisioning at Timor, where he was on good terms with the Dutch governor "for during my stay here I could talk the language fluently." A house was provided for them in which they entertained their guests who "liked our mode of making curries very well." Delano adds that "the manners and temper of McCluer himself were remarkably adapted to conciliate, and invite confidence, wherever he went."

At Timor the Belauans "enjoyed themselves once more on the land." But to McCluer's grief "this was the last land that two of them ever trod upon." Much illness was reported at this time "among men and crew," and McCluer was advised they should drink liquor but not eat the local fruit. These precautions did not prevent the death of Mr. Haswell, "a lad of strong passions"—he who had chased the duck earlier in the voyage from Bombay.

> 21 February 1792. Sent all the sick on board except a Palou girl which was now given over for life, and now we only waited to see the fatal event, when on the 22nd she departed this life and was decently intered in the churchyard followed to the grave by all the gentlemen on shore, and although not a Christian by baptism we read part of the funeral service over her being well deserving it, during the time we knew her she led a life of perfect innocence and simplicity and died like a sleeping infant. The Palou people bore the loss of their companion stoically, and what is contrary to their custom, followed her to the grave without a tear.

The two ships left Timor on 24 March 1792, and reached Christmas Island on 2 April. Here McCluer made the discovery that

smallpox had got on board and unluckily on our Palou
friend, this being a matter of serious consideration we
began instantly on the discovery, to prevent the contagion
from spreading as we had above 20 people on board of both
vessels that never had the small pox, the greatest part of
that description being on board the *Panther*. I ordered all
those from the *Endeavour* who had not ever had the disorder and sent others in their stead from the *Panther*. Being
thus prepared, our Palou friend took his last leave of us,
and went on board the *Endeavour*. Being then the third day
I saw it was a dangerous kind and gave him up for lost, but
as there was a probability of saving him I gave Mr. Proctor
orders to make the best of his way for Bencoolen and there
get some fruits or medical assistance to keep up his spirits. I
sent Mr. White with him being his *Suckalie* [friend].

When on 26 April 1792 the *Panther* rejoined the *Endeavour* off the
coast of Sumatra at Bencoolen, McCluer, to his "sad grief," learned of
the death of "our Palou Ambassador who departed this life the 9th of
the month and as supposed the 10th day of the disorder." Phymoo was
presumably buried at sea. Delano reports, as of 28 April, that they
"lost nearly 20 men in half the number of days."

McCluer moved his ships to safer, that is, healthier waters at Rat
Island near Bencoolen. Here he found it necessary to have the
Endeavour filled with water to rid her of "rats, roaches, ants, and cen-
tipedes that had come on board with the supplies of wood." But there
were still more deaths and McCluer's complement of men was further
reduced when "Captain Faulkes [of the *Asia*] sailed away with ten of
my best hands." A larger Company or naval ship commanded by a
higher-ranking officer could do that; it was common practice, although in this instance the transfer of men had been completed in a
rather underhanded manner without McCluer's prior knowledge or
consent.

In September McCluer was at Batavia and in November at Sooloo
(Sulu), where he was repeatedly asked why he was taking two ships to
the remote Pelews, which offered "no kind of trade and no advantage
or return for coming so far." McCluer replied,

I told them the English Company had no lucrative view in
sending vessels to those islands, but on the contrary were at

a very great expense in fitting them out to carry a present
to the inhabitants as a grateful reward for their kindness to
the crew of an English ship that was wrecked there.

The "reward" was "as much livestock as we could carry for the
Pelew Islands." So much, in fact, that McCluer had to decline a gift of
two horses for want of space aboard his ships.

In January 1793, after "a very tedious passage," the two ships
reached Belau where the two surviving Belauans were returned home
and the cargo of animals offloaded. But the deer, "by being tied by the
legs, never rose after they were landed." And the second day after the
cattle were landed, "two of the cows fell down a precipice and killed
themselves." Then "three of my Ewes, and two of my goats killed
themselves by eating till they burst!" Not a very auspicious finale for
the expedition's last visit to Belau. McCluer, doubtless upset over
these losses, recorded that the remaining animals were "properly
attended by my own boys otherwise I should have lost all the pains I
had taken with them." Whether he had run out of time or patience,
these were the last words McCluer wrote in his journal. To continue
the story we must turn to notes written by the American volunteer,
Amasa Delano.

16

DELANO'S *NARRATIVE*

THE McCLUER expedition occupied little more than two years in the life of Amasa Delano. But when, at the age of fifty-four, he retired from the sea, sorted out his memories, and published his *Narrative of Voyages and Travels,* his experiences aboard the *Panther* and in the Pelews occupied more than seven of the twenty-eight chapters of a book filled with enough adventures for two lifetimes. This is fortunate in that his reporting continues the account of the expedition to its virtual conclusion, whereas McCluer's journal ends at Belau. For the period covered by both Delano and McCluer there is agreement enough on most details and a similarity of views with respect to nearly everything except each other.

Delano seems to have admired McCluer from the time of their first meeting at Macao and often speaks of him in his *Narrative.* But McCluer, the captain, had next to nothing to say about Delano, the "volunteer." Had McCluer known that some one hundred forty years later a Delano descendant would become the thirty-second president of the United States, he might have given the American volunteer more space in his journal. The Delanos of Massachusetts were, according to Samuel Eliot Morison, among that state's most durable seafaring families. On such good authority, and more particularly on the strength of Amasa's own book, it is possible for the people of Belau to know that the first American to set foot on their soil was no ordinary sailor. He was a man of exceptional abilities, and even McCluer finally acknowledged as much. In a letter he wrote to London, McCluer admitted his indebtedness to Delano by stating, "This man proved of great service to us in the course of the voyage, particularly at Bencoolen when every other Gentleman was sick." When Delano departed Belau for the last time McCluer "made him a present of 525 dollars" for his stalwart services.

Born "on the north side of the Blue River" in Duxbury, Massachusetts, Amasa Delano was named for an uncle who had been killed by Indians. His biographical sketch, "written by a friend" and inserted at the conclusion of his *Narrative,* recalls that the young Delano had shunned school in favor of the more exciting pursuits of "fishing and gunning." He first went to sea at the age of sixteen aboard a privateer, the *Mars.* For the next eleven years he alternated his time between trading voyages to the West Indies (plus one voyage to Portugal, which he captained) and working at shipbuilding, in which he gained considerable valuable experience.

In March 1790, at age twenty-seven, Delano sailed as second officer aboard the *Massachusetts,* bound for Batavia and Canton. The owners had expected to trade at Batavia for a cargo of interest to the Chinese, but this had not worked out. Consequently, it developed that the owners' debts could be paid only by selling the ship. The *Massachusetts* was sold for $65,000, and the crew had to find their way home aboard other ships. Delano stayed on at Canton with work repairing a Danish ship that had been badly damaged in a typhoon.

When Delano completed his ship repair work, he went to Macao. There, at the factory of the same Thomas Freeman that Lee Boo had known, he met McCluer, who had just brought the *Panther* to Macao after his first visit to the Pelews. The two became friends, according to Delano, and because McCluer was shorthanded he invited Delano to join his expedition and come aboard the *Panther.* "The service was just that for which I had always entertained a strong desire," wrote Delano, "and I did not hesitate a moment." However, things did not go well at first. "I went on board as a volunteer officer, doing duty as a lieutenant, and subject to none but the Commodore's command. This last article made it very unpleasant to me for a short time, for the Bombay Marine was as regular as any public service whatever. The officers, who were to obey me, did not all think the regulation proper, and were not satisfied. This, however, was but for a short period."

The tide began to turn in Delano's favor when they stopped for wood and water en route to Belau from Macao. Two of his fellow officers conspired to send him off in search of gold. One of them, the surgeon, "Dr. Nicholson," had painted a small rock gold and mixed it with minerals from his medicine chest. They sent Delano off with a guide who spoke no English but would show him where to search for more. Delano, by his own description of the prank, was willingly duped and blamed only himself. When, as the day wore on and his guide obviously knew no more where to look than he did, Delano realized how he had been tricked and resolved to "laugh with the rest" and get in some hunting. He returned from his wild-goose chase with a bag full of exotic wildfowl "of a plumage surpassing in beauty and richness, the finest colours of the mineral kingdom." At the shore he was met by the two culprits, who mingled "much kindness with the trick they had played" on him and greeted him with "every article of food and liquor, which could tempt the appetite, and exhilarate the spirits." Ironically, the merriment ended when Delano was bitten by a large centipede that came aboard with the wood collected that day, and he spent a night of misery bathing himself with "hot vinegar and salt" —salt in the wound indeed.

Not all of the ship's company was as quick to accept Delano or to acquiesce to his authority. On the contrary, some must have resented him deeply. Delano relates that at one point early in the voyage when he was in command of a landing party, some of his men conspired to murder him. His valor in the face of this threat, and other acts of courage, apparently gained their grudging respect and, eventually, their friendship.

Picking up the story of the expedition with the final arrival at Belau (January 1793), Delano gives us more details than McCluer, whose mind, at that time, had apparently become almost totally preoccupied with the animals he was delivering to the islands. Delano, on the other hand, reports that the first thing the men of the *Panther* learned upon arrival was that the premonition of death expressed by Abba Thulle when the *Panther* left Belau in June 1791 had proved all too true. The king was dead. At this time Delano, at least, learned that "Abba Thulle" was a title and not a name. He records it this way: "we inquired, 'who is the King now?' The natives answered 'Abba Thulle.' We said, 'who was King before?' They replied 'Abba Thulle.' " Delano therefore concludes, "The real name of the individual whom we first knew as Abba Thulle, whose likeness is given in this book, and who is spoken of by Wilson, we never discovered."

This matter clarified, Delano goes on to provide his own eulogy for the great king:

In regard to Abba Thulle, the king we first knew in 1791, and who deserves to be called the great, in distinction from all the others who bore that office afterwards, it may be said, in addition to the description already given, that he was not only an eminent warrior, statesman, and sage, but was a most sportive and delightful companion. He was as distinguished for his pleasantry in the hours of relaxation in his house, or among his friends, as he was terrible in the field, able in council, and sagacious in morals. The women of his court wore a species of apron, called a *cray,* which was made of the husk of the cocoanut. They had also ornaments upon their wrists, necks, ankles, and in their hair. With any, and all these in turn, our officers and myself have often seen him, in the flow of feeling and good nature, make amusement for himself, the women and us, without the least offense to any individual. We had become so much acquainted with the language, that we could enter into the spirit of his wit and humour, and were able to find new sources of admiration for his character in his moments of the greatest levity.

One wonders if Keate would have approved of the levity, but Delano, the American adventurer, broadens and illuminates our comprehension of a truly congenial and admirable man.

William Ross and James Mellick, the two boys who had been left behind, had been treated, in Delano's words, "like young princes." During most, if not all, of the nineteen months that the *Panther* and the *Endeavour* had been away from Belau the boys had been separated, one "remaining at Pelew" (Koror) and the other "taken to Artingall." Delano explains: "This separation was not the effect of any hostility to the boys, but of the policy and self interest of the contending parties. Each wished to have some pledge of their attachment to the English, and of the care they had bestowed, during our absence, upon wards left behind." By sharing in the care of the two boys and demonstrating equal affection for them, neither of the opposing sides had reason to claim a monopoly on the friendship of the English.

But Amasa Delano did not linger long enough to enjoy very much of the friendship bestowed by the people of Belau. For whatever reason, and none is given, he changed ships while in Belau and transferred to the *Endeavour,* which, under Captain Proctor, was the first to leave after remaining "about a month only at the islands." He continues his

Narrative, describing a rough voyage from Belau to China until the Asses Ears were sighted and the *Endeavour* anchored off Macao. Then, in Canton in March 1793, he brought "accounts to a close with the English government for my services in the expedition under Commodore McClure." (Delano never seems to get McCluer's name spelled right—a problem familiar to all McClures/McCluers and many others involved in this saga.) By way of payment for his part in the expedition, Delano says, "The chief supercargo of the English at Canton paid me two dollars a day, for two years. This was not the whole time, during which I had been employed by them. But the Commodore had always granted me many privileges, and good opportunities to gain a profit in various parts of the expedition, and I felt no disposition to complain of my wages." With that statement Delano concluded his relationship with McCluer and the East India Company. Wanting to return to America, he found the only ship available to him was the *Eliza,* out of New York and without an experienced captain. Delano was given the position. At this point he sailed away from Macao and out of the context of this book. Although he would eventually return to Canton and sail far and wide in the Pacific, he never returned to Belau.

17

"A SPECIES OF
INSANITY"

WHEN AMASA DELANO parted company with John McCluer at Belau and sailed aboard the *Endeavour* for China, it was understood that McCluer would follow with the *Panther*. In fact, Captain Proctor told John Company representatives at Macao that McCluer would arrive within twenty days. But McCluer had other ideas. Within a week of the *Endeavour*'s departure he announced that the *Panther* would sail without him, that he would turn over his command to Lt. Wedgebrough and remain in Belau!

To answer all protestations, McCluer explained that he had thought the entire matter out at length before making his decision—a decision he said he had "been determined upon" ever since leaving Bencoolen. But realizing that Wedgebrough might be in trouble with the East India Company if a satisfactory explanation was not made for his unexpected and unprecedented action, he wrote several letters, including one to Wedgebrough himself and another to Company authorities in Bombay. In these documents McCluer made it a matter of record that he had acted alone, that Wedgebrough had "used every argument" to dissuade him and was in no way to be held accountable for any part of the decision.

Whatever might have motivated McCluer, he was not going to make a Madan Blanchard of himself. With his letter to Wedgebrough he enclosed a list of items he wanted put ashore for his own use, including 20 muskets, 12 pistols, ammunition, a forge, anvil and bellows, a vice, and a "large frame saw." With these and other items to be mentioned later, McCluer would be far better equipped than his illiterate predecessor—provided, that is, Wedgebrough, after inventorying the ship's stores and consulting with the other two officers of the *Panther,* agreed. Wedgebrough dutifully inventoried, consulted, and agreed—but, with the proviso that McCluer's attorneys in Bombay would reimburse the owners if "the Honourable Company should not be pleased therewith."

McCluer must have been prepared to pay not only for the goods he was, in effect, commandeering, but to pay the much higher cost of sacrificing the remainder of his career with John Company and its Bombay Marine Service. In his letter to Wedgebrough, he put it succinctly: "considering my circumstances and rank in the service, this step will be taken for an act of insanity or the effect of some disorder." Not too many years later, the staid and prestigious British *Dictionary of National Biography* was happy to oblige, stating:

> It would seem that the long and arduous work in New Guinea had weakened his mind, and that he was unable to resist the fascinations of the dusky beauties of the islands. It is only by a species of insanity that his extraordinary conduct and breach of all rules of naval discipline can be explained.

McCluer's own explanation is far more lofty. In his letter to the Bombay authorities he stresses his concern for all of the people of Belau, not just the "dusky beauties":

> From the many contentions, which we in a manner have occasioned by introducing things of value among them, they are now constantly at varience with each other, and are absolutely in need of some person to advise them and regulate their conduct to prevent them murdering each other, this task no one could be better provided for than myself, and I have the vanity to think I have sagacity enough to conduct and instruct the natives in the most useful branch of agriculture, and being well disposed towards me I make no doubt in the plan I have formed to succeed.
>
> A few years of my life for the benefit of my Country and the World in General by enlightening the minds of these People, could not be better employed, and should I fall sac-

rifice to the attempt 'tis only the loss of an Individual, who enters a Volunteer in the Service without any lucrative view, but on the contrary gives up his all to gain the object in question.

Was the object in question gained? Was the plan successful? Were the people enlightened? Who can say? McCluer himself left no final assessment. What he did have to say was hardly optimistic. In a letter dated 23 July 1794, written in Macao after he had left Belau, he summarizes the experience:

The *Panther* sailed away and I remained, with every appearance of domestic pleasure, but, alas, this was not for long duration. I soon became displeased with my situation, in six months I lost five cows and two bulls, also all my Deer & Turkies, the heavy rains destroyed all my young plants; and many of my garden seeds did not come up, and to add to my misfortunes I lost a fine Slave & most of my other boys were affected with Sores owing to their change in food. I also found the supplies from the natives were not so constant when I omitted the ceremony of paying for them, this was remonstrated to the King and Chiefs, but with very little success, we were often but badly provided and frequently felt the bottom of our stomachs, to add to all this, I daily had the mortification to hear the report of chickens stolen, my pigs speared, kids and lambs dying, my fences broke thro' and my plants taken away for nothing else than an idle curiosity, and when I complained to the King of these outrages, he said why don't you put the offenders to death, seeing this being the case I became indifferent and careless, leaving the work entirely to the care of the boys, who were about the 8th month not very able or willing to work, owing to their spare diet, and the natives would sooner starve than till the ground, saying God ordained women for that purpose, and my boys soon imbibed those principles when I withdrew my proper authority from them.

To support my drooping spirits the Supreme Director of Nature ordained I should be father to a fine boy on the 18 Dec., on Christmas Day I named him George being the first of his colour born at Corror.

> I soon changed my amusements from the land to the water, and went on frequent parties with, and without the natives, by this means I became perfectly acquainted with the different channels and made a complete examination of the northern extremes of the group hitherto unknown.
>
> When I formed a Resolution to reside at Palou I did not conceive I was ordained by Fate to an unsettled rambling life; Ternate being only the run of a few days from me, I purposed taking a trip there to hear the news from Europe, and return in the space of one month or two, with this resolution I prepared my boat and took my departure to the sad grief of the natives and the pledges I left behind me.

The grief of the natives and the pledges he left behind might be interpreted to mean that McCluer left Belau without stating his future intentions. Indeed, he may not have known his own mind. He had to get away, to have the news. He may well have found it easier to pretend he was merely off on one of his seagoing parties than to explain his restlessness for things unknown in the islands of Belau. But he was not to get the news at Ternate. After he had set a southwesterly course from Belau, the winds shifted; obeying "the dictates of providence," he changed his course to the northwest "and without any material accident" made Macao.

Having completed this open-boat voyage, McCluer describes it in his Macao letter of 23 July 1794:

> I left those Islands in a six oar'd boat, with only four Malays, who were wrecked formerly on the Islands at different periods, we spoke only the Palou language, which may be supposed was not very perfect on my side being but fifteen months in the practice of it, nor could they steer the boat by the compass, with all these apparant difficulties we reached Macao the 4th of May after a voyage of 19 days and sailed in that time near 2,000 miles the success of this voyage will speak for iteself, nor will I intrude on your patience to peruse a discription of our sufferings during the trip, suffice to say, there were none of us belious [bilious] when we arrived.

The East India Company representatives at Macao could not help but be impressed by this remarkable voyage. But if they admired the courage of the man who brought it off they were less sure of his motives and the conditions of his departure from Belau. They wrote, "there appears to be reason to believe that his situation was not so pleasant as he hoped to find it, and that his departure was private and unexpected by the natives." Which seems to be a euphemistic way of saying he did not want the Belauans to know he was leaving.

In Macao, McCluer arranged for the purchase of a small ship, the *Venus,* "a Snow of 100 tons," with which to sail back to Belau. He also obtained "every useful tree and seed I could procure at Macao." But his next sentence reads, "After doing all I could for the benefit of futurity I proposed a trip to Bombay to hear how my conduct was considered by my superiors there." His plans now seem to call for a return to Palou with seeds and plants and then a trip to Bombay. Perhaps this is precisely what he would have done had not another character entered the story. McCluer writes:

> Being now entirely ready for sea I only waited for a favourable spurt of wind to set off with, but how strangely was I surprised with the arrival of my brother Hydrographer Captain Hayes, in the *Duke of Clarence,* who agreeably acquainted me with his having made a new Settlement only a few days sail from mine, and I having it in my power to furnish this place from mine with stock of various kinds. This meeting seemed to both of us the most fortunate circumstance of ours—

Fortunate, that is, for Hayes, in that McCluer would sail at once and take supplies to Hayes' settlement with only a brief stop at Belau en route. If the meeting was fortunate for McCluer, it was because Hayes' confidence in him gave a big boost to his morale, as indicated in the closing lines of his Macao letter of 23 July 1794:

> Thus far has insanity got possession of me, and I hope the same kind of geni who has hitherto protected me may still attend me while I still continue to deserve the favour. Mr. Hays is also of the opinion that I am still a rational being. . . .

It is as if McCluer had expressed his determination to succeed in some sort of colonizing endeavor, somehow, somewhere, even if he might be a bit mad for trying. The opportunity to become associated with Hayes' settlement at Dorey Harbour on the northwest coast of New Guinea represented a chance for McCluer to parlay his experiences in Palou. And so he returned to Palou, but by the unusual route of crossing the China Sea to Manila and then "thro" the Philippines to Belau—a route which Dalrymple later commented "will be very useful to Navigation."

When he arrived at Belau, McCluer "found everything in a very thriving state, the stock considerably increased." From Manila he had brought "above fifty fruit trees [and] a pair of horses" which were landed safely. Perhaps unwittingly, McCluer had fulfilled one of Lee Boo's wishes: he had delivered horses to Belau.

To care for his "plantation" at Belau, McCluer left "4 Chinese, 2 natives of Bombay, and 4 slaves." With them he left "100 bags of rice, 4 guns and carriages." Then, to use the wording of the *Dictionary of National Biography,* he "embarked his family and property, with men servants and women servants, after the manner of the patriarchs of old" and left Belau never to return again.

Some indication of what transpired at New Guinea is provided by Sir John Hayes' biographer, Ida Lee, who writes that McCluer found "Hayes Colonists in a miserable plight. Several had died and fourteen so weakened by illness they were quite dependant on the kindness of the Papuans." Lee concludes that "McCluer's coming seems to have set the starving colony on its feet again," but it doubtless did little to inspire McCluer to want to stay any longer than necessary or to become further involved. Lee reports, however, that in his efforts to assist Hayes' colonists McCluer made a trip to Geby Island where "he hoisted the British flag on Oct. 25th 1794 and took possession of the Island in the name of King George III." Lee reports that McCluer also made a chart of the island, which lies just to the north of the New Guinea mainland, and presented it (i.e., sent it) to Dalrymple. One wonders why McCluer, who spent a far longer time in Belau and charted it thoroughly, did not "take possession" of anything there other than a small bit of land called Fort Abercromby, even though the former Abba Thulle had on several occasions offered the English the islands he controlled.

Having completed his commission at New Guinea, McCluer sailed to Amboyna, Timor, and Bencoolen. At Bencoolen he met another old friend, Captain Pickett, who was there with the frigate *Bombay.* For reasons not stated, the two devised a plan whereby McCluer would carry Pickett's dispatches to Calcutta and Pickett would take six women on board his frigate and carry them to Bombay, where they were to be placed in the care of Wedgebrough. The six women arrived at Bombay and McCluer arrived at Calcutta as planned. But when McCluer sailed from Calcutta in August 1795, he, his ship, and everyone aboard must have met with the ultimate of misfortunes at sea, for they never reached Bombay and were never seen or heard of again.

Thus ended the career of a man who was surely remembered in Belau for many years, not only because he had carried away Belauans, some of whom may have perished with him, but because of the living evidence of his presence that remained in the islands. In all, McCluer had brought to Belau a total of 9 cows and 3 bulls, 20 ewes and 2 rams, 20 goats, 7 deer, 4 turkeys, 24 ducks, 12 geese, 10 "tame hens and a cock," 6 bantam fowls, 6 rabbits, 2 horses, 4 sows with young, and a boar pig. Although some of these did not survive, some—especially the pigs and fowls—must have procreated their kind all through the years to the present.

But in England and in India McCluer would be remembered for the work he completed before the "species of insanity" struck him. In a footnote to Charles Rathbone Lowe's *History of the India Navy,* a writer reviewing McCluer's work in 1829 states:

> When the works of an individual are carefully preserved and consulted as a standard authority by those who survive him, it is sufficient proof of their excellence, and as much as he himself could desire. Those of Lt. McCluer have stood the test of nearly forty years; the considerable addition they formed to the stock of Hydrographical knowledge, justly entitled their author to the acknowledgements of the Maritime World; and at this distance in time we readily bestow our tribute to the memory of a man who has perpetuated his name by his valuable works.

18

SNOOK'S SWORD

ON 26 JULY 1796, almost a year after McCluer was lost at sea and presumed dead, his will was proved at Bombay Town Hall by the oath of Samuel Snook. Snook had also witnessed the will when McCluer drew it up on the "12th day of February [in the] Year of our Lord one thousand seven hundred and ninety-three." The will had been written and witnessed shortly before the *Panther* departed Belau, leaving McCluer to begin his self-imposed exile. This was, of course, before the child, George, had been born and then named on Christmas Day, 1793. George is not mentioned in the will, but the two orphan boys, William Ross and James Mellick, are, as are a "female named Elizabeth Tennel," and a "child named Margaret by a Malabar mother," and McCluer's own mother, to whom, his will states, "I have remitted home 500 pounds."

Samuel Snook was not named as one of the executors of McCluer's will, but, as events will show, he should have been. Wedgebrough and White, who were named, were seldom at Bombay after returning from the expedition. White himself had only a few more years to live and died on 20 October 1799, aged thirty-two, after "returning sick" from a survey of the Red Sea. Wedgebrough did not fare much better. After commanding a variety of ships and having a trip home to England, he died at Goa of a fever on 14 May 1804, aged thirty-seven. Samuel Snook was named executor in the wills of both men. But before he was to fulfill his unhappy duties on behalf of White and Wedgebrough, he had some unfinished business to take care of for McCluer.

The Belauan women whom McCluer had sent on ahead to be cared for by Wedgebrough until McCluer himself arrived at Bombay became, instead, the wards of the obliging Samuel Snook, who took them in with his family in the village of Magaguam, just outside Bombay. Only three of them had survived. Their names, as spelled by the English, were Cockilla, Cockathey, and Remme. The others, sadly unknown to posterity and even nameless, had fallen victim to that scourge of sojourning Belauans, smallpox.

After the surviving three Belauan women had been in the Bombay area for nearly two years, Snook and a Dr. Helenus Scott approached the East India Company authorities in an effort to have them returned to their home islands. Not long after, Captain Henry Wilson arrived at Bombay with his ship, the *Warley,* destined for Canton. Captain Wilson needed little persuading to agree to take the women on his Indiaman and attempt to return them to Belau en route to China. He agreed, on the condition that Snook accompany him as chaperon for the women and as pilot to navigate the huge ship safely through Belauan waters.

With the approval of his superiors at the Bombay Marine, Snook agreed to go and the *Warley* sailed on 1 October 1797. But Snook's humanitarian mission was not so easily fulfilled. The *Warley* was accompanied by three other large East Indiamen—the *Neptune,* the *Hindostan,* and the *Earl of Abergavenny.* When they reached Belau, the convoy was enjoying such a favorable southwesterly wind that it was deemed unwise to stop and risk losing a quick passage to China. They sailed on and completed what Snook described as "one of the best eastern passages ever made."

After arriving at Macao with Captain Wilson, Snook rented a house and took the three Belauan women ashore "with their necessaries and the presents given them by the Government on leaving Bombay." He then set about trying to find passage for himself and his wards. Finding no captain willing to undertake the mission on agreeable terms, he obtained permission to purchase an inexpensive vessel that might be used for the voyage to Belau. After much investigating in and about Macao, on 5 February 1798 he purchased "a sloop rigged vessel named the *Diamante,* a vessel of about 40 tons" for 2,200 Spanish dollars. At the time of this purchase Captain Wilson was still in the Canton-Macao area and assisted with some of Snook's financial transactions in the use of Company funds.

Snook's orders from the Company's committee at Canton instructed him to return "the three Pelew women under your charge" and then to proceed to Bombay. His orders further read: "Should any Chinese who may have been left in the Pelew Islands be desirous of quitting them and for that purpose apply to you for passage we desire that you will immediately grant their request and carry them to Bombay unless you should in your route touch at any place where they may wish to remain." Although this is presumably a reference to the Chinese left by McCluer, it is also possible that some of the Chinese who were with Captain Wilson on the *Antelope* still remained in Belau. Keate never mentions them after the departure of the *Oroolong*. Whatever obligation Wilson or McCluer may have felt, the Company's attitude seems to have been that the Chinese remaining in Belau could be left on any island they chose.

Samuel Snook sailed from Macao as captain of the sloop *Diamante* on 4 March 1798, but was back seven days later, after encountering a storm that damaged the main boom and parts of the rigging. Without a carpenter on board he was forced back into port for repairs, which he estimated would take "3 or 4 days." When he did get fully underway, he did not reach Belau until 13 July "owing to bad weather and a dull sailing vessel." The time taken for that voyage was an incredible hundred days more than McCluer had needed to cover the same distance in an open boat! But, as Snook later reported to the Company, his pickup crew was hardly the best and several of them he "lost through sickness on the voyage and on arrival at the islands had not a man on board myself included but was in a very weak and sickly state." Snook was fortunate to have reached Belau alive.

The three women were, to say the least, grateful to be home at long last. Snook wrote of the arrival: "Just as the vessel anchored the King came aboard, who seemed pleased to see the people returned to their country again and remained on board all night." The Abba Thulle was also pleased with new presents of "Muskets and Powder." But Snook was distressed to learn that most of the livestock had been either killed by the people left behind by Captain McCluer or allowed to run wild. When he told the Abba Thulle that he was displeased about this because he was badly in need of fresh food, the reply was to the effect that "they were the property of the English as well as the Isle of Oroolong and as Captain McCluer's people belonged to the English he thought they had a right to eat them." To which Snook replied, "The

Company had sent these animals to multiply on the islands and that in case any of our ships touching here might be supplied with some fresh stock." Snook's own immediate needs were eventually provided for when a hog was produced and, more satisfactorily, two bullocks were shot and salted for his return voyage.

A return voyage to Macao rather than a voyage to Bombay it had to be. In his letter to the "Select Committee of Supra-Cargoes" at Canton, Snook explained:

> By the time I arrived [at Belau] the Westerly Monsoon was well set in and the vessel's sails and rigging in bad order and required much repair and being very short of provisions, and so bad a sailing vessel I knew it was impractical either to beat to Amboyna, Molucca or think of proceeding to Bombay, therefore thought it most prudent to wait at the island 'till the Monsoon was nearly over and then return to Macao, being the nearest port I could attempt to fetch.

The Blue-Green Dragon had been up to its tricks again and, together with the slow ship's poor condition, prevented the *Diamante* from reaching Macao before 3 December 1798. With Snook were "two Chinese, one Malay, and two Mallabars [left by McCluer] who had requested passage on the vessel." In keeping with Company instructions, Snook sold the *Diamante* for seven hundred dollars, the same figure that had been obtained for the much smaller *Oroolong*. He also settled accounts with his "7 European and 4 Chinese crew."

Snook had now devoted over a year of his time to the task of returning the three Belauan women to their homeland. He took passage to Bombay aboard H.M.S. *Intrepid,* Captain Hargood, and reached his home on 12 May 1799. In 1800 he wrote a long letter to Amasa Delano recounting events to that time, including White's death and news of Wedgebrough. In 1801 he was made "Master Attendant" for Bombay (a position similar to the U.S. Coast Guard's position of "Captain of the Port"), and in 1805 he was given the same position at Goa, where he remained until 1815.

Finally, one year before his retirement, Snook was made commodore at Surat. His chapter, a final chapter in the events stemming from the wreck of the *Antelope,* closes with a sword of honor he was awarded by the East India Company for his zeal and gallantry at the time he returned the women to Belau.

The sword remained with him to his last days at his home, Iver Elms, in the village of Iver, Bucks., England. He died in 1844. One hundred twenty years later, in 1964, his sword of honor was sold at auction. It was purchased for £370 by an arms dealer who, in turn, sold it to Wilkinsons, the modern-day razor-blade makers, who presented it to England's National Army Museum in Chelsea, London, where it is displayed.

The *Panther*, one of the two vessels the East India Company sent to Palau to carry the news of Lee Boo's death. Sketched by William Henry, who was with the expedition. (Courtesy of British Museum)

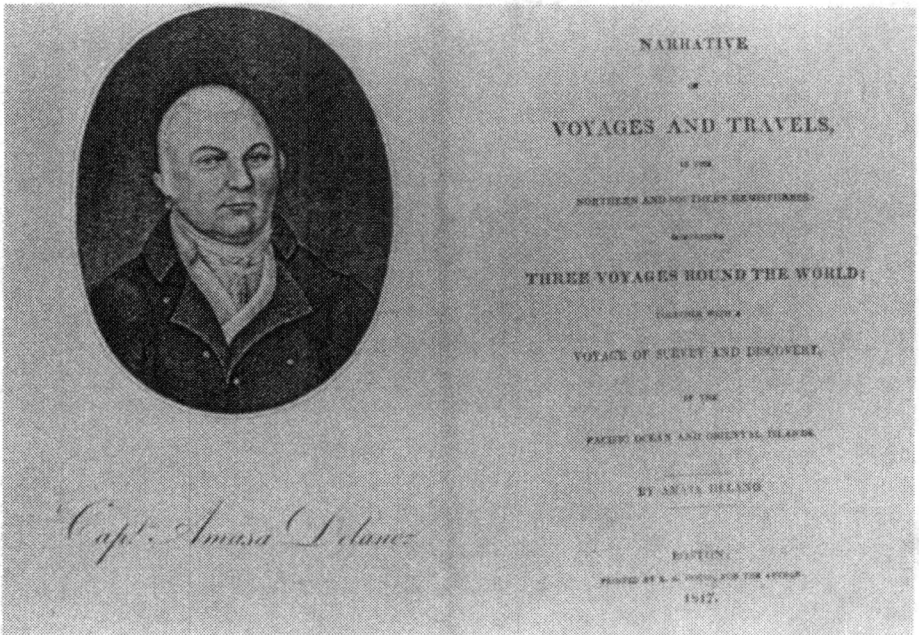

NARRATIVE

OF

VOYAGES AND TRAVELS,

IN THE

NORTHERN AND SOUTHERN HEMISPHERES;

COMPRISING

THREE VOYAGES ROUND THE WORLD;

TOGETHER WITH A

VOYAGE OF SURVEY AND DISCOVERY,

IN THE

PACIFIC OCEAN AND ORIENTAL ISLANDS.

BY AMASA DELANO.

BOSTON:

PRINTED BY E. G. HOUSE, FOR THE AUTHOR.

1817.

Capt. Amasa Delano

Amasa Delano, who sailed aboard the *Panther* with McCluer and thereby became the first American known to have visited Palau. (Portrait from his *Narrative*)

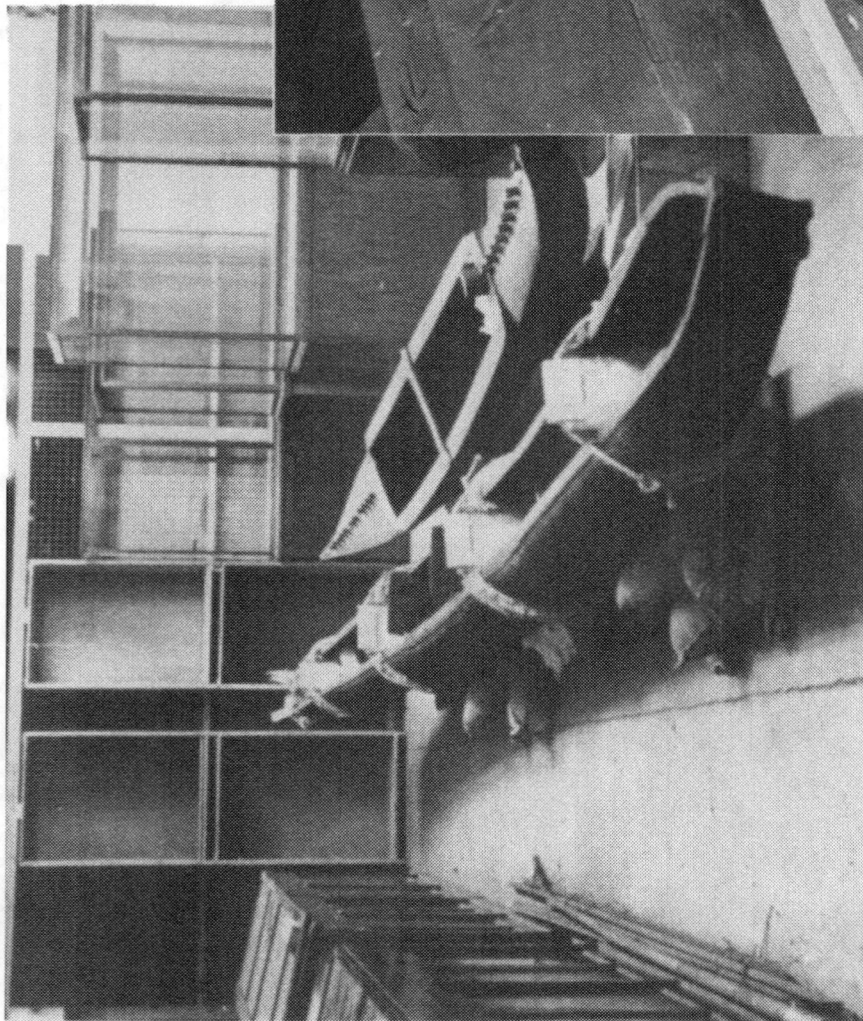

The canoe (left) carried from Palau to Macao by Captain McCluer and then sent on to Sir Joseph Banks in London aboard an East Indiaman. Now kept in storage by the Museum of Mankind, it measures 35 feet, 6 inches in length. (Courtesy of the Trustees of the British Museum)

(*Inset*) Detail of inlay work on side of canoe. (Author's photo)

nvestiture of the Rupac." The honor was declined by McCluer
t carried out upon the wrist of Captain Wilson in the manner
own here by an unknown artist following Keate's description
the awarding of the "order of the Bone." (Courtesy of British
useum)

The Bone itself . . . Quite
possibly the very one forced
over Henry Wilson's hand,
where he was admonished to
keep it. (Courtesy of
Museum of Mankind, Lon-
don)

Some of the artifacts Captain
Wilson brought from Palau, as dis-
played at the Museum of Mankind,
London. (Courtesy of Museum of
Mankind, London)

Gifts received by Captain Wilson from the people of Palau as illustrated in Keate's *Account*. These are now in the Museum of Mankind, London.

This is believed to be Kockywack and the two women McCluer took to Macao where, according to his journal, he commissioned Spoilum, "the famous painter," to paint them in March 1791. The three are doubtless from Palau, but why the artist portrayed them in an island setting so far from the home McCluer returned them to remains a mystery. (Courtesy of Museum of Mankind, London)

This Evening, THURSDAY, Oct. 31, 1833,

Their Majesties' Servants will perform Colman's Comedy of The

POOR GENTLEMAN

Sir Robert Bramble, Mr. DOWTON,   Sir C. Cropland, Mr. WOOD,
Lieutenant Worthington, Mr. G. BENNETT,   Frederick Bramble, Mr. COOPER,
Ollapod, Mr. HARLEY,   Corporal Foss, Mr. BLANCHARD,
Farmer Harrowby, Mr. TAYLEURE,   Stephen Harrowby, Mr. MEADOWS,
Humphrey Dobbins, Mr. BARTLEY,   Warner, Mr. THOMPSON,   Valet, Mr. HONNER
Emily Worthington, Miss E. TREE,   Miss Lucretia Mac Tab, Mrs. C. JONES,
Dame Harrowby, Mrs. BROAD,   Mary, Miss LEE.

After which will be performed (Second Time) a Grand Melo-Dramatic Romance, called

PRINCE LEE BOO.

(Founded on the principal Events in the popular Tale of that name)

THE NEW MUSIC BY MR. B. HUGHES.

The Dresses by Mr. Palmer and Mrs. Coombe. The Machinery by Mr. Saul. The Decorations by Mr. Bradwell
The new and extensive Scenery by Messrs. ANDREWS, MARINARI, ADAMS, FINLEY,
SEWARD, FRANKLIN, HOLLOGAN, and
Mr. STANFIELD.

Lord Arlingford, Mr. THOMPSON,
Mr. Mordaunt, ... (an East India Merchant) .... Mr. YOUNGE,
Waif, (a Cosmopolite) Mr. T. GREEN,
Capt. Wilson, (Commander of the E. I. Company's Ship, 'The Antelope') Mr. MATHEWS
Manning, (his First Mate) Mr. BEDFORD
Jack Blanchard, ... (his Boatswain) .... Mr. T. P. COOKE,
Bill Grummet, Mr. F. COOKE,   Tailor, Mr. HONNER,   Servant, Mr. EAST,
Miss Arlingford, Miss E. PHILLIPS,
Mrs. Fusby, (Captain Wilson's Housekeeper) Mrs. BROAD,
Betty, (her Maid) Mrs. CHESTER,   Mrs. Bates, Miss SOMERVILLE,
Sailors—Messrs. EAST, HENRY, ALLCROFT, BRUCE, BOXALL, BATTEY, DICKINSON, GUNN,
Abba Thulle, ... (King of Pelew) ...... Mr. HATTON,
Prince Lee Boo, ... (his Son) ..... Mademoiselle CELESTE,
Arrah Kooker, (King's Brother) Mr. FENTON,   Artingal Chief Mr. HOWELL,
Artinguls—Messrs. BROWN, BRADY, RUSSELL, STANLEY,
Ulva, .. (a Pelewese, betrothed to Prince Lee Boo) .. Miss H. CAWSE,
Chorus of the Pelewese—Mesdames ALLCROFT, BODEN, R. BODEN, CONNELLY, DALTON,
Pelewese Dancers—Mesdames THOMASIN, FOSTER, FAIRBROTHER, RYALLS, HUNT,

Act I—Sea View on the ISLAND of PELEW, with YAWL on the STOCKS, and

WRECK OF THE ANTELOPE

IN THE DISTANCE.

A MANGROVE IN THE ISLAND OF ARTINGAL.
EXTERIOR OF THE PALACE OF ABBA THULLE, WITH THE SETTING SUN, AND

MODE OF PELEWESE WORSHIP.

A FIATOOKA, OR BURIAL PLACE.

The Cove of Oorolong, with the

LAUNCH OF THE YAWL.

and Departure of Prince Lee Boo for England.

Act I.—CAPTAIN WILSON'S APARTMENT IN LONDON, VIEW OF GREENWICH HOSPITAL.

GARDENS OF CAPTAIN WILSON'S HOUSE.

A VILLA on the Thames, near GRAVESEND, an outward bound

East Indiaman in Full Sail,

STORM, and CLEARING-UP of MIST to a BRIGHT MOONLIGHT.

The reception of PRINCE LEE BOO

Authorises its announcement for repetition Every Evening until further notice.

To-morrow, the Tragedy of MACBETH. And PRINCE LEE BOO.
On Saturday........the Comedy of AS YOU LIKE IT. And PRINCE LEE BOO.
On Monday.....Shakspeare's Play of Henry the Fifth. And PRINCE LEE BOO.
On Tuesday.....The Merry Wives of Windsor. And PRINCE LEE BOO.
On Wednesday,....(in consequence of the great overflow last Evening,) will be repeated
Lord Byron's Tragedy of WERNER.
Warner, Mr. Macready,   Ulric, Mr. King, (his 3rd Appearance at this Theatre)   Gabor, Mr. Cooper

SHAKSPEARE'S HISTORICAL PLAY OF

ANTONY and CLEOPATRA

Playbill of 1833 for the Theatre Royal, Drury Lane. (Courtesy of Victoria
and Albert Museum, London)

Southwark students performing their Lee Boo Bicentennial pageant at the Rotherhithe Theatre Workshop. "Captain Wilson" is reviewing his "troops" after the shipwreck in "Palau." Other scenes were enacted across the street in St. Mary's Rotherhithe as part of the same performance, July 1984. (Photo by D. L. Peacock)

The Rotherhithe pageant also included a parade when performers and audience alike moved from St. Mary's Church to the Theatre Workshop. Floats included the "Antelope" (background) and a whale encountered on the "voyage" to Palau. The whale has just passed the Peter Hills School, where the figures of two students watch from the second floor even as they did when Lee Boo walked these very streets. (Photo by D. L. Peacock)

19

OMAI AMONG OTHERS

LEE BOO was not alone. He was not the first from distant and exotic islands to visit England; nor, of course, was he the last. An ever-increasing succession of Lee Boos have strolled through St. James's Park since "A Prince of Mine" was there in 1784. Thanks to wings of flight undreamed of by Lunardi, modern-day Lee Boos can be seen there, as elsewhere in London, their flight bags bearing the imprint of some remote island airline: Air Nauru, Air Tungaru, or possibly Air Micronesia—the airline Lee Boo would take to begin a trip to London today.

London is as powerful a magnet today as it has been over the centuries, and it has pulled people from all over the world. The impulse to yield to its pull has been as strong as the pull and the impulse to aid and abet has been almost as strong for some Londoners.

Outstanding among the first who were intent on bringing Pacific Islanders to London was Sir Joseph Banks. While collecting his botanical specimens on Cook's first voyage, Banks also collected Tupia and his servant Tayeto, two Tahitians who later died at Batavia (Djakarta) en route to England. Saddened by this, but still determined, Banks had a second chance at the conclusion of Cook's second voyage, when Captain Furneaux returned with Omai, a young Tahitian man whom Banks had met during the first voyage.

On 14 July 1774, just ten years to the day before the arrival of Lee Boo, Furneaux delivered Omai to Portsmouth. Omai, or Mai as he was known among his own people, recognized Banks, who met him at the dock. The two were able to converse well enough to prepare

Omai for presentation to the king, which followed just three days later. Lord Sandwich then took Omai to the palace at Kew where, appropriately, some of the flora on display in the gardens had been contributed by Banks. King George III greeted Omai, gave him a sword, and ordered that he should be given an allowance while in England.

In the months that followed, Omai was invited everywhere, but not before Banks withdrew him from society, had him inoculated for smallpox, and stayed with him until he had fully recovered from the very considerable ordeal. Back in circulation, he was a hit. Sir Joshua Reynolds painted his portrait and Boswell argued with Johnson about the possible advantages, if not the superiority, of the Tahitian way of life as exemplified by Omai. But Johnson, although impressed with Omai, would have nothing to do with such ideas, arguing that bread from the baker was more to his taste than bread from a tree. After nearly two years in England, Omai might have agreed with Dr. Johnson. His sponsors, suspecting that he might be adjusting too well to London life, arranged for him to be taken home.

Ironically, it fell to Captain Cook to deliver Omai to his home islands. Cook had not been enthusiastic about having Omai travel to London in the first place. Omai had wanted mightily to go, Furneaux had apparently been equally anxious to take him, and Cook had not intervened. But Cook would rather have taken Oedidee, a Tahitian who had traveled with him among Polynesian islands as an interpreter. Oedidee, too, had wanted to go to London, and members of Cook's crew had encouraged him with tales of "what great things he would see," leading him to believe that he would "return with immence riches, according to his ideas of riches." But Cook took a far more realistic view, stating, "I thought proper to undeceive him . . . knowing that the only inducement of his going was the expectation of returning and I could see no prospect of an opportunity of that kind happening, unless a ship was expressly sent out for that purpose, which neither I nor any one else had a right to expect."

But here was Cook delivering Omai to the island of Huahine, where he could be left among relatives. Cook had no illusions about how Omai would be treated. He was not of high family, and although he had comported himself well among the high society of London, the many gifts bestowed upon him by the English could only create envy within the higher ranks of his own people. Cook tried to ensure

Omai's survival in spite of these inevitable jealousies by building a European-style house for him, and by supplying him with a garden and livestock. But, sadly, within three years of Cook's departure, Omai was dead.

Some ten years later, when Captain Bligh brought the *Bounty* to Tahiti to obtain breadfruit plants for the West Indies, he talked to "Odiddee who confirmed to me the death of Omai . . . who had lived only thirty months after Captn. Cook left him at Huaheine." Still later, in 1829, William Ellis, a missionary, wrote in greater detail about Omai's return. Cook, according to Ellis, had arranged for the land on which Omai was to live, which consisted of "about 200 yards along the sea shore." Omai's garden had been "enclosed and planted with seeds brought from England or the Cape of Good Hope." Omai had also been given "a breed of horses, goats, and other useful animals." After Omai's death, which by all accounts was from natural causes, most of his possessions disappeared. Ellis was glad to find a Bible said to have belonged to Omai, but he saw little else. Ellis reported, "The spot where Mai's house stood is still called Beritani, or Britain, by the inhabitants of Huahine." If Omai, or anyone else at that little bit of "Britain," had hoped the English would soon return they might well have listened to the words of the poet Cowper:

> Alas! expect it not. We found no bait to
> tempt us in thy country. Doing good,
> Disinterested good, is not our trade.
> We travel far, 'tis true, but not for nought;
> And must be brib'd to encompass earth again
> By other hopes, and richer fruits, than yours.

The problem of returning an island visitor is also illustrated in the story of Aoutourou, another Tahitian, who had been taken to Paris even earlier by Bougainville. Aoutourou is described as being some thirty years of age, of average height, and companionable—especially with the ladies. He is said to have enjoyed dancing, the theatre, and the opera. Although he lived with Bougainville, he is reported to have become well enough acquainted with Paris to go out alone and walk about shopping in the city. But after he had been eleven months in Paris, Bougainville felt that Aoutourou must be returned to his home. This proved difficult in the extreme, and Bougainville had to finance a portion of the voyage himself. Aoutourou never got beyond Madagascar, where he died, possibly of smallpox.

For an American example of these early pioneers of cultural exchange we need look no further than our old friend Amasa Delano. Now with his own ship, Delano was in "Owhyhee" (Hawaii) in 1801. A young man whom he describes as a "king's son" who had taken the name of a Scotsman, Alexander Stewart, asked to sail with him to Canton. This boy and a companion of his received permission to go, but when Delano was well out at sea he found three more boys aboard as stowaways. Delano says that he personally inoculated all of these young men against smallpox. In Canton, Alexander Stewart and his Hawaiian friend were invited to go to London aboard an Indiaman. Delano, remembering Lee Boo's fate there, resisted the idea at first, but eventually gave in on assurances that they would be well cared for and let them go. The last he heard of Stewart he had been "adopted" by a "gentleman of consequence" and had remained in England. One of the other boys, whom Delano named Bill, traveled with him to Boston, where he performed on the stage several times in *The Tragedy of Captain Cook.* He later returned to Hawaii with Delano but did not stay, choosing instead to go to Canton with Delano's brother Samuel, and Delano says he heard nothing more of him.

Then, in what is perhaps the best-known and saddest story of all, Liholiho, King Kamehameha II, traveled to London. His people had been so favorably impressed by the English during George Vancouver's two visits to Hawaii that he had decided to visit England himself. He traveled aboard the *L'Aigle,* Captain Starbuck, reaching England in May 1824. Two months later he was dead from the measles. His wife, Kamamalu, who had made the trip with him, had died six days earlier. Their remains were returned to Hawaii aboard the *Blonde,* Captain Lord Byron, in what Te Rangi Hiroa (Sir Peter Buck) described as "one of the most gracious acts that one country has ever extended to another." There followed a friendship between British and Hawaiian royalty and a kindly disposition between the two island peoples that continues to this day—a friendship made visible by the Union Jack incorporated in the Hawaii State flag.

Aside from Liholiho, questions arise as to the propriety of taking islanders away from their home islands. Should such a practice have been condoned? The explorer Pedro Fernandez de Quiros, whose travels took him through the Pacific Islands, asked the question as long ago as 1605. Writing from Peru to the Archbishop of Lima, he proposed to "bring back here or take to Spain some natives from thence in order that they may become acquainted with and take a liking to our political customs and friendly social relations; that they may learn our language and make use of it on returning to their country . . ." The reply he received from Church authorities stated in part:

> In answer to the first question whether it is licit to take some of the natives from those parts and bring them to territories inhabited by Christians in order to teach them Spanish so that they may act as interpreters, and also that they may observe our manner of living and take a liking to it, this may be done, firstly, in a way of which there can be no moral doubt, namely by blandishments so that they are induced by overtures of friendship and material gifts and drawn either of their own free will or with the consent of their parents, a way in which there would be no injury to them nor breach of any law.

In short, if they want to come and there are no moral or legal barriers, you may bring them.

For their part, the Protestants in England, especially with reference to Omai, expressed regret that more attention had not been given to Christian education. But they did not always fail in this regard. The *London Chronicle* for 1–3 November 1791 carried a "Letter from Winchester" in which was stated that an "African Prince" named John Nambana, "Prince of Robana," had visited Plymouth where he had been shown "the ships, great guns, and other objects of curiosity." This young African is then reported to have made the following observations to his hosts:

> He told them in English, which he speaks with tolerable ease, these things were different to what he was sent to learn; and he was afraid he should not have room in his mind for it all. In the course of the voyage from Africa he was taught to read; an attainment he is fond of, that he is never more gratified than when asked to read in the Testament, which he calls the good book. This untutored African Prince seems to consider those that have the power of imparting knowledge to others, as the first of human

beings; he therefore looks upon a schoolmaster as the most
honorable of all characters. He said, "When I return to
Africa, if I live to succeed my father, I will not be the King
of my people; I will be their school master."

To which the good Captain Wilson might have said, "Amen," but
the wise Captain Cook might have asked, "But how will you
return?"

Perhaps Cook's longer voyages and lengthier absences gave him a
better understanding than most of the anxiety of those who wait for a
voyager's return. Perhaps he empathized more with the parent who
waited at home than with the child who went to sea. And George
Keate, perhaps speaking for Henry Wilson as well, expressed empathy
for the waiting Abba Thulle when he wrote at the end of his book:

> the human mind is far more pained by *uncertainty* than a
> knowledge of the *worst*—every reader will lament, he
> should to this moment remain ignorant, that his long-
> looked for Son can return no more!

When Abba Thulle had asked Captain Wilson how long it would
be before Lee Boo would return, the captain had estimated "thirty
moons, or might chance to extend to six more." Whereupon Abba
Thulle had tied a corresponding number of knots on a line. Keate assumes that Abba Thulle then untied the knots with each passing moon
until there were no more. What a difference it might have made if, at
that time, a George Keate had remained in Belau instead of a Madan
Blanchard. Keate, with his enormous respect for Abba Thulle, would
doubtless have chronicled the aging chief's reactions to the inordinate
amount of time that passed without a word of Lee Boo. And he would
have described for us the abject despair that Abba Thulle experienced
on 3 April 1788, when the first English ship to call at Belau since the
wreck of the *Antelope* came without news or even understanding of
what had occurred there less than four years earlier.

The first post-*Antelope* ship known to have been seen at Belau
proper (in contrast with the islands to the southwest which, although
a remote part of the group, are not germane to the story of the *Antelope*) was the *Iphigenia,* Captain Douglas. The *Iphigenia* had sailed with
the *Felice,* Captain John Mears, but the two had parted at Zamboanga

in the Philippines, from where the *Iphigenia* had sailed prior to reaching Belau. Captain Douglas was en route to the northwest coast of North America to collect furs. Ironically, he had with him some "Lee Boos" of his own, including a Hawaiian whom Sir Peter Buck described as "a Kauai Chief named Tianna (Kaiana), aged 32 and 6 feet 5 inches tall." Just before reaching Belau, a companion of the chief's, a Hawaiian named Tawnee, died and was buried at sea. Kaiana had also been ill, but survived to be returned to his home islands later in the voyage.

When Captain Douglas brought the *Iphigenia* as close to the shores of Belau as he dared approach, he was greeted by men in canoes who shouted "English" and "Moore." In a footnote added after completion of the voyage, it is explained that "Moore" was probably "Mora mey," signifying "in the Pelew language, 'Come to me.' " But at the time Douglas steered his ship past Belau, where "reef appeared within reef," he knew nothing of the *Antelope*, Captain Wilson, or Lee Boo, as the men in the canoes would have assumed he must know. The ship was obviously English; it was even of the size of the *Antelope*, but neither the captain nor any of his crew had any knowledge of the events of 1783.

To quote from the one available account of this visit by Douglas, "One of these boats [canoes?] continued to follow the *Iphigenia* for a long time, and one of the people cried out, from time to time, 'Eeboo, Eeboo,' and exerted himself to the utmost in making signs for them to go back. Indeed, when he perceived that all his endeavors were in vain to persuade them to return, his actions bore the appearance of a man in the most frantic distress." The writer of this account then goes on to explain further that Captain Douglas

> could not know that his countrymen had received every aid, comfort, and kindness which these hospitable islanders could afford; and that the sovereign of them had entrusted his son to the care of Captain Wilson, to return with him to England, to be instructed in the arts and manners of our country. Had he been acquainted with these interesting occurrences, there is no doubt but his humanity would have exerted itself to the utmost, in order to contrive some further communication with them; for who can have the least doubt but that the canoes which followed the *Iphigenia* were sent to receive Lee Boo; or at least, to hear some

intelligence concerning him; and that the native who has been described as calling after the ship, and employing the most frantic actions, when he found that he called in vain, was any other than *Abba Thulle,* the father of the young prince, agitated by the most poignant sensations of disappointment and despair.

This author does not rest the matter here; he goes on, sparing the conscience of his reader nothing, and aims a particularly pointed barb at the corporate body of the East India Company:

> As no attention whatever had been then paid by the East India Company to Abba Thulle, for the kind and humane treatment afforded by him to the crew of their ship the *Antelope,* he may be supposed to have been suffering, for too long a time, the alternate impressions of hope and fear. It may therefore be conceived what his feelings were, when he first saw the distant sails of the *Iphigenia* whiten in the sun. It may also be imagined with what haste his canoe was launched from the beach to bear him to the ship, and how swiftly she was driven on to receive, as he might hope, a son, who was returned with the various knowledge and attainments of Europe, to adorn and improve his own country. But it is difficult to conceive, as it would be impossible to describe, what such a mind as his must feel, when the *Iphigenia* proceeded on her way, and the people on board, occupied in avoiding the surrounding dangers, were as inattentive to his distress, as they were ignorant of the cause of it.

Where was Blanchard when he was needed? Had he reason, perhaps, to prefer that this English ship sail on and leave him alone? Might he have preferred to think that ignorance is bliss? That the English need not know of him, and the people of Belau need not know whatever melancholy news the English might have of Lee Boo? We will probably never know. And we cannot know the anguish Abba Thulle must have felt at encountering Englishmen aboard an English ship to whom the name of Lee Boo meant nothing.

For Abba Thulle there was only one Lee Boo and the only absolute certainty about his trip to England was that he had not returned.

20

TARTARY, SURAT,
OR THE PELEWS

HOW COULD the Abba Thulle of two hundred years ago
know that not every Englishman had heard of Lee Boo? How
could he have known that not even everyone in London had
heard of Lee Boo, or of Omai, for that matter? Indeed, many more
than these two could have come and gone and the general populace
would hardly have noticed. But there were those for whom the islands
they came from represented a special challenge. Witness the words of
the Reverend Mr. Burder of Coventry who informed his colleagues
that there is

> a new world—a world of islands in the vast Pacific Ocean
> —some of them as promising in the disposition of the peo-
> ple, as in the appearance of the country.

The Reverend Burder's words to the "professors of the Gospel"
whom he would have "do something immediately" did not go
unheeded. The "Rev. Messrs" and just plain "Messrs" who read his
sermon then gathered at the Castle and Falcon, an inn on Aldergate
Street, London. Over a period of nearly five days they met at the inn,
listened to each other's sermons at various churches and, on the fifth
day, 25 September 1795, at the Castle and Falcon, they obliged the
Reverend Burder by "unanimously" resolving that

> the first attempt of this Society shall be to send Missionaries
> to Otaheite, or some other of the islands of the South Sea,

˙and also that Missions may be, as early as possible, attempted to the Coast of Africa, or to Tartary, by Astracan, or to Surat, on the Malabar Coast, or to Bengal, or the Coromandel Coast, or to the Island of Sumatra, or to the Pelew Islands.

To the question of another speaker, "Am I my brother's keeper?" more than enough men, some with their wives, eventually stepped forward to answer in the affirmative and volunteer to go forth. And to the question "who is my neighbour?" apparently those who inhabited the farthest islands qualified to be treated as neighbors and, in time, to be brought into the fold.

Later, the Reverend Thomas Pentycross confronted the skeptics, real or imagined, dead or alive:

> May we not justly challenge infidelity to propose a greater good to mankind than the Gospel of Jesus Christ? Spirit of Hume, the subtil; spirit of Rousseau, the fanciful; spirit of Voltaire, the cowardly, tho' daring! . . . Moses' opponents! Tell us what you can suggest for the happiness of the world equivalent to the Gospel? What book like the New Testament can you put into the hands of poor pagans in the South Seas?

One does not have to be an infidel to wish that those challenged could have answered from their graves. Perhaps native islanders would have been referred to books that might help them to cope with the missionaries. More probably the subtle Hume, the fanciful Rousseau, or the cowardly tho' daring Voltaire would simply have pointed out that the "Godly men," to borrow McCluer's phrase, had the cart before the horse, in that the islanders had not yet been taught their letters. Rousseau in particular could have been counted on to say a great deal more about how people learn, whether on a pagan island or a Christian continent.

But first these teacher-preacher professors of the gospel had to get to the islands. The London Missionary Society was founded on the premise that they would find a ship and send missionaries to the Pacific Islands. As it happened, they found a captain before they found a ship. Another Wilson—James Wilson, unrelated to Henry—stepped forward. This Wilson had been twenty years in India, had returned to enjoy his retirement in England, was converted, read an article about the society's plans, and volunteered. The ship that was needed that "the voyage might be completed, if the Lord of the wind and seas smile on our attempt" materialized as the *Duff*, a ship not unlike the *Antelope*.

Less than a year after the "Rev. Messrs" had resolved to take action, the *Duff* sailed down the Thames with its hymn-singing party of thirty men, six women, and three children. (Of the men, only four were ordained ministers; five were carpenters, two bricklayers, one smith, etc., but all were listed as missionaries.)

The voyage began on 10 August 1796. Captain Wilson had intended to follow a route similar to that taken by Captain Henry Wilson, but the closer he got to Cape Horn, the more he disliked the weather he encountered. He reversed his course and took the more favorable winds toward the Cape of Good Hope. Sailing south of Australia and New Zealand, he did not turn north until he reached the longitude of Tahiti. He then sailed among the islands that Captain Cook had coincidentally but conveniently named the Society Islands "because of their contiguity." The *Duff* dropped anchor at Matavai Bay in Tahiti on 6 March 1797, and her first unordered consignment of missionaries and missionary helpers was delivered.

By the time James Wilson brought the *Duff* into Micronesian waters eight months later, he had parceled out all of his missionaries. It had been left to his discretion whether he would reserve any "Godly men" for Belau, but his instructions had apparently prejudiced him against this by stating, "Suppose that, by a new Chief having arisen with less favourable dispositions than the father of Lee Boo, or through any other cause, you should be prevented from leaving our breathren there, with perfect satisfaction to yourself and them, what would be the effect?" The effect would have been to require the *Duff* to double back to Polynesia, and although James Wilson did not want to take that risk, he did feel obliged to call at Belau en route to Canton.

Unlike the *Antelope*, the *Duff* raised Belau from the east and Captain Wilson found himself approaching the largest island, Babeldaob, on 5 November 1797. Even though he says he did not have McCluer's charts with him, James Wilson somehow knew that he was off the coast of Artingall, the home of Abba Thulle's arch rivals to the north of Koror. Some two hundred persons soon gathered on the beach, and although the weather was not good and a storm threatening, three canoes made their way to the ship. As the Belauans called out to the men on the ship, Captain Wilson thought he heard the name of Abba Thulle spoken but not the name of Lee Boo. He strained to listen and had Keate's "Vocabulary" in his hands but found it of little help. He did understand that the men in the canoes were imploring him by word and gesture to proceed to an anchoring place with the obvious intention that he should seek shelter from the impending storm and stay awhile. But one Wilson upon the reefs of Belau was enough, and James Wilson was not going to imperil the *Duff* by anchoring or lingering about with a storm at his heels. However, the *Duff*'s first mate, still another Wilson—William—wrote that this premature departure was:

> much regreted by us, as it had all along been the Captain's intention to stay here a few days, for the purpose of learning what we could of the inhabitants respecting the expediency of settling a mission among them; and to prepare the way for Missionaries, by distributing some useful articles retained in the ship for these and the Feejee people, from a hope of being favoured at both places with safe anchorage and friendly intercourse; but for the present voyage, we concluded every thing of this nature at an end, and proceeded to make the best of our way to China, cherishing the hope of there receiving letters from our dear friends in England, to whom we now thought ourselves drawing near, though still at the distance of many thousand miles.

The *Duff* sailed on after only the briefest contact with people whom its captain had hoped to serve. Although the brevity of the stay was regretted, William Wilson's comments about those he had seen were not very complimentary. Based on his brief observations, he felt that the people of Belau, along with the other people of the Caroline Islands that the *Duff* had contacted, were not to be compared favorably with the people of Polynesia, who were of larger stature and more impressive physically. To which readers of Keate's book can be heard to say "O, ye of little faith!" for the strength of the people of Belau, as exemplified by Abba Thulle and Lee Boo, was one of character and it is upon character, surely, that a missionary might find the rock upon which to build.

But even the voices of praise for the Polynesians soon had to contend with letters and reports from those now living in the islands, those whom the *Duff* had deposited and others, who wrote back to London describing the work that was needed to win the inhabitants from their wicked ways. Familiarity breeds contempt. The islands that wishful thinkers wanted to think of as newly discovered Edens were now being described as tropical hells. It is almost as if they believed the devil were island born and islanders his slaves. Bernard Smith, in his *European Vision and the South Pacific,* illustrates how the tide had turned:

> Many who in their youth had wept like Coleridge over the tomb of Prince Lee Boo, paradigm of the natural virtues, came in the end to give their pennies to the missionary societies to save the people of the Pacific from their natural vices, and to agree with Coleridge that "Christianity brings immence advantages to a savage."

It is doubtful that any pennies collected in England ever benefited the people of Belau. Similarly, pennies collected in New England Sunday schools went, primarily, to purchase and support a series of sailing vessels all named *Morning Star* that served missionary efforts in the Marshall Islands and the Eastern Caroline Islands, but did not reach Belau. Instead, Spanish priests, presumably operating on a penny budget of their own, pioneered efforts on behalf of Christendom in Belau. The priests and Protestant missionaries from Germany, followed by Jesuits and Maryknoll sisters from the United States, made major contributions, especially in the field of education—teaching the people their letters and building schools for that purpose. For example, Father Edwin McManus, S.J., of Brooklyn, New York, compiled the *Palauan-English Dictionary,* which, after being edited and expanded by Dr. Lewis S. Josephs and the Belauan linguistic scholar Masa-aki Emisiochel, ran to some 455 pages when published in 1977. Anyone who ever heard Father McManus speak Belauan with his rich Brooklyn accent can appreciate what a monumental achievement it was for him to have compiled a dictionary without a background in linguistics. What a joy it would have been to Captain Wilson and to George Keate to compare it with their "Vocabulary of the Pelew Language" which appears at the back of Keate's book. They would have been pleased to learn that their modest effort was not so far off the mark after all.

And how pleased the Rotherhithe captain and the London poet would have been to learn that one of the words in their "Vocabulary" has been retained as the name of a street in Rotherhithe. This came about in 1912, when the London County Council endorsed the recommendation of the Bermondsey Borough Council and authorized the renaming of that portion of Neptune Street that lies closest to St. Mary's as Rupack Street. The city fathers sought to honor both Abba Thulle, "Rupack or King of one of the Pelew Islands," and the people of the Pelews by renaming one portion of Neptune Street "Rupack" Street and the other "Pelew" Street. Only the "Rupack" renaming was carried out. For unspecified reasons, the renaming in favor of "Pelew" was never effected.

"Rupack," the street sign, is fixed to the side of a pub: The Neptune. The pub faces Brunel Street, named for the famous engineers, Sir Marc Isambard Brunel and his son Isambard Kingdom Brunel. It is said that the Brunels worshipped at St. Mary's during at least some of the many long years it took them to build a tunnel under the Thames that is still being used today by Rotherhithe-London commuters. Their tunnel, in turn, inspired another tunnel, this one for vehicular traffic, and it was this second tunnel that severed Neptune Street and created the need for a renaming. That was in 1908. A short time earlier, in 1907, Reverend Edward Beck's book about his Parish of Rotherhithe had been published, briefly retelling the story of the *Antelope,* Abba Thulle, Captain Wilson, and Lee Boo. Fresh from reading this recounting, the authorities made the decision that resulted in the naming of Rupack Street.

No wonder the poets, the essayists, and the dramatists are inspired by all of this. Whereas Abba Thulle knew nothing of London save that his son died there, he is remembered at the pub Neptune where nothing is known of Belau. The missionary efforts conceived at the Castle and Falcon on Aldergate Street never reached Abba Thulle's Belau, but the most renowned *rubak* of all is remembered at the corner of Brunel and Rupack streets, only a few steps away from where Lee Boo lies in his sober grave.

21

THE HAPPY ENDING

WHERE does the story of Lee Boo and the shipwreck of the *Antelope* end? It does not end. Only individual participation in the never-ending continuum of events ends. Everything that is written, everything that is revealed helps to keep the story alive. Oddly enough, very little of it is fiction, which, judged by the earliest contribution by a novelist, is just as well.

In 1809 a work of fiction appeared in London bearing the title *The Adventures of Madiboo, a Native of the Pelew Islands.* The anonymous author assumes that his readers have already read Keate, would rather think of Lee Boo as still living, and would want to know what happened to Blanchard. The story begins with Blanchard, a tear on his cheek, waving goodbye to his fellow Englishmen as they depart in the *Oroolong*. Blanchard adopts an amiable boy named Madiboo before being killed in a raid he led—victim of a spear gone astray. Madiboo then meets an Irishman named Mooney, is taken to Europe aboard a French privateer, and falls upon hard times in Spain, where he is regarded as a vagrant. When asked if he has relatives, he replies, in effect, "Why yes, my Prince who lives in England and my King who will make me a nobleman if I return." This unlikely story is met with derisive laughter and Madiboo is thrown into prison. Somehow he meets and falls in love with a girl named Laura but is separated from her in his attempt to reach England, where he is shipwrecked on the coast of Cornwall. He goes to London to try to find Lee Boo. Laura reappears. Madiboo has a duel with her boyfriend and kills him. Betrayed, he goes off to the West Indies. While at sea his ship is consumed in flames; Madiboo jumps to a passing ship, and who should be aboard but his old friend, Mooney. Madiboo eventually gets back to London on an American ship, finds work, finds Laura, but never finds or even sees Lee Boo. At the happy ending, he is set to marry Laura with, apparently, no further thoughts of Lee Boo or of returning to the life of a nobleman in his homeland!

Such cavalier treatment of historical fact is not unusual in fiction, but more often than not it does a disservice to Pacific Islanders. A Madiboo, real or imagined, then or now, may well wish to visit Europe, but to suppose that he would search there for a place to spend the rest of his life rather than return to his homeland is not credible. Conversely, to imagine, as so many authors do, that a European would find lasting happiness in the islands is to ignore the reality of a Blanchard, a McCluer, and any number of others who met sad endings. But the more serious reality ignored by the author of Madiboo was Lee Boo—the one real Belau Islander in London; dead or alive, he would not have been all that difficult to find. He was not found, presumably, because finding Lee Boo in his grave would have marred the author's concept of a happy ending. Yet the reality of Lee Boo's death cannot be written away, nor should it be. Smallpox was one of the realities of the age in which Lee Boo lived. Thousands upon thousands throughout most of the world died of the disease. Had he not traveled away from home, Lee Boo might have been spared, but in time the disease traveled to the islands and did its devastating work there, as elsewhere, until finally conquered some one hundred ninety years after his death.

The happy ending to the story of Lee Boo and the wreck of the *Antelope* is not to be found in London or in the islands the English called Pelew, but in the village where Captain Wilson retired—Colyton, in the land of Devonshire cream and strawberries. If the novelist needs a happy ending, let it be found there, with the captain as overlord of his own Oroolong House.

If Henry Wilson deserved a happy ending, so did Lee Boo. But who would begrudge the captain what his protégé could not have? Certainly the captain was entitled to his last years of contentment. Here was a man who may have been the first East India Company captain to have circumnavigated the globe, even though a shipwreck intervened and he had to complete the voyage in a ship that was not his own. In his little village he would almost certainly have been the only one to have accomplished such a feat. Whereas his fellow villagers could only read of the voyages of others, Henry Wilson could reflect on his own. Frequently he must have dwelt on "his" islands of Pelew, and especially his Oroolong. One wonders if he took the gift of the island seriously. Presumably not. In any event, no Englishman has since been known to live on it again, not even for three months. But Henry Wilson was more interested in the people he had known there: Abba Thulle, Raa Kook, Arra Kooker, and the others. The sincerity of his interest was demonstrated when he commissioned his son-in-law, John Pearce Hockin, to write the *Supplement* to Keate's *Account* that would assure Keate's readers that Abba Thulle had not been forgotten. In the *Supplement,* everyone is accounted for, including Madan Blanchard, whose death was certainly not a happy one, whatever the specific cause.

If Lee Boo were to have his happy ending he would, one presumes, have had to return to his home islands, as did Omai. But in reality both endings were unhappy: Lee Boo went too soon to a grave too far from home, and Omai went to live a few pathetic years among people who coveted his possessions but not his knowledge. Yet who can blame them for coveting Omai's treasure trove of souvenirs that included a hand organ, a puppet show, a coat of mail, a suit of armor, and a menagerie of livestock—cattle, sheep, geese, turkeys, and three horses. Although he would have loved to return home with even one horse, Lee Boo was a practical person who might have been able to put the things he had learned abroad to creative use. The more modest souvenirs he would have brought home would have presented less cause for jealousy. Because of this, the prospects for a happy ending were much brighter for Lee Boo than for Omai, had he returned in time to be reunited with the Abba Thulle who sent him.

A vision of Lee Boo returned to his islands is possible if one remembers those, such as Kockywack, who did return. Lee Boo, too, would have been surrounded by those eager to hear his stories. The telling would have taken many days and nights. In addition to his knotted cord, he would have used any number of other mnemonic devices to trigger his memory, even printed matter. We can see Lee Boo proudly seated next to Abba Thulle, turning the pages of a London newspaper and describing what the people of England did, what they talked about, and what absorbed their interests. It would not be as totally foreign to Abba Thulle as might be supposed. There were, for example, frequent advertisements offering turtles for sale, even as there might have been in Belau, had newspapers then been printed there. Whatever Abba Thulle did not readily comprehend, Lee Boo would have set out to explain. In time Abba Thulle's understanding of the ways of the English would have sharpened his insight and his reputation as a statesman would have grown. Lee Boo, whatever his evolving role, would have enhanced that reputation. Visiting ship captains would have been impressed and almost certainly the Wilsons—father, son, and brother—would have made every effort to call at Koror if they could have expected Lee Boo to be there to greet them.

But if Lee Boo *had* returned after an absence of some two years, as did Omai, would he have forgotten how to be a Belauan? Hardly. He would not have forgotten Belauan traditions, customs, or protocol. He would not have forgotten the preparations required for a proper feast, the seafood preferred, where and how such things were caught. (It might be noted here that the frequent requests for additional time that Abba Thulle made of the visiting English, especially prior to their departures, would almost certainly have been prompted by the need to collect and prepare the requisite foods for auspicious occasions, as well as the need for time for people from throughout Belau to gather together.) Lee Boo would not have forgotten the parts of a canoe, which must have been as well known to a Belauan boy as the parts of an automobile or a bicycle are to the youth of England or America today. He would not have forgotten the deference paid to older people and persons of rank, or the place of children in society. Nor would he have forgotten the songs, chants, and legends of Belau, including some of those still told as stories and depicted on story boards today. And, to mention but one thing more, he would certainly not have forgotten how to throw a spear, for, as Keate observed, he practiced the art with young Harry at Rotherhithe.

Can it be said that what Lee Boo learned in England would have contributed to the life of his people? Assuming that he could have taught his peers their letters, what use would that have been without a more generous supply of reading matter than he would have been able to bring with him? Beyond ephemeral entertainment, it is difficult to imagine how more than a chosen few would have benefited, except in such ways as somewhat enlightened leadership might have provided.

Of course Lee Boo would have seen to the planting of his seeds, and some of them, under the watchful care of his female relatives, might

have grown and given him pleasure and, as they multiplied, pleasure
to others. Gardening was women's work in Belau and not one of the
masculine pursuits that would have been expected of him. Better that
he should be a craftsman who wore his adze proudly on his shoulder as
did his father. Perhaps he would have fashioned a bower of bamboo in
the style he observed on the island of St. Helena, but he had not
learned how to build a permanent house of solid walls, and had he
returned he could only have described such buildings and let his friends
marvel at his knowledge of such things.

But it did not happen. Lee Boo did not return and what Abba
Thulle learned of Lee Boo's adventures abroad and his life in London
would have come from his talks with McCluer, White, and Wedgebrough, none of whom were in London with Lee Boo. Abba Thulle
would have learned more from a reading of Keate's book. Perhaps the
copy that was delivered by McCluer was translated for him. No doubt
Henry Wilson would have thought of this and arranged for the book
to be delivered to Abba Thulle after inscribing it for him. The inscription might have read:

> To: The Honourable Abba Thulle
>   Rupack of Pelew
>
> May this book serve as a record of our meeting and as a tes-
> tament to our friendship. I only wish Lee Boo could have
> brought it home and translated it for you. How proud he
> would have been to do that—he wanted to teach you and
> all of the Rupacks what he had learned. He may not have
> learned all that you wished for, but he learned enough to
> bring honour to your islands. What a very fine young man
> he was. He had much of your wisdom and courage. He
> died a better man than I—so brave, so thoughtful of others;
> and his last thoughts were of you and his beloved Pelew.
> He thought you knew what was happening to him and he
> was sorry to bring you grief. I am sorry too. But please
> know that his example of unselfish kindness and comrade-
> ship will never die, even as it most assuredly will live in the
> heart of your most grateful friend,
>
>> Henry Wilson, Esq.
>> Commander
>> The Hon. Company's Ship *Warley*

Just as Lee Boo was not restored to his islands, the island life he knew cannot be restored—even by the powers of imagination. It is difficult enough to attempt a description of Belau today. Now, perhaps, fiction is required; the reality is too complex for most of us, the truth often too unbelievable to be accepted as the truth. Blanchard and McCluer were not the last of their kind. Anyone can believe that a Blanchard would remain behind in Belau, but it stretches credulity to say that a McCluer would do the same; it does not matter that he really did—it remains implausible.

Nor would it seem plausible that two more disparate characters than the Polish scientist Jan Stanislaus Kubary and the Irish-American adventurer David Dean O'Keefe would reach the islands at about the same time, eighty years later. Kubary arrived in Belau in February 1871; O'Keefe was mysteriously cast away on the island of Yap ten months later. Kubary had given up medical studies and left Poland and then Germany for political reasons. He was sent to the Carolines to collect specimens for a private German museum. While he collected he studied the island people and earned their respect, if very little in the way of monetary reward. O'Keefe, on the other hand, involved himself in collections of quite a different kind and earned money for himself and his island hosts. He helped the Yapese by acquiring a ship with which to transport the large grindstone-like discs that were quarried in Belau and used in Yap as prestigious "stone money." In exchange, O'Keefe was granted a favored-merchant status that gave him a virtual monopoly on Yapese copra production. While O'Keefe prospered as a trader throughout the islands, Kubary collected, recorded his observations, and remained poor. O'Keefe became known as His Majesty O'Keefe; Kubary's painstaking work in Belau and among other Caroline islanders eventually earned him the title Father of Micronesian Anthropology. In the end, both men died in the Western Pacific after living lives filled with the stuff island legends are made of.

It would take a master storyteller to do justice to these real-life characters who held sway in the islands when the setting remained roughly the same as it was in Lee Boo's time. Perhaps the last chance for the British to render such a description was missed in 1890 when Robert Louis Stevenson sailed from Sydney aboard the *Janet Nichol*. His cruise took him into Micronesian waters, but no further than the Marshall Islands. Had it been possible, he would have gone further. We have his word for it that he would have liked to sail on into Lee Boo's islands when he wrote in *The South Seas,* "It was my hope, for instance, to have reached the Carolines."

Perhaps Stevenson had heard of the Scotsmen who preceded him. In addition to McCluer there was Andrew Cheyne, whose checkered career as a trader ended in Belau in 1866. Cheyne once drafted a petition requesting Her Britannic Majesty to "take the Pelew Islands under the Protectorate of the Crown of Great Britain." In so doing he invoked the name of Captain Wilson and reminded the British Government that Abba Thulle's domain "has always been an asylum for shipwrecked people." But Cheyne himself was no castaway. He was, in fact, too much the ruthless empire builder and was murdered, having too often offended the incumbent Abba Thulle. Unfortunately, the Abba Thulle also lost his life as a consequence.

Stevenson may also have known of another ship that sailed from Sydney just seven years earlier: HMS *Espiegle,* Captain Bridge. Sir Cyprian Bridge was a man well suited to a mission to Belau. He knew of the often violent rivalries that had plagued the islands, as first reported by Henry Wilson. Instead of siding with Abba Thulle or his adversaries, as so many of his predecessors had done, he persuaded the highest ranking chiefs of Belau to come aboard his ship and sign a peace treaty. Bridge, who later became an admiral, wrote in his memoirs that he was much pleased to have accomplished this "within a day or two of the Centenary of the loss of the HCS *Antelope,* whose Captain took Prince Lee Boo to England." He also made it clear that this was no small event in his life, for along with many schoolboys of his generation, he had read *The History of Prince Lee Boo,* had been moved by it, and remembered it well. He must also have considered that the major contribution the British had made in those one hundred years was the introduction and provision of firearms, which, in effect, had prolonged and intensified the violence he now sought to end. And he might also have been saddened to think that after a century Lee Boo's people had still not learned their letters, his peace treaty having been signed with the *X* marks of the Abba Thulle and the Reklai.

A copy of Admiral Bridge's peace treaty was placed among the historical papers at the Public Records Office in London; yet Belauans lived at peace long after that document had been forgotten. By World War II, with decades of peace behind them, the people of Belau might have wished that the great powers themselves had signed such a treaty and lived up to it instead of bringing their modern wars to the little islands of the Pacific. Not only was Belau, especially the island of Pele-liu, the scene of some of the bloodiest battles of that terrible war, but the Belauan people were not allowed to inherit the city the Japanese had constructed on Koror. In an end-of-the-war act of irrationality, the city was destroyed. It confounds our comprehension of reality, but some of the ruins and a few of the buildings remain to testify to the truth.

Some of the Americans who came to the islands after the war lived and worked in the few Japanese buildings that had been allowed to stand; others occupied the corrugated metal quonset huts that for some twenty years represented the best nonindigenous housing on the islands. Meanwhile, the islanders were building Japanese-style rectangular houses as well as learning their letters. Those who had learned Japanese between the wars now learned English as a third language.

The former League of Nations mandated islands became a United Nations Trust Territory. On Koror the United Nations flag flew every day, not just on those days every three years when a United Nations mission visited to invite petitions and to determine whether the Trusteeship Agreement was being adhered to—missions that always included a member from Captain Wilson's British Isles.

Under the Trust Territory administration, Belauans enjoyed greater and ever-growing autonomy and the consequent feeling of greater intrinsic worth found expression in the respect shown to the United Nations on each 24 October, United Nations Day. Representatives from all over Belau came to Koror to compete in athletic events, exhibit varied crafts, perform their traditional arts of song and dance, and listen to the oratory of both hereditary and elected leaders. On Koror, the organizers would often begin the day with a parade.

The United Nations Day parade of 1953, for example, had a historical theme. Leading the parade were older men of Belau representing the precontact era before the coming of foreigners: *rubaks* walking proudly with the traditional adze on their shoulders, some, if not all, of them tattooed, all dressed only in loin cloths and carrying their betel-nut bags. The men were followed by older women wearing traditional apron-like fiber skirts and chanting as they walked. Then came a float, a replica of the *Antelope*. Although Spanish ships had appeared at Belau long before it, the *Antelope* was featured as Belau's preeminent early encounter with foreigners. Walking beside the float were figures intended to represent Captain Wilson and his crew, nondescript only for want of costuming for an eighteenth-century ship's company of sailors. Clearly, however, the next group in this historical procession were "Spanish," in clerical habits appropriate to the nineteenth-century period when the Spanish were predominant in the islands and concentrated on Christianizing. Then came "German" administrators, dressed immaculately in white, depicting the early twentieth century period, prior to World War I. The "Japanese" who came next were represented in larger numbers, commensurate with the vastly greater influx of foreigners who came from Japan to colonize the islands during the period between the wars. Belauans had no trouble at all in depicting the Japanese; some wore clothing they had worn during the Japanese period and many wore military uniforms left behind at the end of the war. The postwar American administration was represented by some American children marching with the Belauan children to symbolize the modern era in Belau.

The passing parade of Americans who came and went in the 1960s and 1970s was exceeded only by the numbers of Palauans themselves; more of them went abroad for educational opportunities, proportionately, than did any similar island people. Some of them returned with teaching credentials, some with medical training, some prepared for the civil service, some for business, and some with degrees in law, engineering, or medicine. New schools were built, new additions made to the hospital, and, most spectacular of all, a new bridge, said to be the world's longest prestressed concrete bridge, connected the islands of Koror and Babeldaob and the domains of Ibedul and Reklai.

At one point in the recent history of Belau it was even seriously proposed, though not by a Belauan, that the northernmost portions of the islands be made into a "superport"—a gigantic storage place designed to serve the insatiable oil needs of the Japanese. The mere proposal of a scheme so tempting to a people who no longer have any appreciable mineral resources of their own created new conflicts within Belau, dividing those who would sacrifice island beauty for material gain from those who would hold on to the homeland known to their ancestors.

With such serious intrusions into the way of life known to Lee Boo, one must have comic relief. Fittingly, foreigners have sometimes obliged. Outstanding among those of recent years were the American film star Lee Marvin, the Japanese actor Toshiro Mifune, and the English director John Boorman, who came to Belau in 1967 to film the movie *Hell in the Pacific*. It was fitting that the movie should be special, in that the cast consisted entirely of Marvin and Mifune fighting a duel of wits as opposing stragglers at the close of World War II. The islands near Oroolong provided a unique setting. The theme was serious, but the Belauans who assisted with the filming reveled in the experience. How delightful to create a scene then discard it in favor of another, and another, with cold beers in between and another day's wages assured. Marvin became enamored of the islands for a time and took to fishing there. He was popular and doubtless could have made of himself another McCluer, had he been so inclined. By contrast, most of those involved in making the film were not inclined to the more rugged island life. They brought their own chartered ship, the *Oriental Hero*, which came not from Canton or Macao, although its owners were in Hong Kong, but from Japan. There was no hotel in Belau at the time large enough to accommodate everyone. Today they could be accommodated at a hotel overlooking some of the islands that were the setting for their movie. Today they would not need to bring their own doctor—the staff at MacDonald Hospital on Koror, some of whom were trained at the Medical College in Fiji and some of whom were graduated from the University of Hawaii's School of Medicine, could provide ample care. In short, Koror today could provide all of the necessary amenities, including even a museum and a library for cultural pursuits.

Appropriately enough it is in museums and libraries that Lee Boo has been best remembered and best of all in that monumental institution, the British Museum, which also houses the British Library. Here, in the library, one can see all of the editions of Keate, many editions of *The History of Prince Lee Boo*, the novel *Madiboo* (rarely seen elsewhere), and perhaps more important, McCluer's journal and his hydrographic works. Separately housed in the nearby Museum of Mankind, the Museum's Ethnographic Department mounted a bicentennial-year exhibit centered on the artifacts that Captain Wilson brought back to England—gifts from the people of Belau. Included were the large bird-shaped tureen, carved of wood and inlaid with mother-of-pearl, from which Wilson and his men had imbibed, an inlaid ''sword,'' and a bone of honor—perhaps Wilson's. Above these items were two of Devis' original sketches, one of Lee Boo and one of Arra Kooker. Portraits of Abba Thulle and Ludee hung nearby, along with the Belau Island sketches of White, Wedgebrough, and Henry Wilson, Jr.

In all, it is as though the people Lee Boo knew best had gathered for a reunion and brought with them their most precious Belauan possessions. Only George Keate was missing and some of those who entered the story after Lee Boo's death, notably John McCluer. But the painting McCluer commissioned of Kockywack and his two female companions was there as painted, it is assumed, by Spoilum during McCluer's first trip from Belau to Macao. Another item, also related to McCluer's trip to Macao, was too large to display and must be seen in the museum's storehouse. How it came to England is worth explaining.

From the Downs on the Thames estuary on 22 April 1792, a letter was sent to Sir Joseph Banks signed by a Captain Cummings who had "just come in before a strong gale." The captain reported that "the Chief Supercargo at Canton had given me leave to offer you the King of the Pelews Proa, which was brought to China by Captain McCluer last year. She is hewn out of one tree like the South Sea Cannoes about forty feet long and has paddles spears etc etc belonging to her." In another letter Captain Cummings adds, "All the apparatus is with the canoe, and Captain Wilson's brother has offered to rig her." What may have transpired afterward—whether Matthias Wilson rigged her and even sailed her on the Thames—is unknown. But the canoe is in the British Museum's storehouse, as well preserved as any Pacific Island canoe could be that traveled so far so long ago.

And what of the *Antelope*? Does anything visible remain on the reefs of Belau? No, but there are those who say they have seen a mound of coral covering the spot where the *Antelope* was wrecked. Under the mound, in and around the skeleton of the ship, the coral may have captured lead weights, an anchor, cannon shot, and what might be left of the *Antelope*'s copper-sheathed hull. Some ships similar to the *Antelope* were said to have a "specie well" where valuables were kept. But Captain Wilson and his men had ample time to remove anything of value. Had anything of the sort remained, Wedgebrough and White would have known and would have given the matter their attention when they returned with McCluer, but they did not. In fact, they did not even mention the wreck, as though it were no longer a subject of interest to them.

By now the *Antelope*'s depleted treasury of colored cloth and trinkets and the mundane stores within her holds have long since been scattered and consumed by the breaking surf. Yet some small evidence of what happened on that fatal reef must meet the eye there or along nearby shores. Chinaware from Macao and Canton, for example. Beachcombing the area, one does find seaworn bits of porcelain. Some of them may be beachworn reminders of the *Antelope*. Some of them may be all that is left of the china used by Blanchard and McCluer, fragments from their teacups, empty for so long and now broken.

Are these bits and pieces all that remain of the entire affair? Did the wreck of the *Antelope* leave no lasting mark? Captain Wilson's copper sign on Oroolong did not last, nor did the guns that Blanchard was to care for—their barrels doubtless beaten into fish hooks and spears when gunpowder gave out. The islands themselves were untouched except for a few felled trees soon replaced by inexorable tropical growth. But Captain Wilson made his mark in other ways. Even today the title of Captain is sometimes heard when a term of respect is needed. The shipwreck and its aftermath was as exceptional an experience for the people of Belau as for the men of the *Antelope*. Seeds of learning were planted that have never stopped growing. Belau was better prepared for the coming of the Spanish, the Germans, the Japanese, and the Americans. And Belauans moved faster into the twentieth century than other peoples of the Caroline Islands. As if drawing inspiration from Lee Boo, Belauans seem also to travel farther. The England that sent forth the sailors who discovered Belau is now being discovered by the Belau Islanders. The reigning Abba Thulle has visited London, as has his traditional rival, the incumbent Reklai of Melekeok. Lee Boo's tomb has been visited and revisited.

The story does not end. The people of Belau, having learned their letters, are writing chapters of their own. The new republic has issued commemorative stamps picturing Lee Boo, Captain Wilson, and Abba Thulle. And in 1984 the people of Rotherhithe remembered Lee Boo, "the Black Prince." They honored him in their schools, at their civic center and at St. Mary's. Whereas one might expect Lee Boo to be remembered in his home islands, there would be little reason to expect England to remember him well enough to tell his story on national television. But this was done in the bicentennial year of Lee Boo's stay among the people his father would have him emulate. In London little that is worth remembering is allowed to be forgotten, not even a stranger from a distant and unknown island.

22

POSTSCRIPT TO LEE BOO

IN MY OPENING LETTER, Lee Boo, I mentioned that two plays had been staged in your honor. They were performed in 1833. Some of your old schoolmates may have attended. If they did they must have enjoyed themselves. The Surrey Theatre's production was "received each night . . . with the most unanimous approbation, and the excellence of the music and scenery . . . elicited general applause." The audience was presented with three scenes:

> The Island of Oroolong, in the Pelew Islands, and a View of the Pacific Ocean.

> The *Antelope* Repaired, and Departure for England.

> And, a Grand and correct View of Plymouth Harbour! With arrival of Prince Lee Boo in England!

Of course the *Antelope* was not repaired, and you did not land at Plymouth but at Portsmouth. But it is the way of the world of entertainment to make of such events what they will. This is called dramatic license and in this case it permitted your role to be played by a "Miss Vincent"! In the cast you were joined by your father, Captain Wilson, Raa Kook, Arra Kooker, and twelve fictional characters, including a person, presumably female, named Zittilee who was described as "an European, wrecked on the Isle of Oroolong when a child." In the first scene the composers have you and Zittilee sing a duet, "The Bright God of Day Illumines the West." And in the second act, in the Captain's cabin, the two of you sing "Love's Alphabet."

Just as you wanted to return to Belau to teach your people their letters, it has occurred to me that, were it possible, what a delight it would be to have this play performed in Belau today! In fact, I have been asked what a company of players might expect if they were to travel to Belau for that very purpose. In the first place, the cast would not need eight months or more to travel by sailing ship but could travel all the way from London by jet airplane—not a balloon, but a coach that flies—all the way to Belau! They would land at the airport at Airai where they would be met by the Abba Thulle of today, the Ibedul, that is. There would be hundreds if not thousands of people there to greet them, and they would be seated in modern motor-driven coaches that can carry many passengers. (There are no horses in Belau today, but many of your people have seen them and some have ridden them, just as you did.)

The arriving cast of players would be driven across the bridge that connects Babeldaob with Koror—a bridge even longer than those spanning the Thames! Once in Koror, they would stay at a modern inn, with fine beds in private rooms and a large dining hall. But the food would almost certainly be brought to them in the traditional way, by women of Belau carrying trays on their heads.

The play would be performed in a modern auditorium at a school that teaches young people like yourself (and others from the islands to the east) the skills of the carpenter, the builder, the plumber, the electrician, and the welder—skills unknown to you or even the people of London in your time. The construction of buildings with solid walls and ceilings is no mystery to these young people. And, yes, the school teaches agriculture, including methods of planting a variety of seeds and the care of livestock. But, like all Belauans, the students would love to see the "shew." It would be a grand holiday for them.

At some time during their visit, the cast would be taken to see the island of Oroolong, and then, it must be hoped, to Artingall (Melekeok) or to one or more of the other communities to the north. Although the people of Belau have lived at peace for many, many years, it is still a matter of tact that, whenever possible, whatever is brought to Koror should be shared with its former rivals.

In boats similar to the *Antelope*'s longboat, but with motors attached, the cast would be taken through the mangroves of Airai, past Ngchesar, and on to Melekeok. Arriving at the pier they would be greeted by a reception party, and everything would be the same as in peaceful visits of the past. Drinking coconuts would be opened with consummate skill, the self-contained cup placed in the hands of each arriving actor. No better drink for its time and place could be provided. The cast would rest in the little house at the ocean end of the pier. They would talk of the boat ride in the hot sun, the fish seen, the fish caught, and then, of the need to get their equipment and gear to the *bai*. Children would appear to carry the duffel, young men to carry the heavier pieces. The walk along the well-trod path above the shallow waters would begin. The cast would be walking along the same long pier that the men of the *Antelope* saw. They would soon arrive at the home of the village chief for the customary courtesy call, but a voice would call out urging them to proceed at once to the *bai,* where everyone, including High Chief Reklai, would be waiting. On they would go to the *bai.*

Picture the scene: The cast is guided through the village and is soon facing the front of the *bai* with its painted symbols of stories told here and in *bais* of the past before anyone present was born. They pass through the opening in the *bai*—the doorway without a door—which, like a cathedral, is always open. Inside, they walk with slightly stooped shoulders to avoid hitting the beams overhead. Everyone is assigned a seat—seats not already assigned by protocol and custom that require no theatre manager's seating chart. The cast is shown to the place in the *bai* that has been left clear for a stage. The floorboards here are made of the hardest *dort (Intsia bijuga)* wood and polished to a sheen by those who have sat on them before.

Once everything has been made ready and everyone is seated, the Reklai speaks to the *rubaks* and all others present, reminding them that they are gathered to see a play about the visit of the first Englishmen and about Lee Boo. Heads nod in agreement: *"chochoi"*—yes, we are ready. Betel nut is visible; the older men sit with their betel-nut baskets in front of them, and chewing accoutrements assembled at their feet. It is going to be a long evening and they are prepared. The Reklai asks that the play begin.

The visiting actors perform the first act in which the English find themselves on Oroolong, which is represented on a painted backdrop. At first the audience is silent, then murmurs of approval are heard, and finally applause when the first act is completed. While the scenery is being changed, trays of food are passed in through the windows of the *bai* by the women who have prepared it. Taro, balls of tapioca, lobster, reef fish, chicken, bananas, papayas, and other fruits adorn the trays. There is an intermission while everyone eats. But for the cast, who are anxious to get on with the second act, it is more a matter of nibbling now and eating later.

The second act takes place at the dockyard at Oroolong, with the men of the *Antelope* at work on their boat. The English depart, and Lee Boo says good-bye. By now every window of the *bai* is filled with onlookers awaiting the third act—the arrival of Prince Lee Boo in England. The scenery depicts a ship tied to the dock with a grand view of the harbor in the background. This triumphant scene is followed at once by the grand finale, with all the cast assembled for a last song.

The play is over; the children are asleep in their fathers' laps. Lee Boo is in England, and it is late at night, but the Reklai rises and invites the cast to take time to relax and enjoy more food; then, if they are willing, he would like the play repeated. And so it would go until after repeated performances everyone was exhausted. Finally rolls of mats would be brought and the *bai* would be vacated for the privacy of the visitors. Perhaps the young woman who played the role of Zittilee, the girl on Oroolong, would unroll her mat and find written on her pillow the words, "There is a Lee Boo in London, and there is a Lee Boo in my heart."

Next morning, after a bath in the stream and trays of fresh food, the party would pack and leave to return to Koror where everyone would want to hear how the performance had been received. From Koror, they would cross the bridge to the airport at Airai and take off again in the jet. With the miracle of flight they would soon be back in London, but the visit to Belau would not be forgotten—just as you are not forgotten. Your memory now a part of their memories, they would visit St. Mary's Rotherhithe and deliver messages in song—songs you inspired. Your courage, your kindness—the message of your life—is still being received. You should have had many replies.

NOTES

Introduction.   Whereas much of the research for this work was, of necessity, conducted in London, it has been a Pacific islands readership for whom I have aimed. Although I hope I have been diligent in my research, I did not want to be pedantic in presenting the material. Nonfiction books treating Pacific Island subjects have all too often been esoteric tomes of far more interest to the writers' colleagues than to the general reader—in the islands or elsewhere. The shelves of the Pacific Islands Central School, for example, were once weighted with scholarly works far better suited to the needs of the faculty than the interests of the student body. I did not want to add another. At the same time I wanted this to be a work that Micronesian students both at home and abroad could refer to in their own research and writing, without fear of contradiction. Although I have searched out, verified, and accounted for the data I have used, I did not employ footnotes, believing that they would tend to intimidate the very readers I was most anxious to attract. Instead, I have provided the notes that follow.

1   LETTER TO LEE BOO

Dr. Johnson's Letters.   The quotation, "We shall receive no letters in the grave," appears in most if not all editions of Boswell's *Life of Samuel Johnson.* See, for example, p. 371 of Dell's Laurel Classic edition.

Lee Boo the best remembered.   Those who know more of Omai than of Lee Boo may have doubts as to who is best remembered. My own views are developed in Chapter 19 and in my notes to that chapter. I might add that no history of Omai was published, like the one of Lee Boo, which was persistently and widely published for two-thirds of a century following his death.

The Lee Boo plays.   For a description of these, see the Postscript and accompanying notes.

Lee Boo's funeral. The "great concourse of Parishioners" and other details can be found in the Reverend Beck's book about the Parish of Rotherhithe (see Bibliography).

Brook Watson, M.P. According to the *Dictionary of National Biography, 1921–1922,* Vol. 20, Watson was "elected M.P. for the City of London on 6 April 1784, and held the seat till 1793 and was elected Lord Mayor of London in November 1796." For more on Watson, see Chapter 13.

Lee Boo's epitaph. For the entire text of the epitaph, see Chapter 14. It was "written by Brook Watson" according to *Gentleman's Magazine,* Vol. 58, No. 1, Part 2, July 1788, p. 631.

Coleridge and other poets. For poetry inspired by the story of Lee Boo, see Dapp's work and also Fairchild's *The Noble Savage.* Coleridge's poem is entitled "To a Young Lady with a Poem on the French Revolution."

George Keate. Keate's life and works have been described in scholarly detail by Kathryn Gilbert Dapp in her dissertation, *George Keate, Esq., Eighteenth Century Gentleman.* His *An Account of the Pelew Islands* ran to five editions, plus pirated editions, and was translated into French, Italian, German, Spanish, Swedish, Russian, and Dutch (hereafter referred to as Keate's *Account*).

Rupack Street. For details, see Chapter 20.

E. M. Forster. Forster's "A Letter to Madan Blanchard" was written in 1931. The copy I have used appears in a collection of his essays, articles, broadcasts, etc. entitled *Two Cheers for Democracy,* pp. 309–318.

Ships named for Lee Boo. The English ship that was named for Lee Boo and sailed for Honolulu less than ten years after his death was the *Prince Lee Boo,* according to Kuykendall and also according to W. B. Broughton, but an unsigned article in *The Friend* (June 1862) refers to it simply as the *Lee Boo.* Kipling named "a Chat-ham boat" the *"Prince Leboo"* (p. 65 of *Captains Courageous*).

Abba Thulle's visit to London. The incumbent "Abba Thulle," Ibedul Yutaka M. Gibbons, visited London in December 1983, attended the opening of the Museum of Mankind's Micronesia exhibit, and visited Lee Boo's tomb at Rotherhithe.

Smallpox and Lee Boo. Please see the notes to Chapter 14.

2 ROTHERHITHE'S CAPTAIN WILSON

Robinson Crusoe and Henry Wilson. To those for whom the name Robinson Crusoe evokes more than a book once read, I recommend Walter de la Mare's *Desert Islands and Robinson Crusoe.* Although Rotherhithe's Captain Wilson will not be found in any of the 58 pages of text or 229 pages of notes, kindred souls will not be disappointed. Nor would Henry Wilson have been disappointed with de la Mare's encyclopedic ruminations. Although he may have thought himself too fortunate to be put in company with Robinson Crusoe, he had a crew member who thought of himself in that light. But we do not know if Henry Wilson gave the matter any thought at all and that is probably the least of what we do not know about this captain who survived shipwreck so successfully.

Captain Wilson's career.   Fortunately, it is possible to trace Henry Wilson's career at sea by use of Hardy's *A Register of Ships* in which ship's officers are also listed. The award of 500 guineas, also including "a piece of plate" valued at 50 guineas, is mentioned on p. 123 of the appendix to Hardy.

The Wilson home in Rotherhithe.   Henry Wilson's family and his home in Rotherhithe are mentioned briefly in Beck's history of the Parish. (For a description of the house and neighborhood, see the end of Chapter 11 and notes to that chapter.)

Mayflower associations.   Rotherhithe's *Mayflower* associations are described in Mary Boast's substantial pamphlet entitled, *The Mayflower and Pilgrim Story, Chapters from Rotherhithe and Southwark.*

Henry Wilson's friends.   Our only clues to Henry Wilson's friendships, other than those among his fellow officers at sea, have been provided by Keate, who tells us that it was Brook Watson who introduced him to the captain.

George Keate.   Further information on Keate is provided in later chapters of this book, and for information on Keate's book, without which most of these lines could not have been written, see the notes to Chapter 15.

Oroolong House.   I am much indebted to Mr. Nevil Dickin of London whose correspondence has provided me with most of what I know of the Wilson family genealogy and of Oroolong House, about which I will have much more to say in Chapter 21.

The Admiral Linois affair.   It was on Henry Wilson's last voyage but one that he participated, with his ship the *Warley*, in the action that repulsed a French fleet under Admiral Linois in the Straits of Malacca in February 1804. The circumstances are described in a number of sources. My own favorite is the somewhat fictionalized account provided by Captain Marryat in *Newton Forster or, the Merchant Service* (pp. 302–306) in which Marryat states, "I do not know on record any greater instance of heroism on the part of British Seamen." Although that is a deliberate exaggeration, Captain Wilson did receive his 500 guineas, a very great deal of money in those days, and a sword of honor for his part in the affair.

Henry Wilson the man.   Although neither George Keate nor anyone else has provided a description of Henry Wilson, C. Northcote Parkinson, in his *Trade in the Eastern Seas,* has provided an unexpected clue to Captain Wilson's character in describing an earlier phase of the same voyage that later encountered Admiral Linois. It seems that Wilson and some of the other captains would sometimes intentionally lag behind or otherwise display an independent spirit when sailing in an East India Company convoy protected by a Royal Naval vessel. Rear Admiral Sir Thomas Troubridge, irritated by such mischievous conduct on the part of some of the Indiamen, wrote several letters of protest in which Wilson's ship the *Warley* is specifically cited. Parkinson, on p. 314, goes on to explain that the *Warley*'s conduct under

Captain Wilson in this and related matters "seems less a symptom of incompetence than of a sense of humor." Competent or not, and his many successful voyages surely prove his competence, it is nice to think of Henry Wilson as a man with a good sense of humor; it must have stood him in good stead in the islands where, above all else, it is the quality of character most to be desired.

3 JOHN COMPANY'S *ANTELOPE*

Ship losses. 1782 and 1783 were particularly difficult years. Cotton, in his *East Indiamen,* p. 135, lists ten ships lost in that short span of time and the list does not even include the *Antelope* which was excluded from most such lists simply because it was not an Indiaman but a packet ship. Averaged over a much longer period the losses were not so staggering but bad enough: *Hardy's Register,* pp. 360–363, indicates 160 Indiamen lost between 1700 and 1818.

Lloyd's. For what I needed of *A History of Lloyd's,* I used Wright and Fayle's book by that title which, as the subtitle indicates, covers the period *From the Founding of Lloyd's Coffee House to the Present Day* (1928). It is ironic that merchants and ship owners who made their fortunes in tea remained addicted to coffee until well into the eighteenth century when, like Dr. Johnson, they took more enthusiastically to tea.

In search of the *Antelope.* My search for the origins of the *Antelope* began at the National Maritime Museum at Greenwich and at the modern home of Lloyd's Register in London. At neither place, however, could I learn the meaning of "Nwbry." It was a librarian at Newbury, England, who suggested that I might be searching on the wrong side of the Atlantic and recommended trying Newburyport, Massachusetts. This was of particular interest in that in reading Amasa Delano's *Narrative* I had noted his claim to having known the *Antelope* when it was the *Franklin,* and that he had been on board it in Boston Harbor at some unspecified time prior to his visit to Belau. As if to reassure a doubting reader, Delano went on to say that he had known the *Franklin* cum *Antelope* well enough to make a miniature model of it which he presented to Abba Thulle. Unfortunately, both "Franklin" and "Antelope" were so commonly used as ship names that searching lists, indexes, directories, and the like results in little more than frustration. In time an opportunity arose to visit Newbury, Massachusetts, where the best I could do was confirm that the *Antelope/Franklin* could very well have been constructed there. To make a long story short, I finally corresponded with a variety of authorities, all of whom agreed that "my" ship must have been constructed at Newbury, Massachusetts. Howard I. Chapelle of the Smithsonian Institution, for example, wrote, "I am quite sure your *Antelope* was built at Newbury (now 'Old Newbury'), Massachusetts." And, Philip Chadwick Foster Smith, Curator of Maritime History for the Peabody Museum of Salem, Massachusetts wrote, "I think it is most certain that the marking of 'Nwbry' refers to Newbury or Newburyport, Massachusetts."

The *Antelope's* dimensions. To estimate the length and breadth of the *Antelope* I worked from figures found in Goldenberg's *Shipbuilding in Colonial America* for a ship of almost identical size built at Philadelphia in 1775. Captain Bligh's description of

HMS *Bounty*, a vessel of similar size: "Her burthen was nearly 215 tons; her extreme length on deck, 90 feet 10 inches; extreme breadth, 24 feet 3 inches; and the height in the hold under the beams, at the main hatchway, 10 feet 3 inches" (Bligh's *The Mutiny on Board H.M.S. Bounty*, New American Library edition, 1961, p. 13). Similarly, the *Bounty* carried a total of 44 officers and men; the *Antelope* carried 50 including the Chinese supplementary crew.

The log of the *Antelope*. This can be seen at the India Office Library in London where it is identified as L/MAR/B/570A. It documents the period from 31 December 1781, the date the ship was "launched Deptford," to 4 June 1783, the date it anchored at Macao Roads. The log for the voyage from Macao to Belau has not been found.

East India Company—sources. I have used, primarily, C. H. Philips' *The East India Company 1784–1834*; the works of C. Northcote Parkinson; Morse's four-volume *Chronicles of the East India Company Trading to China, 1635–1834*; Gill's *Merchants and Mariners of the 18th Century*; and that outstanding work with so much packed in a small space, Cotton and Fawcett's *East Indiamen: The East India Company's Maritime Service*.

Dr. Johnson's tea. The quotation in which Dr. Johnson describes his addiction to tea is found in the *Literary Magazine* vol. 2, no. 12, 1757, as quoted in the *Oxford Dictionary of Quotations*, p. 278.

4 THE *ANTELOPE*'S SECRET VOYAGE

The route taken. The secret nature of the voyage of the *Antelope* and especially the rationale for the route taken is explained by E. C. Pigou, who was one of the Company's agents residing at Macao. His notes, correspondence, and records (India Office, Factory Records, G/12/77—Consultation Book) including correspondence with Chinese authorities at the time of the *Antelope*'s arrival at Macao contain such words as "while the War continues with France, Spain, and Holland it becomes indispensibly necessary to have such vessels [as the *Antelope*] for conveying intelligence to us of the Company's intentions, as well as the motives of the enemy" and because of the war the Company's ships "are obliged to take another route different to what they did in time of Peace" and that "the Company had a good reason to expect a great many more ships in China last year, that one object for sending the Packet [the *Antelope*] was to know what was become of these ships . . ."

Exploration. The principal reason to believe that the *Antelope* was charged with a mission to engage in some explorations is the presence on board of two draftsmen and the artist Arthur William Devis. Instead of returning to England after the shipwreck of the *Antelope*, Devis went to India where he established enough of a reputation to merit 35 pages in Mildred Archer's book, *India and British Portraiture*. In introducing her section on Devis, Archer explains that Devis was needed on the voyage to "prepare coastal profiles as aids to future navigation" (p. 35). Captain Wilson's log of the *Antelope* indicates that Devis did, in fact, engage in such work along the coast of Patagonia and at least one of his charts has been preserved.

Antelope records.   Records showing who signed on, whether at Gravesend or at Falmouth, can be seen at the India Office Library along with records of how much "impress" (advance) pay each received and what arrangements were made for "absence" pay to relatives while crewmen were away from home. Also at the IOL: the log of the *Antelope* as quoted in this chapter.

White and Wedgebrough: The two school boys, Robert White and John Wedgebrough (whose surname is spelled three different ways in the various records and accounts—I have chosen, normally, to use Keate's spelling of "Wedgebrough") were signed out to Captain Wilson at Christ's Hospital, London, on 3 August 1782 (School Register, Guildhall). It may be of more than passing interest to note that other captains including Captain Cook had earlier obtained or sought to obtain students from this school. (See Bernard Smith's *European Vision . . .* , p. 76; Smith also gives some background for Christ's Hospital on p. 9, stating that the "Drawing School" was attached to the "Mathematical School.")

Arthur William Devis.   What is known of his life both before and after the wreck of the *Antelope*, but especially after, can be found in both Archer and Pavière. That he was "invited" to make "coastal profiles" for which he was to be paid "one hundred guineas" is a matter of record—India Office Marine Records L/MAR/B/570C(I) as cited by Mildred Archer.

Samuel Kelly.   He who was "applied to" and offered a position as one of the mates aboard the *Antelope*, recorded the incident at Falmouth on p. 57 of his book, *An Eighteenth Century Seaman Whose Days Have Been Few and Evil*. The incident is of interest because it not only confirms the presence of the *Antelope* at Falmouth in July 1782, but also illustrates the point that only men of rather substantial economic means could afford to equip themselves to serve as officers aboard East India Company ships —men who, as Parkinson explains, "came from the middle class." (Parkinson has an entire chapter on the subject of the EIC's Maritime Service in his book, *Trade in the Eastern Seas*.)

EIC uniforms, salaries, rates of pay, etc.   Parkinson, in the chapter cited above, provides details on the dress of EIC officers and seamen as do, also, Cotton and Fawcett, and Hardy. Rates of pay for the period 1782–1789 are shown in Gibson's *The Story of the Ship*, as well as in Parkinson's chapter.

Gratuities in lieu of private trade.   The practice of permitting private trade or private "venture" which made it possible for captains of the large Indiamen to carry as much as "92 tons" of their own cargo (combined with that of their top officers) is clearly explained in Parkinson's *Trade in the Eastern Seas*, pp. 198–205. Captain Wilson and his officers were paid "Gratuities in lieu of private trade" according to entries in the Court of Directors Minutes for 18 January 1782 (IOR Marine Records, L/MAR/1/36, No. 21).

Provisions and treasure. The log of the *Antelope* reveals that provisions began arriving while the ship was still in the Thames, the first being "bread and beef for present use." Guns had been boarded at Deptford, gunpowder at Gravesend. "Wet provisions" and "dry provisions" are not defined but the "wet" presumably included water, rum, beer, brandy, vinegar, oil, and lime juice. The "dry" provisions must have included the ubiquitous sea biscuits which were being mass produced in London, as well as bread, flour, dried peas, dried beans, and oatmeal. Livestock and the more perishable provisions must have been taken on at Falmouth shortly before sailing. The intriguing entry in the log, "received on board 2 small boxes of treasure," is not explained. However, it follows the words, "the Captain arrived from London," and one might conclude that Captain Wilson returned to Falmouth on 12 August with articles of trade obtained from the Company's warehouses. If something of greater value were implied, presumably the words "specie" or "silver" would have been used, although that remains a possibility.

Barker's cabin. Captain Wilson's reactions on finding caches of liquor and tobacco within the walls of his second mate's cabin are not surprising in light of the fact that some captains refused tobacco aboard ship entirely (Cotton and Fawcett, p. 77) and although officers may have been permitted their own private stock of spirits they were expected to drink in moderation and be alert at all times.

5 OPIUM AND THE BLUE-GREEN DRAGON

Chinese attitudes. The background and rationale behind Chinese attitudes toward all foreigners is well explained in J. L. Cranmer-Byng's introduction to *An Embassy to China*, the journal kept by Lord Macartney during his embassy to the Emperor Ch'ien-Lung in 1793–1794.

As to the Chinese obduracy in refusing to accept packet ships as non–cargo-carrying vessels and nothing more, Danton, in *The Culture Contacts of the United States and China*, states on p. 19, "The Chinese could see only two reasons for leaving home and coming to China: one was to bring tribute, the other was for gain." Presumably the *Antelope* had arrived at China for neither of these two purposes and was, therefore, an enigma to the Chinese.

Chinese refusal to admit the *Antelope*—sources. All the quotations I have used regarding the experience of the Company's agents in trying to obtain permission from the Chinese for the *Antelope* to refit and restock have been taken from the India Office's "Factory Records" G/12/77, and (virtually the same information) from Volume 2 of Morse's *Chronicles of the East India Company Trading to China*. (Although it is not mentioned in the text, it is of interest that the only message delivered by the *Antelope* to be mentioned in the available records simply relates to the quantity of Singlo tea that it was considered wise for the Company to purchase that year. If that is all, it can be said that the *Antelope* was lost for the want of tea, or, more precisely, out of the Company's determination to control the quantity of tea exported to England.)

Opium.   The subject of opium is extensively treated in volume 2 of Morse. The *Nonsuch* arrived at Macao from Calcutta with a cargo of 1601 chests of "Patna Opium" (p. 77) and disposed of 200 chests at Canton (p. 78) even though the English knew that trade in opium was officially prohibited and that the *Nonsuch*'s cargo of opium was "contraband" (p. 77). When the *Antelope* appeared eleven months later, "because of the voyage of the *Nonsuch* in 1782 with a cargo of opium" the authorities had "become more rigid in their treatment of ships which professedly brought no cargo" (p. 87). A careful reading of Morse's Chapter 37, "A Speculation in Opium, 1782," and the following chapter, "Relations of Supercargoes and Merchants, 1783," can leave little reasonable doubt that the Chinese suspected the *Antelope* may have been carrying opium, just as had some other English ships, especially the *Nonsuch*, and as had many "country" ships that traded between India and China but were not East India Company ships. The entire background of the Company's relationship to opium is fully described in the first 60 pages of Owen's *British Opium Policy in China and India*, including an account of the *Nonsuch* and a reminder that even Robinson Crusoe participated in two voyages that carried opium to China!

Chinese as crew.   The practice of employing Chinese aboard Company ships is well described by Cotton and Fawcett in *East Indiamen*, pp. 58–59. The Chinese and Lascars (on ships bound from India) were so commonly used that the Company maintained boardinghouses in London where they were lodged when waiting for a return passage. In the interest of obligating ship owners to employ entirely British crews, the Chinese were not supposed to work on the outward voyages from England, but so many men were lost on long voyages, either through "running" or by death, that crews had to be augmented for the homeward voyage to England. Cotton and Fawcett explain that even ships outward bound often carried a mixed lot, including a variety of Europeans as well as some Chinese and Lascars. Henry Wilson, too, had to put the Chinese to work and, therefore, arranged for them to be paid when he reached Macao. Then, just before departing Macao, he gave advance pay to those who were taken on to assist him with the return voyage from Macao to London.

The Blue-Green Dragon.   I am indebted to Per Collinder's *A History of Marine Navigation* for my introduction to the blue-green dragon and for my reference to the "heat equator."

The Eastern Passage.   Parkinson, in *Trade in the Eastern Seas*, describes the Eastern Passage on p. 118 and states that it was another Wilson, captain of the Company's ship *Pitt*, who "discovered some such possibility in 1758."

The *Antelope*'s homeward route.   The fact that Keate found no reason to comment on Captain Wilson's route upon departure from Macao would seem to indicate that it was not a point of interest, that it was to have been nothing more nor less than a routine return voyage from Macao to London via the Cape of Good Hope. Pavière, on p. 104 of his book, *The Devis Family of Painters*, states that Devis was to "pursue a voyage round the world in the *Antelope*, Capt. Wilson." If the *Antelope* were to circumnavigate the globe it would obviously have had to return, as all Company ships did, by way of the Cape. Kingston, in his "Wreck of the *Antelope*" (Chapter 10 of

Shipwrecks and Disasters at Sea) gives the *Antelope* a vague bit of itinerary when it sailed from Macao "with dispatches for the Company's settlements in the East Indian Archipelago" but he provides no authority for his statement. In summary, there is little doubt that Captain Wilson was taking the Eastern Passage, from which he would have entered the Indian Ocean and returned to England by the usual route.

The *Antelope*'s voyage: Macao to Belau.   From the time of the *Antelope*'s departure from Macao we have only one source of information: Keate's *Account*. My quotations from that point to the end of the chapter are, therefore, from Keate except for the reference to the "heat equator."

6   KELLY WAS WRONG

Keate and Rousseau.   Keate's life and works have been described by Dapp in *George Keate, Esq., Eighteenth Century Gentleman*. In Dapp's view Keate's "Rousseauism" surfaced long before he met Captain Wilson or before he had heard of Belau. In his *Short Account of Geneva*, 1761, and his *Alps*, 1763, he had deplored the evils of "civilization" and in *Sketches from Nature*, 1779, he had kind words for a life of "simplicity." But Dapp found Keate to be less than a "true primitivist" for he spoke of some primitive peoples who lived "under that darkness and absolute barbarism from the sight of which humanity gladly turns aside" while others, including, presumably, the Belau Islanders, according to Keate, "unaided, unassisted but by mere natural good sense, have not only emerged from this gloomy shade, but nearly attained that order, propriety and good conduct which constitute *real* civilization." Dapp concluded that Keate's *Account* must have "satisfied" the believers in Rousseau, the "Noble Savage," and the "Children of Nature." Apparently the French agreed. M. J. Brez, the translator of a 1792 version of Keate's *Account*, dedicated his work to "a little friend" whom he urged to become as nearly like *"l'amiable Lee Boo"* as possible and, according to Dapp's reading of the introduction, "he extolls Keate's work as corroborating the theories of the *Contract Social*."

Samuel Kelly.   From what he wrote of himself, Kelly lived a life that was neither as short nor as evil as the title of his book would have us believe. Between the time of his first encounter with the *Antelope* at Falmouth in 1782, and his purchase of Keate's book in 1793, he had sailed from England to New York, Florida, Jamaica, Barcelona, Malaga, Ireland, and three times to Philadelphia where he saw Ben Franklin walking the streets, "a gold chain around his neck," and George Washington "in black velvet address the Senate." Back in England, he also walked the streets of Rotherhithe where, unfortunately, he did not encounter Captain Wilson, who could have enlightened him with regard to the shipwreck, but Wilson left on his second voyage as captain of the *Warley* on 22 January and was gone all of the remainder of 1793, the year that Kelly obtained his copy of Keate.

Kelly might also have improved his perspective of the *Antelope*'s fate if he had read, among many other works, a volume entitled, *Adventures of British Seamen*, in which the presumed editor, H. Murray, put together in one binding the story of the *Antelope* as abstracted from Keate, the story of another English ship, the *Boyd*, and the mutiny-bound *Bounty*. The point of it all is, in this context at least, that Captain

Wilson and his men were very fortunate indeed, unlike most of those on the other two ships, especially the crew of the *Boyd*, many of whom were killed by natives of New Zealand.

Keate and Kelly.   Both Keate and Kelly might have altered their views if they had actually been with Captain Wilson. Keate doubtless wanted to believe that remote Pacific Islanders lived a life of innocence, a life to be admired by men such as himself who inhabited cities where crime and poverty abounded. Kelly, on the other hand, had lived a life at sea and was thankful to have survived its many perils. He was glad he had been spared a misadventure which he apparently assumed to have been far worse than portrayed by Keate. The truth, of course, could not rest entirely with either Keate's wistfulness or Kelly's misconceptions. Few islands could qualify as the paradise Keate envisioned, and few island people felt compelled or much inclined to live up to Kelly's worst fears. What Wilson and his men found in the islands they were thrust upon would, however, lend more support to Keate's wishful thinking than Kelly's misgivings. They were to see some brutality but they were also to experience acts of kindness and compassion performed by a rational people living a life-style almost ideally suited to their island environment. The island complex that Henry Wilson and his men came to know may not have seemed a perfect paradise, but there is no evidence to suggest that any other place they had seen in their world travels would have been preferred as a place to be shipwrecked and at least one among them ultimately preferred it to that "other Eden, demi-paradise . . . England."

First contact.   Had there been any hostile intent in the first contact, the Belau Islanders would have approached the Englishmen's island of refuge with a hundred or more canoes and several hundred men in a manner that Captain Wilson's men were later to see demonstrated. There may well be some question as to what the Belauans expected to find as a result of the shipwreck or what they might have contemplated doing with the Englishmen if they had been unarmed. But whatever their intentions, as the English were to learn, it was not the Belauan way to make a sudden attack without warning and it was not in their minds to carry out wholesale slaughter. The taking and displaying of an occasional head as a symbol of the righteousness of superior power and authority had served their purposes just as it had served English purposes. (The similar practice of displaying heads at London's Temple Bar continued, according to Piper, until 1745—five years after Henry Wilson was born.) Kelly, who probably never saw his own countrymen commit such acts, may have been repelled by Keate's description of the cruelty inflicted on a few Belauan prisoners by Abba Thulle's men. Today, of course, such acts are only a memory—a memory preserved on the "story boards," the unique Belauan art form that owes its origins to the artwork displayed on the gable boards and cross beams of the traditional or community meeting house, the *bai*.

Malayan "linguists."   It is not too surprising that Malayan sailors were present in Belau before the arrival of the *Antelope*. They were said to have been shipwrecked just as the English had been. Even in relatively recent years Indonesians have been known to appear in Belau as a result of some misadventure. Nor is it very surprising that Captain Wilson had someone with him who could speak Malayan. McCluer was instructed to employ "linguists" and Parkinson points out in his *Trade in the Eastern Seas* that East India Company ships often had a mixture of nationalities among the crew, although the two countries from which they were principally drawn were India and China. Tom Rose apparently combined the linguistic skills from both areas, being from Bengal and having lived in Macao.

7 YOUR ENEMIES ARE OUR ENEMIES

Why take sides? Why should Captain Wilson have so readily agreed to risk providing armed assistance to a people he little knew against a people he knew not at all? If Keate had provided his readers with more than the briefest description of Oroolong, his position would have been more clearly understood. We are told only that the island's most distinguishing characteristic was a cove that was surrounded by rather rugged terrain. Why we are not told more is a mystery. A modern English sailor would very likely describe the shore or flat land area of the cove as being roughly the size of a football field—although, of course, not the same dimensions. This was the area the English fortified and used as their camp and boatyard. But describing the cove tells only part of the story. Like most island areas of Belau, Oroolong was not a single island but rather a tightly knit complex of small islands that on modern detailed maps, is shown to consist of three separate islands and some thirteen islets, some of the latter being no larger than a single plane tree in St. James's Park. Oroolong itself was very roughly a mile long and a quarter of a mile wide, rising to a height of about four hundred feet. In all, this island complex offered numerous hiding places for an invading force. Wilson and his men could not help but have realized that in such an environment they could not have defended themselves indefinitely without an ally familiar with the terrain. Even if they could, they would have perceived that they could not survive on the meager rations they had rescued from the wrecked *Antelope*. The vegetation on the Oroolong islands and islets, although lush, could hardly have supported one Robinson Crusoe, not to mention fifty. The sketches of Henry Wilson, Junior, do not even show coconuts. To have survived, a Robinson Crusoe would had to have been a very resourceful fisherman and shellfish scavenger. To make life bearable, Providence would had to have given him a female Friday to plant his taro and prepare it as his "daily bread." The taro (which Keate seems determined to refer to as "yams") and the fish provided by the Belauans were crucial to the survival of the English and although Captain Wilson could not have known in advance just how much help he could expect from such an ally, he could and presumably did reason that a friendly, cooperative relationship would ensure survival.

Oroolong, the island(s). For a fuller description of Oroolong, see Osborne, *The Archaeology of the Palau Islands.*

A typical day. For my description of a typical day on Oroolong I culled Keate's chapters for the activities of the English during their time on the island.

Treatment of prisoners. Some of those on the scene were repelled by the cruelty to prisoners taken in the heat of battle. Although this may have been the only practice that was truly offensive to the English, it was, if accurately reported, grim indeed. One prisoner was beaten to death with his own severed arm, and another had his hand removed in order for his captor to obtain a prestigious bone bracelet. Abba Thulle, while not necessarily condoning the brutality, did explain that they had given up holding prisoners in captivity because they had too easily escaped, returned to their home villages, and provided the enemy with vital military intelligence. When the English protested, Abba Thulle offered to turn any future prisoners over to them and let them decide their fate. Captain Wilson, of course, declined the offer. It might be added that the captain himself never observed these practices, having never accompanied any of the military expeditions. If he had, he might have been able, as an older man, to have put them into broader perspective if he remembered the English practices of beheading, "branding with a hot iron," and "in the case of women, there was even burning alive," according to Besant in his *London in the Eighteenth Century*. I might add in this context that I do not entirely agree with the thesis that it serves little purpose to point out that the practices of one society may be as bad as those of another. No society can profess perfection, but we need not silently condone what we do not approve. No man of whatever culture should be immune to an examination of his own conscience. Captain Wilson was a man who did not himself practice cruelty and therefore could, in good conscience, protest those acts of cruelty practiced by others. We do not know if the same can be said of all his men.

The *Oroolong*.   I am puzzled by Keate's description of the vessel the English built, later to be named the *Oroolong*. Keate describes her as being "one sixth" the size of the *Antelope*. Were that the case, she could not have been much over fifteen feet long. I believe that she must have been at least twenty feet long and closer to one-fourth the size of the *Antelope*. She was also very broad abeam if we can believe young Harry's illustrations of her.

8   MADAN BLANCHARD AND LEE BOO

Madan Blanchard and Lee Boo.   Most of the material for this chapter has been abstracted from the first edition of Keate's *Account*, chapters 18 through 21, except for the quotation from the book review, which appeared unsigned in *Gentleman's Magazine and Historical Chronicle*, Vol. 58, 1788, part 2, pp. 629–631, in which the reviewer goes on to express

> regret that the curtain is perhaps forever dropped between King Abba Thulle and the world . . . Pity but the Hon. Company . . . would send Capt. Wilson, or an officer equally proper, to revisit his old friends in the India Archipelago, and make them some return for their hospitable treatment of him; and that some Englishman, better calculated than Madan Blanchard, who preferred staying there to returning to his native country, would go and indulge that taste for natural society which it is the fashion of modern philosophy to prefer to political society, and man in a state of nature to man in proper cultivation.

The reviewer saw merit in the exchange not only as evidence of the hospitality of the Belauans but of the confidence they had in Captain Wilson:

> Nothing can be a stronger proof of the engaging dispositions of this new people than the circumstance of Madan Blanchard, one of the crew of the *Antelope,* determining to stay behind, and to end his days with them; more especially when we are told that he was universally liked by the rest of the ship's company; so that his determination could not be the result of any pique against his comrades. And the mutual confidence which was established is clearly demonstrated by the King's permitting his son to come to England with Capt. Wilson.

The Bone of Honor.   The bone is a vertebra taken from the spine of a dugong, the shallow-water mammal often described as the inspiration for the original mermaid. If Keate were alive today he might also have added that not many modern-day Wilsons are likely to receive "the order of the bone" in that the defenseless dugong, once common in the waters inside the reefs of Belau, is now a rare and endangered species. I saw only one dugong in my five years in Belau, although I did see a bone of honor bracelet being worn by at least one old *rubak.*

Blanchard's fate.   The end of Blanchard's story did not come until 1790 and then did not become known to the world outside Belau until 1803, when Hockin's *Supplement* to Keate's *Account* was published with the fifth edition. The story, or what is known of it, is included in Chapter 16.

"A Letter to Madan Blanchard."   I would feel remiss if I did not mention E. M. Forster's essay again. It is required reading for anyone with more than a casual interest in Lee Boo. Although the "Letter" threw no new light on the subject, it put Lee Boo in the spotlight again and thereby Forster helped as much as any man of letters could to keep Lee Boo's name and memory alive for another century. Forster's essay was written just one year after the publication of de la Mare's *Desert Islands and Robinson Crusoe,* which was an amplification of a lecture de la Mare gave in 1920 to the Royal Society of Literature of London. Whether or not Forster heard the lecture or read the book, he is mentioned in de la Mare's introduction, and his essay on Blanchard and Lee Boo is a not dissimilar treatment of a similar theme. Even if only coincidental, the connection is worthy of note.

9   FAREWELLS AND FIRST KNOTS

The Englishmen depart.   The scene of the *Oroolong* departing Belau was graphically captured by Henry Wilson, Junior, in two illustrations that mysteriously did not appear until the fifth edition of Keate's *Account.* In one of these the care that Abba Thulle took to ensure a safe passage through the reef is conveyed by a group of his men seated on an outcrop of the reef where, presumably, they could point out the channel. In the other, billows of smoke emanate from the deck of the *Oroolong,* indicating that a cannon—probably a swivel gun—has been fired as a salute to the people of Belau. In both there are many canoes surrounding the *Oroolong*.

The voyage of the *Oroolong*.   George Keate had remarkably little to say about the voyage of the *Oroolong,* considering the opportunity it presented for him to praise the men of the *Antelope* for their boat-building accomplishments, and Captain Wilson for his navigational skills. But, like so much of the entire story, Keate remains our only reliable source and all quotations appearing in this chapter have been taken from his *Account.*

Lee Boo's line of memories.   Because Keate does not mention each and every instance in which Lee Boo must have knotted his cord, I have taken the liberty of assuming that if an island or a ship merited a knot, so would a horse or a unique building as encountered by Lee Boo somewhat later in his travels. For those desiring a stricter accounting of how such mnemonic devices were used in Belau, I recommend Dr. Robert K. McKnight's *Mnemonics in Pre-literate Palau.*

Englishmen in Macao/Canton.   My source for stating that the English could enter and leave their compound at Canton only by water is Parkinson's *Trade in the Eastern Seas,* p. 60. Other authors have also described the confined conditions under which foreigners had to conduct their business at Canton. Foreigners lived a somewhat cloistered life inside their factories. (It should be understood that the term "factory" refers only to the facilities of the factor—the agent or supercargo—and has nothing to do with manufacturing as is often connoted in today's usage.) The agents were not even permitted to bring their wives to Canton; all foreign women were very strictly forbidden. Consequently the English spent as much time as they could at Macao, where they maintained homes, going upriver to Canton only during the winter months when the tea was ready to be purchased and the ships from England came in with the last of the southwest monsoons in September and October. They stayed at Canton just until the last of their Indiamen had sailed with the northeast monsoon, which required a departure before March. Whereas the *Antelope* had arrived at Macao in June, the off season, the *Oroolong* was fortunate to arrive on the last day of November, just in time to catch Indiamen departing for England in December.

A farewell to Oroolong footnote.   Somewhere, although I cannot remember where, I have read that the vessel Captain Wilson and his men built was originally destined to be named the *Relief.* If true, the original name would have reflected the condition the men of the *Antelope* found themselves in—a condition from which they sought relief. The change of names was doubtless agreed to in order to be amenable to Abba Thulle, who suggested it, but it also spoke to their condition at the time they left Belau; they were willing, if not eager, to honor the name of the island that had sheltered them.

By good fortune, Oroolong was an island the people of Belau did not need, but it was just right for the English, with its protected cove that afforded an almost ideal place for them to build their boat. Had they landed on Abba Thulle's home island of Koror, or at the home village of his arch rivals at Artingall, the story might have been different as indeed it was for some of the castaways who came later—long after the close of these events. (See, for example, Holden's *A Narrative of the Shipwreck, Captivity and Sufferings of Horace Holden and Benj. Nute,* as well as Captain Barnard's *Naked and a Prisoner.*)

The *Antelope* affair demonstrated that the proper stance for a shipwrecked crew was to be at least once removed from the centers of activity where territorial lines are so well drawn as to permit few if any infringements, however innocently committed. In this sense, the men of the *Antelope* did not "cross the beach" (to use Greg Dening's phrase), from which there may have been no return. They were also wise to decline Abba Thulle's offer to remove themselves and their material goods to his home island.

Years later, at Oroolong House, living in retirement and voluntarily removed from the scenes of his active life, Captain Wilson no longer sought respite from long and arduous voyages into alien lands; he had found relief—its name was Oroolong, and it was near the sea.

10 THE NEW MAN

The American "Flowery Flag Devils."   The most readable and best illustrated work I have found for the period of American entry into the China trade, and coincidentally for the period of Lee Boo's visit to Macao and Canton, is Tamarin and Glubok's *Voyaging to Cathay,* upon which, along with Henderson's *Yankee Ships in China Seas* and Danton's *The Culture Contacts of the United States and China,* I based my opening paragraph. Tamarin and Glubok have the Americans called the "New People" by the Chinese and their new nation "the flowery flag kingdom." Henderson has them called the "New People" and the "Flowery Flag Devils," and Danton states that the Americans came to be known as the "Hua Ch'i Kuo"—"the Flowery Flag Country," or "the New Nation" (p. 170).

Lee Boo—the New Man.   Keate reports Lee Boo described as the "New Man" and provides the picture of the Portuguese ladies admiring Lee Boo's tattooed hands.

Lee Boo in Macao.   The description of Lee Boo's days in Macao is abstracted from Keate. Also used were correspondence between Captain Wilson and the "Council of Supra Cargoes" at Canton, informing them of the wreck of the *Antelope;* the council's subsequent instructions to him; the rationale for auctioning the *Oroolong* at Macao rather than at Canton; and related matters, including an itemized statement of expenses, one of which was "Cloathing for two boys, Apprentices to Captain Wilson and also the Man from Pelew" (India Office Factory Records G/12/77 and G/12/79, India Office Library).

Lee Boo aboard the *Walpole.*   Lee Boo's remarks to Captain Wilson upon sailing aboard the *Walpole* are taken from Keate, but for a description of a typical voyage up the Pearl River from Macao to Canton I have relied primarily on Tamarin and Glubok, including the statement that children had buoys tied to their backs to prevent drowning.

Lee Boo at Canton.   Canton—what foreigners, including Lee Boo, could see of it—is well described in Morse and MacNair's *Far Eastern International Relations,* Chapter 4. The statement that the EIC's factory was more of a palace than a warehouse is taken from *Trade in the Eastern Seas,* p. 60, where Parkinson provides the description of a "critic writing anonymously in 1812." "Foreign Life at Canton" is also the subject of Tamarin and Glubok's Chapter 7. Lee Boo's comments on it are all, of course, from Keate.

Foreign factories at Canton.   The factories at Canton where foreigners lived and worked during the winter months are described by Morse and MacNair, p. 61, and by Parkinson in *Trade in the Eastern Seas,* pp. 59–63, as well as in Tamarin and Glubok's Chapter 7. Although perhaps not referring to the same factory building as Lee Boo saw, British affluence is well described in Morse and MacNair's statement (p. 61) that "at a dinner on New Year's Day, 1832, a hundred guests sat at table in the spacious dining room of the English factory."

The Indiaman *Morse.*   The tonnage of the Company's ship *Morse* is found in H. B. Morse, *Chronicles . . . ,* Vol. 2: *East India Company's Ships at Canton, 1775–1804.* The *Morse* was the largest ship to call at Canton in 1783.

Lee Boo aboard the *Morse.*   All details of Lee Boo's voyage to England aboard the *Morse* are from Keate and from the log of the *Morse.*

A footnote for researchers.   The English were some one hundred fifty years ahead of the Americans in establishing trade by sea with the Chinese and they were almost a hundred years ahead in establishing a trade at Canton. By the time the Americans arrived in 1784, all of the procedures, protocols, and practices required by the Chinese were old hat to the English, whereas everything was a fresh, new experience to the Americans. This was a blessing for me in that when I turned to American sources after reading British descriptions, I found a number of writers who provided a picture of the situation at Macao and Canton as it must have existed at the time Lee Boo visited—and did so with far more attention to detail than British authors writing of the same period. The Chinese welcomed the Americans, who spoke the same language and displayed the same customs as the British, with whom they had learned to deal, and for whom they now recognized a potential competitor who could offer new items of trade—ginseng and furs, to name but two. They seem to have been glad to have these "new people."

11   A HOUSE "RAN AWAY WITH BY HORSES"

By coach to London.   To retrace Lee Boo's route from Portsmouth to London today one must walk, drive, bicycle, or take the train. It could, I suppose, be done on horseback, but hardly by coach. Coaching days have been gone for more than a hundred years, more's the pity. They were colorful days if one can believe the literature. The "Land Frigate" that traveled the Portsmouth Road is described by Margeston in *Journey by Stages.* The fullest description of the route, the hazards of travel, etc., is found in Tristram's *Coaching Days and Coaching Ways.*

The route, the speed of the coach, and related information are found in Bates'

Directory of Stage Coach Services but because this refers to a somewhat later period, the stops en route vary slightly from those listed by Tristram. Besant's *London in the Eighteenth Century* also includes information on travel by coach and the customs related to it. Those interested in the subject might also read the accounts of visitors to England during this period, especially Moritz, who walked through much of England in 1782, and La Rochefoucauld, who visited England in the same year as Lee Boo, 1784. In particular, *Journeys in England, An Anthology,* edited by Jack Simmons, should be consulted for contemporary comments of the English themselves, including the quotation describing the coach as a "purgatory." In an excerpt from *Tom Brown's School Days,* Thomas Hughes describes the experience of traveling "outside" (on the roof of, instead of inside a coach): "there was the consciousness of silent endurance, so dear to every Englishman—of standing out against something, and not giving in."

No. 28 Paradise Row. In finding the location of the Wilsons' residence I was first assisted by the Reverend Beck's history of Rotherhithe Parish, which gives the street —Paradise Row—but not the house number. For that information I am indebted to Nevil Dickin, who searched leasehold records and rate (tax) payment documents, which established the Wilsons' home to have been at No. 28 Paradise Row. The house stood much as it had when Lee Boo was its honored guest for almost another two hundred years, until in 1977 it was removed to make way for a new gate to Southwark Park. The park now occupies many acres of what were, in Lee Boo's time, gardens and fields to the south of the Wilsons' home. My description of the house is based on copies of photographs obtained for me by Mr. Dickin; the view from Lee Boo's window is based on maps of the period.

12   LEE BOO'S ROTHERHITHE

The frozen river. As a result of a frost, the Thames was known to freeze "once in a hundred years or so" according to Besant who, on pp. 441–442 of *London in the Eighteenth Century,* describes the scene. Considering the tides, it seems incredible to me that this could happen, especially "both above and below the bridge." But it did happen just four years after Lee Boo's visit of 1784, in the winter of 1788–89, when, beginning "on the 25th of November" the river froze over and remained frozen until "early in the new year." The people who lived along the Thames made it the occasion for a fair and put up booths on the river, including one in which a printing press turned out ballads and broadsides to sell for souvenirs. "There were shows of all kinds, theatres, puppets, music, eating, drinking, dancing—an orgy which the Lord Mayor would find it difficult to stop" (Besant, p. 442). In a description of a similar frost on the Thames, Pritchett, in *London Perceived,* includes "horse-coach races." Too bad Lee Boo missed it all.

Southwark's coat of arms. The coat of arms of the London Borough of Southwark is shown and described in Mary Boast's *Southwark, a London Borough.*

A riverfront walk. For Thames riverfront scenes of the sort that would have confronted Lee Boo I consulted many sources, several of which are listed in the Bibliography. My own favorite, although from a slightly later period, is Captain Marryat's *Jacob Faithful*, Jacob having been a young man of approximately Lee Boo's age, who spent most of his youth on the river as an apprentice to boatmen and watermen. In order to describe a walk along Rotherhithe Street, "the essential walk" according to Pevsner, I have relied primarily on Mary Boast's three books (see Bibliography) and William's *South London*. For the names of streets and specific sights to be seen by Lee Boo and Captain Wilson I have used the Bermondsey section of Horwood's map of 1799 which, I was assured by a Bermondsey librarian, was highly reliable: "Just refer to Horwood's map of 1799; everyone knows Horwood, although Bermondsey is in pretty much by accident—they didn't care very much about us down here." However, during World War II, the Germans cared. The docks of the area that were a blessing in Lee Boo's time and for many generations thereafter became something of a curse to the people of Rotherhithe as the Germans made them their target. Many nearby houses and buildings were bombed, but, miraculously enough, none of the landmarks related to the Lee Boo story: not the church of St. Mary's, not Lee Boo's tomb—although there appear to be shrapnel marks on one side—and not the house in which the Wilsons lived, even though the house next door, number 29, was blitzed, as is shown on the Ordnance Survey map of 1950.

The tides.   For informative data on the tides along the Thames I have used Jefferies' *The Port of London*, which, in the convenient Jackdaw format, provides information on both historical and modern aspects of the river's commerce.

St. Mary's Church.   The parish church of St. Mary's Rotherhithe (Church of England) is described authoritatively in the London edition of *The Buildings of England* by Pevsner but is most frequently mentioned in a wide variety of publications as a landmark for sailors and as a pleasant sort of church-in-the-vale among mountains of warehouses by present-day writers. (See, for example, Fletcher's *London's River* in which the author, who once lived in Rotherhithe, provides a double-page sketch of the church as seen from the Mayflower Pub across the street.)

13   LEE BOO'S LONDON

Captain Wilson's uniform.   Parkinson, on p. 197 of his *Trade in the Eastern Seas*, provides a fuller description of the "full uniform" that Captain Wilson would have been expected to wear when "waiting on" the Court of Directors of the East India Company. To describe what I could of Lee Boo's outfit I used the watercolor portrait rendered from memory by Keate's daughter, Georgiana, which is in the possession of the John Harvard Library, Southwark.

East India House.   Although Foster's *The East India House* provides most if not all of what one might want to know, Philips' *The East India Company, 1784–1834* was more useful for my purposes because it provided a precise description of the buildings and facilities as of the year 1784, Lee Boo's year.

The Tower of London.   My description of the Tower as it was when Lee Boo was in London has been drawn from a variety of sources and checked against the London Ministry of Works publication *The Tower of London*.

The Thames below London Bridge.   The single most cogent source for my purposes, when including illustrations, is Eric de Maré's *London's River: the Story of a City.* The description I have provided is drawn from many sources and confirmed on p. 33 and some of the pages that follow.

The drowning waterman.   The story of Captain Wilson's lecture and Lee Boo's reactions after seeing a waterman taken from the Thames at the point of drowning is told in most if not all editions of the *History of Prince Lee Boo,* although, mysteriously, it does not appear in Keate's *Account* from which nearly everything else in the "little histories" was taken.

The Peter Hills School.   It is a shame we cannot assume that Lee Boo attended school here; the building is "right" and the location across from St. Mary's is perfect. But, even though the building existed then as we see it today, Pevsner, on p. 63, states that it did not operate as a school until 1797—thirteen years too late for Lee Boo.

Lee Boo's schooling.   To understand the sort of schooling Lee Boo would have been exposed to, I used Marshall's *English People in the Eighteenth Century,* and Tompson's *Classics or Charity?* among others, including Besant and Marryat.

Reading.   For an example of visitors being impressed with the English as readers, see Moritz's *Journeys of a German in England in 1782,* pp. 42–44.

Lee Boo at home with the Wilsons.   To rise at dawn and retire at dusk would have come as naturally to Lee Boo in London as at home in Belau, although the men of Belau were governed in their waking hours as much by the tides as by the sun. In London, candlelight was still the principal means of illumination. "It was still a time of grievous darkness," wrote Besant, adding, "I doubt if, in the ordinary household the family lit more than one candle at a time," and going on to provide tables showing the number of candles Londoners purchased.

Besant, in *London in the Eighteenth Century,* also explains that lacking indoor plumbing, "in courts and alleys, where there is only one water-tap for all the people, women get up at 4 in order to secure, before the others come out, a supply for the whole week." Presumably in the Wilson household this would have been a duty of a housemaid, as would the task of caring for the chamber pots and the more pleasant chore of collecting the milk and bread delivered to the door. Coal was also delivered and burned for heat: "2 fires in winter, one in summer," and there were Wilson fireplaces enough to keep Lee Boo warm.

The food the Wilsons ate would not have differed in substance from that of their neighbors or most Londoners. The difference between the classes, as explained by Besant, was one of both quality and quantity. The rich ate and drank in the evening until they could or would eat or drink no more. The Wilsons, however, at the time of Lee Boo's visit, presumably ate in moderation, as befitted their relatively modest income. Only after Henry Wilson's later financial rewards from the private trade of a captain of an Indiaman would the family table and sideboard have groaned with the weight of more food than could be decently consumed, if indeed this charitable Christian family indulged in anything approaching gluttony even then.

George Keate and family.   I am indebted to Dapp's *George Keate, Esq., Eighteenth Century Gentleman* for most of the information I have garnered about Keate's career, his marriage, his home, and his friendships, including that with Voltaire. Brief biographical sketches are to be found in such sources as the *Dictionary of National Biography*, but nothing I have found after long searches provides more than a fraction of the information made available by Dapp's work. (The British Museum does have some of the Voltaire–Keate correspondence, but little more.)

London street scenes.   Although my descriptions are based on wide reading from countless sources, I must credit Besant's *London in the Eighteenth Century* as being most helpful.

Dinner at the Keates'.   Besant, using the diary of Catherine Hutton, who visited London in 1778, describes a setting that may very well have been duplicated at the Keates' party: "The dinner, served at three, consisted of salmon at one end of the table, served with fennel-sauce, melted butter, lemon-pickle, and soy; at the other end a loin of veal roasted, with kidney beans and green peas. In the middle stood a hot pigeon-pie with yolks of eggs in it. After this course appeared a ham and chickens; when these were taken away there followed a currant-tart. After the cloth was removed, gooseberries, currants, and melon were placed on the table with wine and cider." (Presumably it was at this point in the order of things that Lee Boo almost committed his breach of etiquette with the cherries.) After this sumptuous meal, the ladies "retired," and, "at five o'clock they sent word to the gentlemen that tea was ready." This most likely would have been the time when Lee Boo, "at teatime," made his enquiries of the lady who had earlier left the company feeling faint. Besant adds, redundantly, "It was a time of great eating as well as great drinking."

Prisoners and crime on the Thames.   The sight of hulks serving as prisons is described in Lewis' *Three Tours Through London*, p. 45, and is also mentioned in many other works, including Besant's. The shadowy characters who worked the Thames, the river pirates, and their many accomplices are described in detail in Colquhoun's remarkable book, *Treatise on the Commerce and Police of the River Thames*, p. 316.

St. James's Park.   Just about everyone who has written about London, whether native or visitor, has had something to say about the parks. St. James's Park, because it bordered the king's palace of the day, was the premier park at the time of Lee Boo's visit. Everything I have mentioned that Lee Boo could not help but see has been mentioned by a variety of writers commenting on the period. For example, Archenholz, who visited some ten years after Lee Boo, is quoted regarding the grass in St. James's. Again, however, Besant's *London in the Eighteenth Century* has probably been the most helpful, although the information is scattered under such chapter headings as "The Parks," "Holidays," and "Amusements, Cock Fighting, etc."

Lunardi's balloon.   The London newspapers were liberally sprinkled with news of Lunardi and his balloon, much of which Lunardi submitted himself via advertisements prior to his flight. For what actually happened, I have relied for the most part on Gardiner's *Man in the Clouds*. Sir Joseph Banks let his feeling be known in a letter to Sir Charles Blagden dated 22 September 1784 (Royal Society Library, Blagden Letters, 29). Banks wrote, "It does not appear that Lunardi has made one real observation to assist the science of Meteorology or indeed anything more than his predecessors in the Art of delivering themselves over the command of the winds." And in another letter, "It is wondrous how many people have been tolerably at their ease in the air without making one observation worth a groat" (Banks to Blagden, 12 October 1784). Similar comments on Lunardi and others who soon took to the air are from Horace Walpole's published correspondence, edited by W. S. Lewis (p. 447 of Vol. 33, Walpole to Lady Ossory, 23 October 1784).

The king in view. The quotations describing the activities of the king (at Parliament; observing the anniversary of his accession and coronation, etc.) are from the *London Gazette,* various issues, August through November, 1784. If Lee Boo saw the king, his reaction may have been no more noteworthy than that of Besant's diarist, Catherine Hutton, who wrote that she walked the Mall for three hours on a Sunday waiting for a chance to see the king. "At last he came out, with the Queen, in three chairs, preceded by the footmen and the yeomen of the Guard. The King looked sour, and his face was red and bloated. He took no notice of the people, who bowed to him as he passed along. The Queen, for her part, affably returned the civilities of the people" (Besant, p. 401).

Brook Watson. The only biography I could find of this man, whom I would have thought merited the attention of more than one biographer, was a short study by John C. Webster. He is, of course, in the *Dictionary of National Biography.* He also figures prominently in Wright and Fayle's *A History of Lloyd's* where he was, for several crucial years, Committee Chairman.

The pleasure gardens. As indicated in the text, it was Besant, again, who provided the quotation for a visit to the Thomas Keyse's Pleasure Garden in Bermondsey, near Rotherhithe (*London in the Eighteenth Century,* p. 423).

14 THE LAST KNOT

Smallpox. In a Dublin edition of *The History of Prince Lee Boo,* the editors added a postscript informing their young readers that Lee Boo would not have died in London if he had "arrived in England some years later." Because the disease was "seldom seen" at the time the editors were writing (1820), they describe it as "a disorder which breaks out in sores over the whole body . . . the face swells . . . and yet the most skillful physicians know no cure for it. . . . If it is of the malignant kind, and it often is so, it carries off the young and strong, if mild, and the patient recovers, it sometimes leaves large scars and marks on the skin, and not infrequently deprives him of sight." They then provide a bit of history explaining that prior to the late 1790s the only preventative or immunization known was by introduction of variolus material from one person to another (variolation). According to the essay, this resulted in serious illness and one death in three hundred, which apparently was too much of a risk for most people, who took their chances of catching smallpox and thereby running the far greater risk of death that occurred in one in six cases. After Jenner's vaccination (inoculation with cowpox) was introduced (Jenner published his findings in

1798—see Cranmer-Byng's *An Embassy to China)*, the risk was reduced (according to the essay) to one in "fifty-four thousand." It is on the basis of these figures, doubtless combined with their own observations, that the editors state that had Lee Boo been in London after Jenner's work had been introduced and widely accepted—say in the early 1800s—he would have been vaccinated and spared. In this sense, he arrived in London just fifteen to twenty years too soon.

However, Banks arranged for Omai to be inoculated (by variolation) ten years before Lee Boo's arrival (see Chapter 19), and both McCluer and Delano gave tangible evidence of advocating inoculation when possible. Why not Captain Wilson? Keate does not say. We are only told repeatedly that Lee Boo was kept from crowded places where he might catch an infectious disease. In a city where, according to the essay quoted above, two thousand people died of smallpox every year prior to 1802, this was a considerable gamble—and, as it happened, not as good as the gamble of one in three hundred that Banks took on behalf of Omai. However, Keate does state that Captain Wilson had smallpox very much on his mind and that it was a disease "which he purposed to inoculate the young Prince with, as soon as he had acquired enough of our language to be reasoned into the necessity of submitting to the operation; judging, and surely not without good reason, that by giving him so offensive and troublesome a distemper, without first explaining its nature, and preparing his mind to yield to it, it might weaken that unbounded confidence which this youth placed in his adopted father" (p. 347). Perhaps, in the last analysis, it can only be said that the captain waited too long.

The short description of the history of smallpox immunization up to the time of Lee Boo and then, a little later, the period of Jenner's work that I have used are found in the notes provided by J. L. Cranmer-Byng in *An Embassy to China,* in which he explains that inoculation (variolation) probably began in China and "spread westward via Russia and Turkey." When "between 1817 and 1826," Jenner's work had reached China and won acceptance, "the wheel had thus come full circle."

Lee Boo's funeral. Because Lee Boo died of smallpox it is doubtful that his funeral would have been in any sense routine except in comparison with others who died under similar circumstances. His body would have been interred as soon as possible.

The usual lying-in-state at home was probably forsaken to protect the health of the mourners. But the Wilson house would almost certainly have displayed black, the required color of mourning. Everyone in the household would have worn black for several days at home and at the funeral service.

Because Lee Boo had been treated as one of the family it is probable that Besant's description applies: "The good people of London made a funeral the occasion for displaying, as much as possible, the respectability and the wealth of the family."

Lee Boo's last carriage ride may have been in a hearse painted black, the horses black or white and black. Even "the church was hung with black." And, Besant continues,

> At the funeral the mourners were presented with black scarves
> and weepers, black cloaks, black gloves, and rings; everybody
> carried a sprig of rosemary, which was thrown into the grave;
> and as the funeral was generally conducted at night, the mourners

wore long black cloaks, black gloves, and scarves; they carried torches which, after the service, they put out by knocking them on the ground.

Archenholz describes the entire procedure somewhat differently and perhaps a bit closer to the circumstances that prevailed for Lee Boo:

> The relations of a person newly dead, are spared the melancholy duty of laying him in the earth. An undertaker is sent for, he is told the day, the hour and the place of interment, and the sum destined for the purpose. He takes care of everything. His people come and examine the dead body, then dress it in woollen agreeable to an ancient law, made to give encouragement to these manufacturers. A coffin is provided, the bearers and carriages arrive, the bells toll, the body is buried, and the undertaker, after having defrayed the expenses, comes next day with his account which according to custom is not paid till Christmas or the New Year. (p. 223)

However many of Besant's or Archenholz' descriptive details were followed for Lee Boo, we can be sure of one thing—Lee Boo would have been dressed in wool, for it was the law (Statute 30 Car. 2. ft. 1.c.3., according to Rees's *Cyclopaedia*) and still applicable into the early 1800s.

15 McCLUER'S JOURNAL

Keate's *Account* was first "printed for Captain Wilson, and sold by G. Nicol, Bookseller to His Majesty, Pall Mall" and must have sold very well. The first edition was published in mid-1788; then a second edition was required and a second printing of the second edition before the end of the year. There followed third and fourth editions in 1789. The demand must have been enough to justify two apparently unauthorized editions in 1788 and a French edition; in the following year, an unauthorized edition was printed at Perth, Scotland, another in Philadelphia, and two separate printings in Basle, plus the first German edition. The demand persisted for many more years and through many more spurious editions, translations, and abridgments, many of which shamelessly omitted crediting George Keate with authorship of the original work, although Henry Wilson is, of course, mentioned, at least in the texts, and it is under his name that some editions are located in library catalogs. One of the early editions even attributes sole authorship to "One of the Unfortunate Officers" who is not named for the very good reason, as Dapp points out, that "his" account is a thinly disguised copy of Keate. Moreover, the translation for one of the French editions, presumably the two-volume 1793 edition, has been attributed to Honoré Gabriel Riquetti, Comte de Mirabeau, the renowned orator of the Constituent Assembly in the crucial days of the French Revolution. The attribution is made by the British Library, the Library of Congress, and the *Dictionary of National Biography* (under the entry for George Keate).

The recommended edition is the fifth, 1803, which includes Hockin's *Supplement* in one volume (although it was also published separately) and thereby provides the essentials from McCluer's journal as an immediate and highly desired sequel to the Lee Boo story. (See Bibliography.)

The East India Company's delay in getting the word of Lee Boo's death to the waiting father, Abba Thulle, is explained in all of its complexity on pp. 89–95 of Howard T. Fry's "Alexander Dalrymple and New Guinea" (*The Journal of Pacific History*, vol. 4, 1969).

The East India Company's directive instructing the authorities in Bombay to send two ships on an expedition which would include a visit to the "Peeloo Islands" ran to 35 paragraphs and was signed by Henry Dundas, 1st Viscount Melville, as president of the board (India Office Library: E/4/1006 *Bombay Dispatches*, 5 Nov. 1789–3 June 1790, p. 129).

McCluer's hydrographic works, which gave "full testimony" to his "competent abilities" and led to his selection as head of the expedition, were *An Account of the Navigation between India and the Gulph of Persia, 1786*, and *Description of the Coast of India, 1789*, both of which had been published by Dalrymple. They may be seen at the British Museum. (See Bibliography.)

McCluer's letter to the Bombay authorities, in which he made a strong plea for better pay for his subordinate officers, and the reply that summoned him to a board meeting to be reprimanded, are found in India Office Library, Range/342/Vol. 12/p. 447. An entry noting that the reprimand had been carried out is on p. 455.

The Bombay Marines' organization, function, etc. is described on pp. 46–50 of Parkinson's *Trade in the Eastern Seas*.

Relationships between Dalrymple and Cook. See Fry's *Alexander Dalrymple and the Expansion of British Trade*, in which is developed not only this relationship but Dalrymple's relationship to the McCluer expedition.

The *Panther*. An illustration can be seen on p. 250 of Chatterton's *The Old East Indiamen*. By William Henry, the draftsman sent by the Company to serve with McCluer's expedition, the sketch was actually made later, at Suez Harbor in 1794. For my description of the *Panther* I am indebted to Nevil Dickin. (As an India-built vessel that, so far as is known, never voyaged to London, it is not listed in Lloyd's Register.)

McCluer's journal can be seen at the British Library Manuscript Department where it is identified as "Additional MS 19301." For the most part, I have used a microfilmed copy at Hamilton Library, University of Hawaii. Because the journal has been preserved, it is possible to know John McCluer better than any of the other principals involved in the entire *Antelope*/Lee Boo saga. Reading his own words, although possibly not in his own script—for journal manuscripts were often copied by clerks—I found human qualities that, by contrast, Keate did not attribute to Wilson. For example, McCluer sometimes procrastinates, and when he makes decisions, some of them seem to run counter to his better judgment. He is even sometimes frivolous, as when he recorded the story of the duck that went overboard and was devoured by the shark; it is unlikely that Wilson would have recorded the incident. Most telling-ly, however, he is the only one of all those who had anything to say about what tran-spired in the Pelews who even hints that the men may have had sexual intercourse!

For the researcher, there are problems with McCluer's journal. It diminishes as the expedition progresses; McCluer seems to lose interest; his notes fall off, are fewer, and less precise. Fortunately, we can compare it with Delano's narrative, which pro-vides some of what McCluer omitted but possibly would have mentioned in the ear-lier stages of the expedition. In fact, months go by with few or no entries in the jour-nal. During the last six months we are not certain where he is or what he is doing. Events are also recorded well after the fact—that is, he may be writing an entry on the tenth of the month telling us about something that happened on the first; then in the next sentence he has moved right on to the end of the month.

Lastly, in this context of McCluer's journal, I should mention that the copy I have used contains marginal notes that there is reason to believe were made by Dalrymple. Most of them tend to be critical—of small matters, for the most part—but in one instance McCluer is accused of failing to follow his instructions, which one suspects is correct.

McCluer's age and the ages of the other officers and all such details are provided from the journal unless a different source is specifically cited.

Belauan canoes.   After arriving at Belau and upon moving up to Koror, McCluer noted in his journal that canoes "shoot past them like so many porpoises." This is apparently not an exaggeration. David Abeel in *Journal of a Residence in China and the Neighboring Countries* offers a similar description of canoes "feathering the ocean, and advancing in pursuit. . . . The performance of their canoes and the skill and dexter-ity with which they manage them are surprising. They come dancing over the waves like 'fairy sprites,' and with a velocity which demands a stiff breeze . . . for a ship to equal" (pp. 57–58).

Blanchard's death.   I know of no way to reconcile the curious fact that McCluer's account of Blanchard's death differs so significantly from all others (Delano's in par-ticular). McCluer does mention that there had been fighting with "Pillilew" which, according to other accounts, contributed to Blanchard's demise, and he had chosen a girl whose father had been killed "in the conquest." (However, that could have been an earlier battle and not the one in which Delano reports that Blanchard lost his life.) The mystery remains. Whom to believe? McCluer, who seems forthright on other matters, may have been concealing the truth in this instance, but I hardly think there was reason for evasiveness in a journal entry he would assume likely never to be seen by the people of Belau and only by too few Englishmen to hurt British pride.

Kockywack and Lee Boo—"adopted" sons.   This bit of information, even if fully correct, is not as significant as might be supposed because in Belauan culture heredi-tary titles are not passed from father to natural son. Ironically, the English may have been more accurate when they applied the appellation of "Prince" to adopted rather than natural sons of Abba Thulle.

McCluer's New Guinea survey.   For background and for a full description of the role played by Dalrymple, see H. T. Fry's *Alexander Dalrymple and the Expansion of British Trade*. See also his article, "Alexander Dalrymple and New Guinea," *The Journal of Pacific History*, vol. 4, 1969.

The Dutch and their spice.   See Parkinson's *Trade in the Eastern Seas*, pp. 346–347.

Delano's observations re Bligh and Edwards.   See p. 103 of Delano's *Narrative* which puts the *Panther* at Timor shortly after Edwards. See also Delano's Chapter 5 for more on Bligh, the *Bounty*, and the mutineers.

16 DELANO'S *NARRATIVE*

The *Narrative*.   Amasa Delano did not publish his *Narrative of Voyages and Travels* until 1817, some twenty-five years after he had parted company with McCluer. Correctly assuming that his readers would doubt that he could retain so much detailed information by memory, he explains, on p. 197, that he had in his possession copies of the journals of the *Panther* and the *Endeavour*. This would go a long way toward explaining the close similarity between his observations and those of McCluer, although Delano adds a good deal more than is found in the pithy writing style of McCluer's journal. Would that we knew where the two journals used by Delano could be found today.

Delano, the man.   Samuel Eliot Morison's reference to the Delano family is found on p. 21 of his *Maritime History of Massachusetts*. McCluer was fortunate to have had Amasa Delano along, although, on the evidence of his journal, he may have been slow to recognize his good fortune and the men of the *Panther* were apparently slow to accept the stranger into their company. They may have had a point. Delano, at least in the earlier portions of his book—those dealing with Belau—comes across as more of a boy scout than the man of the world he later became. He seeks adventure, is prepared for adventure, volunteers for it, and therefore sometimes falls prey to the pranks the more cynical play on eager tyros—as when the men of the *Panther* sent him off on a wild goose chase in search of gold. But however naive Delano may have been in the beginning, by the time he parts company with the English at Canton he has had high words of praise for McCluer and his fellow Bombay Marines and apparently the feeling was by then mutual, as is witnessed by McCluer's words of praise for Delano, quoted at the beginning of the chapter from a letter McCluer wrote to John Morris dated 10 February 1793 (India Office Library, Range 342/Vol. 16, p. 806).

It is too bad that Amasa Delano is probably best remembered as the man who unwittingly supplied Herman Melville with the basis of his story *Benito Cereno*. (Melville took it from Delano's 18th chapter.) But history has put Amasa in good company. The most famous Delano of them all, Franklin Delano Roosevelt, so the story goes, once wanted to borrow a copy of Amasa's book, but the conservative Delano to whom he wrote put the book in a museum where it would be out of the liberal president's reach! Presumably the Library of Congress was then asked to supply a copy of what was then a fairly rare book, but one that has since been reprinted. (The story is briefly told as a footnote to the preface of *Melville's Benito Cereno, a Text for Guided Research* by John P. Runden.)

Apparently Poe also borrowed for his *Narrative of Arthur Gordon Pym*, which is based on Benjamin Morrell's *Narrative of Four Voyages to the South Sea and the Pacific,* as is explained by Richard Wilbur in his introduction to the 1973 Godine edition of Poe's novel.

The two boys left in Belau.   William Ross and James Mellick have the distinction of having remained in Belau longer than any other Englishmen up to that date—nineteen months. Unfortunately, nothing is known of their later life. Inexplicably, Delano refers to one of them, James Mellick, as "Terrence"—possibly a nickname. By whatever name, and they doubtless were given Belauan names as well, it is a pity that their experiences are not recorded.

17 "A SPECIES OF INSANITY"

The decision to remain in Palou.   One would have to search further than I have done to find another example, in fact or fiction, of a man who, without warning, gave up his ship and the command of an expedition in order to see what a Crusoe could do with servants and plenty of arms and tools among a friendly people who, in his eyes, needed the help he thought himself capable of providing. That McCluer was prepared to go it alone "independent of the natives" is expressed in a letter to the governor general (of Bombay, presumably) dated 23 July 1794, in which he explained that he had enough of what he might need to last "two years." In the same letter he said that the people of Belau had "rejoiced" in his decision to remain among them— all except the high chief of Koror (the Ibedul/Abba Thulle) who feared that if McCluer died the English might "turn their enemy." Wedgebrough assured the chief that in that event McCluer's papers would tell the story and that he need not fear.

That the decision came as a surprise to the men of the expedition is best verified by Proctor's letter to the chief of the Select Committee at Canton, dated 15 February 1793, in which he stated that McCluer would be arriving in China in "about twenty days" (India Office Library Factory Records, China, Canton Secret Committee Consultations, G/12/103, p. 244).

That he acted alone and that Wedgebrough had "used every argument" in an effort to dissuade him is stated in McCluer's letter to John Morris dated 10 February 1793, written at "Coorora, Fort Abercrombie,"—one of the letters he wrote announcing and explaining his decision to remain in Belau.

That McCluer anticipated his decision would be "taken for an act of insanity" but was one he had "been determined upon . . . ever since I left Bencoolen" is expressed in his letter to John Wedgeborough [*sic*] dated 2 February 1793, and included in Hockin's *Supplement* to Keate's fifth edition. And that Wedgebrough agreed to McCluer's requests with the proviso that if the "Honourable Company should not be pleased therewith, that they should be accounted for by his [McCluer's] attornies" is also found in Hockin, as is the statement that "a boat" was left for McCluer—presumably the boat he later used for his voyage to Macao.

Overall, McCluer's most complete statement explaining his actions at the begin-ning of his stay in Belau is contained in his letter to John Morris, dated 10 February 1793 (India Office Library, 342/Vol. 16, p. 806).

Departure from Belau and voyage to Macao.   Similarly, the best statement sum-marizing his fifteen-month experience in Belau and his open-boat voyage from Belau was written after his arrival at Macao (India Office Library, Range 342/Vol. 19, p. 397—McCluer to Governor General, 23 July 1794). The Company's cognizance of his arrival at Macao and their doubts as to his motives for leaving are documented in the China Factory Records entry for 4 May 1794 (India Office Library G/12/108, p. 42).

McCluer's future plans.   His purchase of a vessel and his intentions to sail to Bom-bay are also documented in the letter of 23 July 1794, Macao, as is his reference to his encounter with Captain Hayes, and his statement, "thus far has insanity got posses-sion of me."

Dalrymple's comment on McCluer's route: Macao to Belau via Manila.   The com-ment is found in the Melville Papers (MS 1068, ff. 86–92, National Library of Scotland) as is the statement that horses were delivered to Belau from Manila and supplies provided for those left behind in Belau.

The McCluer-Hayes connection.   For more of the background that led up to this impromptu connection see *Commodore Sir John Hayes, His Voyages and Life, 1767–1831,* by Ida Lee (Mrs. C. B. Marriott).

Geby Island claimed for King George.   Lee also purports that McCluer took posses-sion of Geby Island in the name of King George (ibid., p. 155).

McCluer's loss at sea.   Mentioned in a variety of sources, none of which differ as to what his fate must have been. Perhaps the closest to the scene was Samuel Snook at Bombay, whose long letter to Delano (pp. 74–76 of Delano's *Narrative*) relates what is known of the circumstances.

McCluer's "insanity."   Was it real or feigned? Was he speaking facetiously when referring to his own insanity, or was he ill? My own view is that he may well have been ill but that his mind was reasonably clear. I also see him as a character in a play by Pirandello who has almost convinced himself that if enough people thought him to be mad, he must, in fact, be mad. But, to the last, he was trying to prove them wrong and had he not been lost at sea he might well have succeeded.

A further note on sources.   The three principal sources relating to McCluer's deci-sion to remain in Belau, his experiences there, and his subsequent actions are:
1. The India Office Library's "Factory Records" of the East India Company operations at Canton (G/12) and Bombay (Range/342).
2. Hockin's *Supplement* for which Rev. J. P. Hockin used much of the same mate-rial as has been preserved by the India Office Library. In addition, because he was Captain Wilson's son-in-law, Hockin had access to some letters, especially those from Wedgebrough and White, which seem to have disappeared.

3. The National Library of Scotland's Melville Papers—especially MS 1068, ff. 86–92, which is an extract from McCluer's letter of 21 December 1795 to Dalrymple, sent from Bencoolen and annotated by Dalrymple. (Melville had retired from high office with the East India Company and Dalrymple had sent copies and extracts of letters he had received from the field that he thought would interest his superior emeritus. Some of this material has survived longer than the originals, which presumably remained in London.)

Finally, Dr. Howard T. Fry's 37-page bibliography at the close of his *Alexander Dalrymple and the Expansion of British Trade* is also very helpful to researchers seeking to understand the broad context within which the McCluer drama was enacted.

18 SNOOK'S SWORD

McCluer's will.   A copy of McCluer's will is reproduced in *The Memoires of a Bombay Mariner* by Andrew Dunlop and gives every evidence of being authentic.

White and Wedgebrough.   For the dates and circumstances of the deaths of White and Wedgebrough I am indebted to the researches of Nevil Dickin.

The Belauan women.   For the names of the Belauan women and for verification of other facts relating to their stay in Bombay and their return to Belau I have used Snook's letter to Amasa Delano as reproduced in Delano's *Narrative.*

The ships that accompanied the *Warley.*   Although Snook provides the names of the three ships, he does not mention that on board one of them, the *Earl of Abergavenny,* was one John Wordsworth who later, in 1805, became captain. John Wordsworth was the brother of the poet William Wordsworth. Parkinson, in *Trade in the Eastern Seas,* pp. 376–377, gives a brief description of John Wordsworth's career, which ended in tragedy shortly after he succeeded to the command of the *Earl of Abergavenny.*

The *Diamante.*   The name and description of the ship Snook purchased for the voyage to Belau is provided in a letter and an enclosure with that letter dated 5 February 1798 (India Office Library, China Factory Records G/12/119, p. 125). Snook's orders are found in the same source (p. 146).

Snook's voyage to Belau and return to Macao.   Snook's report on his voyage to Belau is found at the India Office Library (China Factory Records, G/12/122, letter dated 3 December 1798, written at Macao and addressed to R. Hall, President of the Select Committee, Canton). Enclosed with the letter was a document entitled "Proceedings of the Sloop *Diamante.*" Also, the settling of accounts, payment of crew, etc., are found in the same source (G/12/125—Snook to Hall and enclosure "Bill No. 4").

Snook's sword.   For the discovery of Snook's sword and for information relating to what is known of the final chapters of Snook's career and his life in retirement, I am again indebted to the researches of Nevil Dickin. The sword itself is illustrated and described in a brief article in *Country Life* (1 Oct. 1964, p. 840).

19 OMAI AMONG OTHERS

Omai.   The definitive history of Omai is McCormick's. In the popular jargon, everything you ever wanted to know about Omai can be found in his *Omai, Pacific Envoy.* McCormick also has something to say about Aoutourou and others but, very disappointingly, nothing about Lee Boo. However, it was reassuring to find on the last pages of this scholar's work the comment that although he had tried to treat the subject exhaustively (and succeeded admirably in my view) he still found, after completing his manuscript, that previously unknown information about Omai had come to light.

Cook.   His statement, "I thought it proper to undeceive him . . ." is from Beagle-hole, p. 400, and footnote 2, same page, Vol. 2.

Bligh.   The Bligh quotations are from his *The Log of the Bounty.*

Ellis.   William Ellis, the missionary, is quoted from his *Polynesian Researches During a Residence of Nearly Six Years in the South Sea Islands.*

Cowper.   The lines are from the poem "The Task," which is found in many editions of Cowper's poetry and in many anthologies.

Aoutourou.   His story is told by both McCormick and Dodge.

Delano.   His "Lee Boos" are described in his *Narrative.*

Liholiho.   For my short summary of this well-known story I have used Peter H. Buck's *Explorers of the Pacific;* the quotation is from p. 92.

Quiros.   The answer Quiros received to his question concerning the propriety of taking islanders from their homes is found in De Munilla's *La Austrialia del Espíritu Santo,* vol. 2, pp. 315–316.

Abba Thulle's "long-looked for son."   Keate's phrase was more perceptive than he could have known. A former student of mine from Belau once related that he could remember his grandmother retelling stories that had been told to her of how Abba Thulle had posted people to keep watch for a returning English ship that might bring the Lee Boo who never came home.

Iphigenia.   The *Iphigenia* affair that resulted when Captain Douglas sailed past Belau without stopping is described in Meares' *Voyages Made in the Years 1788 and 1789 . . . ,* and the quotations are from pp. 294–298. A similar visit by the *Alexander,* Captain Shortland, stopping briefly and "evident(ly)" at Belau is described in *The Voyage of Governor Phillip to Botany Bay,* edited by Auchmuty. Shortland's visit came five months after Douglas' and the circumstances were similar in that Shortland knew nothing of the *Antelope* affair and, therefore, made no effort to call on Abba Thulle. He later regretted this because his crew was in urgent need of fresh victuals, which he was unable to obtain from the Belauans he contacted in the northern sector of the islands.

For further reading. Fairchild's textbook treatment of the subject, *The Noble Savage,* includes everyone who might qualify as a Noble Savage, with a great deal about Lee Boo, whom he compares favorably with Omai.

Anyone engaged in researching an Omai or a Lee Boo will sooner or later (and the sooner the better) discover a little book of Tinker's, *Nature's Simple Plan,* which is a delight to read, no matter what aspect of sojourning islanders one might pursue.

Dodge, in *Islands and Empires,* devotes the better part of a chapter to Omai, Lee Boo, Aoutourou, and others, collectively.

For those who might wish to know more of visitors to London, Benjamin Bissell's *The American Indian in English Literature of the Eighteenth Century* is recommended.

Finally, visits of islanders to the great cities of the world became less rare after the eighteenth century. As Greg Dening points out in *Islands and Beaches,* islanders "had their beachcombers too [who] left their islands on ships and landed on Aoe's (alien) beaches in London, Boston, New York and Paris." But, as Dening states, this was later—after the early ambassadors had been feted and the novelty of their visits had worn thin. Furthermore, the earliest visitors were invited guests; some of those who came later, like Delano's stowaways and those who were taken against their will, could hardly have expected a royal welcome.

20 TARTARY, SURAT, OR THE PELEWS

The Reverend Mr. Burder's words heeded at the Castle & Falcon. The quotations near the beginning of the chapter are from the London Missionary Society's *Sermons Preached at the Formation of the Missionary Society,* a compilation published in 1795, the same year the "Reverend Messrs" met to express their resolve to send forth missionaries. Much of the same information is to be found in Lovett's *History of the London Missionary Society, 1795-1895.* Even now, the sermons make good reading and they surely must have been delivered with a great deal of conviction and inspiration for so much to have been accomplished in such a short time. The "Pelew Islands" are mentioned several times as potential targets for missionary efforts and it is, therefore, quite remarkable that this objective was never met. (It was not unusual for the clergymen to meet at an inn. Moritz fell in with a minister who took him to such a meeting at an inn during his travels in England in 1782.)

The resolution. Specifically, the resolution "that the first attempt of this Society shall be to send Missionaries to Otaheite . . . Tartary, Surat, or The Pelews" is found on pp. 26–27 of the introduction to the *Sermons.* This resolution was later expressed more realistically (in Captain James Wilson's instructions) to read "that a mission be undertaken to Otaheite, the Friendly Islands, the Marquesas, the Sandwich, and the Pelew Islands."

Pentycross's challenge to infidelity. The Reverend Pentycross's challenge to "infidelity"—spirit of Hume, Rousseau, Voltaire, etc.—is found on p. 61 of *Four Sermons Preached in London, at the Second General Meeting of the Missionary Society,* which, in the edition I have used, is bound with the earlier *Sermons* cited above.

The *Duff* at Pelew.   For information on James Wilson and the voyage of the *Duff* I have used Lovett's *History* and Wilson's own *A Missionary Voyage to the Southern Pacific Ocean,* in which the quotations regarding the *Duff* at Belau are found. It is difficult to establish authorship of the comments recorded at Belau, except that the statement "as it had all along been the Captain's intention to stay here a few days" makes it clear that it was not James Wilson writing, but most probably his first mate, William Wilson, according to various authorities.

Abba Thulle, Lee Boo and the *Duff.*   I once spent a day at what was then the London Missionary Society Library trying to determine what influence, if any, the examples of Abba Thulle and Lee Boo may have had on the decision to send the *Duff* on its first voyage. I was told that there could have been no such influence. However, a reading of Captain James Wilson's instructions from the Society would indicate otherwise. He was told, with reference to Belau, "The character of the natives furnishes a *strong inducement* to establish a mission among them . . ." [my emphasis] but his instructions went on to caution that, on the assumption he had rounded the Horn and would be contacting the Belau Islands last, he might have found it more expedient to drop off all missionaries before reaching the homeland of Abba Thulle and Lee Boo. Although the route was not as anticipated, the result was the same: he was out of missionaries before he reached Belau. It is ironic that the people of Belau, whom the Society had held in high regard on the strength of Keate's *Account* (plus possible personal testimony by some of the men of the *Antelope* who had been there), came to be described by William Wilson, on very short contact, in less-than-flattering terms. Consequently, one presumes, the effort to establish a mission in Belau was not further pursued.

Familiarity breeds contempt.   That the early enthusiasm for Polynesian and other Pacific islands soured to varying degrees after missionaries reported home is reflected in letters and journals quoted in the *History of the London Missionary Society.* The same point is made by Bernard Smith, among others, in his *European Vision. . . .*

Morning Stars and missionaries to Micronesia.   The earliest voyages of the *Morning Star,* the American missionary vessel, are described in the *Story of the Morning Stars, the Children's Missionary Vessels,* by Bingham. Other missionary efforts in Micronesia are selectively and ably documented and illustrated in Hezel and Berg's *Winds of Change: A Book of Readings on Micronesian History.* (See also Hezel's *The First Taint of Civilization.*)

Rupack Street.   The naming of Rupack Street is documented in the (then) Metropolitan Borough of Bermondsey's *Minutes of the Proceedings of Council, 1912–1913,* p. 317. As engineers, the Brunels gave Rotherhithe what must have been one of its rare moments of glory. There, at Cow Court, in March 1825, to the peal of church bells and with great fanfare, work began on the first tunnel under the Thames. Sir Marc Brunel laid the first brick and his son, Isambard Kingdom Brunel, laid the second, with such luminaries as the Duke of Wellington and Sir Robert Peel looking on. But it took eighteen years and twenty-three days to complete the 1200-foot tunnel after many delays and interruptions, during which time, at Rotherhithe, Isambard Kingdom also worked to devise a "gaz engine." When completed, the tunnel connected

Rotherhithe to Wapping on the north bank of the Thames, and was inspected by Queen Victoria, who walked through it, followed by some "fifty thousand" people. For the complete story see John Pudney's *Brunel and His World*, from which the quotations here were taken, and Sandstrom's *The History of Tunnelling*.

21 THE HAPPY ENDING

The Adventures of Madiboo.   Similar to *The History of Prince Lee Boo* in format, *The Adventures of Madiboo* was doubtless created and published to capitalize on the popularity of the Lee Boo story then being so widely read. Another much more recent work of fiction is *Aye, Aye, Sir!* by LaRocque DuBose, which is a story for boys—a retelling of the *Antelope*-Lee Boo story with characters added, omitted, or, like the incidents described, juggled to suit the purposes of the author, which were, as he stated, to show relationships between fathers and sons—primarily Captain Wilson and young Henry Wilson. A copy can be seen at the Library of Congress in Washington, D.C.

Pacific Islanders in fiction.   A number of works treat this subject. One of the best is J. C. Furnas' *Anatomy of Paradise*. I agree with Furnas when he deplores the misplaced romanticizing found in most writing with island themes, and at the same time recommends the writing of Robert Louis Stevenson, both fiction and nonfiction, as the best introduction to the islands.

The happy ending: Wilson and Oroolong House.   Of all the memorabilia relating to the story of Lee Boo and the *Antelope*, Oroolong House is the most alive after all these years. It sits almost in the heart of the little village of Colyton near the southern coast of England. Its unsuspected existence was brought to my attention by Nevil Dickin, who discovered it on a pilgrimage to Captain Wilson's tomb. Having found the churchyard where the captain is buried, Nevil was walking back to the bus stop, his head bowed against a pouring rain, when he chanced to look up at the precise moment that he was standing in front of a building clearly labeled Oroolong House. He knocked at the door but found no one at home. Later he met the current occupants, and still later he and I called on them together. They knew the story and welcomed the additional information we were able to provide. It is as happy a home now as it must have been when Captain Wilson sat before his fireplace in the winter and in his garden in the summer. Its many rooms provided ample space for the grandchildren with whom the captain spent his last years. Henry Wilson, Junior, lived on there after the captain's death and the Wilson name was honored and respected in the community. As the Wilson girls married and moved away they carried with them their grandfather's curiosities from Belau, but they left behind the name that symbolized the happy life they had known there.

Hockin's Supplement.   Henry Wilson's daughter, Christiana, married John Pearce Hockin, a clergyman. Inspired by his wife and commissioned by his father-in-law, this Oxford-educated young man wrote the supplement that appeared as an addendum to the fifth edition of Keate in 1803. (Some copies were also printed separately.)

The supplement was an attempt to bring Keate's readers up to date on events since Lee Boo's death. Hockin succeeded in this and, for better or worse, emulated the style of George Keate.

Omai and Lee Boo compared.   Although a comparison is difficult, my contention that Lee Boo stood a better chance of having a happy ending is compounded of many things, not least the fact that he made better use of his time in London. The *Gentleman's Magazine* reviewer of Keate's *Account,* who must have been in London when Omai was there, and then, later, when Lee Boo was there, found Lee Boo to be "an amiable, sensible youth" who, in a "short time [made] a much better use of his natural talents than Omai in a far longer." And, I would add, for that reason and because he died in London, he is better remembered there, his memory having been preserved by Keate and the little histories written in his honor. Had Lee Boo returned to his home island he might well be less remembered in London but better remembered in Belau.

If Lee Boo had returned.   For an engrossing discussion of what a Pacific Islander might have learned that would be of use to him when he returned, see McCormick's chapter 12, in which the debate that ensued after Omai left London is fully documented and explored. Much of what was said of Omai would apply to Lee Boo, and some of the fundamental issues raised as to what constitutes a proper education for a Pacific Islander are still being debated today. The only difference is that the present-day Omais and Lee Boos who have returned are leading the discussion and facing the fact that not all of the knowledge that has been traditionally respected in the islands can be learned from books—at least not until those books have been written and published. Happily, some of this is being done today in Belau by Belauans; some such work has been sponsored and encouraged by the Education Department and other agencies of the Trust Territory Government for many years, and major contributions have been made by such modern-day missionaries as Father Francis X. Hezel, S.J., of Truk and Father Edward A. Soucie, S.J., of Pohnpei. Even an occasional "outsider" makes a contribution that is meaningful in this context—most recently, R. E. Johannes with his *Words of the Lagoon: Fishing and Marine Lore in the Palau District of Micronesia.*

The parts of a canoe.   When I was in Belau working with Belauan educators we devised a test to see how well students could name the parts of a Belauan canoe. Whereas in the 1950s young male students could name most of the individual parts, it is my guess that students of today would fail the same test. But they would probably score much higher in naming the parts of a car or an outboard motor.

Kubary and O'Keefe.   For a description of Kubary's work in the Caroline Islands—primarily Belau and Pohnpei (where he died)—see Spoehr's *White Falcon.* For a fictionalized life of O'Keefe see *His Majesty O'Keefe* by Klingman and Green. And for the roles both men played in the history of Micronesia, see Hezel's *The First Taint of Civilization.*

Andrew Cheyne. For this trader's early work in the western Pacific see *The Trading Voyages of Andrew Cheyne 1841–1844*, edited by Dorothy Shineberg. Both Cheyne's work and Shineberg's outstanding introduction refer to the *Antelope*, Captain Wilson, and Abba Thulle.

Admiral Bridge. On pp. 300–302 of *Some Recollections*, published in 1918, Admiral Sir Cyprian Bridge records how he brought about a peace treaty between "Abba Thuol" and "his enemy 'King' Aracklye" of Melekeok on what was, by happy coincidence, the hundredth anniversary (plus one day) of the wreck of the *Antelope*.

The destruction of Koror. At the close of World War II, the American occupation forces authorized the destruction of most of the Japanese buildings, thus leveling what had been a thriving city, even though it had served Japanese interests. When I first went to Koror in early 1953 we lived for a few months in one of the few remaining Japanese-built houses. The concrete foundations of others were everywhere to be seen. Why so many were leveled after the war (a war in which the Belauans had been innocent bystanders and long-suffering victims) remains a mystery to me. Perhaps the best-known source in which the matter is even mentioned is Trumbull's *Paradise in Trust*, p. 134. For a description of the Japanese years, I recommend Hatanaka's "Micronesia under the Japanese Mandate, 1914–1945," a 16-page introduction to her *Bibliography of Micronesia Compiled from Japanese Publication, 1915–1945*. See also Mark R. Peattie's forthcoming book *Nan'yo: The Rise and Fall of the Japanese in Micronesia, 1885–1945* (Pacific Islands Monograph Series no. 4, Honolulu: University of Hawaii Press). For a concise description of Belau at the peak of the Japanese era (1940) I recommend McKnight's six-page essay, "Nanyo Paradaisu: Images of Life in the Western Carolines."

The passing parade of expatriates. Employees of the American administration of the Trust Territory of the Pacific Islands remained in the territory for an average of about three years, which, it was often said, was not long enough. But it was just as strongly argued that some of us stayed too long. In my own case that was for a total of twenty-five years. We went first to Belau, via Honolulu and Guam, in 1953. We were a family of four with daughters aged five and one. We remained for five years without taking the customary "home leave" to which we were entitled at the completion of each two-year period, because travel over such long distances in the 1950s was not a vacation for young children. After graduate study, I resumed employment with the Trust Territory Government on Pohnpei, where we remained for seven years, followed by fourteen years at Trust Territory Headquarters on Saipan in the Mariana Islands. With the advent of jet travel in the 1960s, we normally took our home leaves, and sometimes included a stop in London where we visited Lee Boo's tomb and began the researches herein culminated.

The Koror-Babeldaob bridge. Completed in 1977, this prestressed concrete bridge with its 790-foot main span was at the time, according to the *Micronesian Reporter* (First Quarter, 1977), the longest bridge of its kind in the world. It replaced a ferry and so enabled a much faster flow of traffic from the capital (Koror) to the airport at Airai at the southern end of the big island of Babeldaob, where an airstrip longer than any that could be accommodated on Koror receives modern jet planes.

The superport.   The idea of a "superport" for Belau was a hotly contested issue in the mid-1970s in Belau, although the idea did not originate there. Most of the debate was conducted outside Belau and created a considerable body of literature, much of it ephemeral, and most of it, correctly in my view, opposed to the idea.

Hell in the Pacific.   The filming of the Marvin-Mifune movie also provided a windfall of material for the *Micronesian Reporter* which at that time was being staffed by Peace Corps volunteers. For the results of their exemplary work, see Vol. 16, No. 2. Marvin, incidentally, may have learned the Lee Boo story while in Belau. In an article in the November, 1970 issue of *Esquire Magazine,* the author describes a dog in Marvin's California home by the name of LaBoo and quotes Lee Marvin as referring to the dog as the "Black Prince!"

British Museum's Micronesia exhibit.   The Museum of Mankind opened its exhibition entitled "Pattern of Islands: Micronesia Yesterday and Today" on 14 December 1983 with the Ibedul and two others from Belau in attendance. At the opening, Assistant Keeper Mrs. Dorota Starzecka gave credit to Nevil Dickin for the help he had provided in the form of his research findings and for his long-standing support of the exhibition.

Banks and the Belauan canoe.   Captain Cummings' letter to Sir Joseph Banks dated 22 April 1792 is found at the British Library Manuscript Department (BL ADD MS 33979, 153–154).

The *Antelope.*   Does anything remain? A son of the Abba Thulle (Ibedul) of the early 1950s told me he had seen the remains of the *Antelope.* My friend and mentor, Dr. William Vitarelli, had the same information. He and several Belauan friends dove three times on the site of the wreck without succeeding in locating anything, even though some of those in the group claimed to have previously seen the "mound" that represented what was left of the *Antelope.*

Belauans moved faster into twentieth century.   Although it is a generalization for which the usual exceptions must be allowed, the people of Belau have been quicker, on the whole, to adopt Western ways and to take advantage of educational and commercial opportunities than any of the other people of the Caroline Islands. Whether this relative precociousness should be attributed to their industry and ambition or to a more thorough exposure to Western and especially Japanese culture can be left to the social scientists. My own view would be that it is primarily the former. In my teaching at the Pacific Islands Central School the Belauans, as a group, excelled in academic initiative and attainment at least in the 1950s and 1960s and for so long as the school maintained its pan-Micronesian character. I always felt privileged to have at least one "Lee Boo" in each of my classes although they were not all from Belau. Obviously other island groups had their promising young men and women as well. Many of these former students have advanced in professional careers and not a few returned to their home islands to teach their own people their letters. But, again, as a group, none have traveled further and pursued their careers more widely than the Belauans. Finally, and in the context of those who have learned their letters, I cannot help recalling from my library experience with these students that those who borrowed (and presumably read) the most books have since advanced the furthest in their chosen fields of endeavor.

Belauans visiting London.   When such leading Belauans as the Ibedul visit London it normally is a visit made in conjunction with an official trip to Europe, the United States, or the United Nations. When the Ibedul visited in December 1983 he had just been to Sweden where he received an award for his efforts to keep Belau nuclear free.

Visiting the tomb of Lee Boo, "the Black Prince."   It is easy, I now know. But on a first visit to London in 1961 our taxi-driver guide had difficulty finding the church, much less the tomb. But the rector of St. Mary's understood at once why visitors from the Pacific Islands had knocked at his door. "You've come to see the Black Prince," he said, and took us to Lee Boo's tomb. (I was surprised to hear Lee Boo referred to as "the Black Prince," and it was not until years later that I read in Mary Boast's Mayflower booklet "Chapters from Rotherhithe and Southwark," p. 26, that "local people still point out, what they call, 'the black prince's tomb.' ") On subsequent visits to St. Mary's I have simply taken "the tube"—the East London section of the Metropolitan Line—under the Thames via the Brunels' tunnel and, upon emerging at Rotherhithe, walked along Brunel Road to the pub Neptune, turned right on Rupack Street, which very shortly joins Mary Church Street, where, after a few steps, Lee Boo's tomb can be seen in the churchyard, standing alone. But Lee Boo is not alone for, as inscriptions at the side of the tomb explain, the Wilsons' son, John Kenderdine, is buried there too—joined, years later, by his mother Christiana Wilson. The captain, too, it is said, wanted to be buried here but died too far away to make that possible. His tomb, in Colyton, is truly alone.

Belauans write chapters of their own.   Most germane is the three-volume history compiled by the Palau Community Action Agency under the direction of Katherine Kesolei who, for long years, worked to collect and edit the tapes of oral histories that contributed to this unique work.

Commemorative stamps.   Late in 1983 a set of eight postage stamps was issued to commemorate the bicentennial of Captain Wilson's stay in Belau. Four of them featured individual portraits of the captain, Lee Boo, Abba Thulle, and Ludee as taken from Keate. The other four stamps in the set presented scenes of Belau, also taken from Keate. For further information, see the London weekly, *Stamp Collecting*, of 15 December 1983.

Rotherhithe remembers Lee Boo.   In April 1984 an exhibition was mounted at the Rotherhithe Civic Centre as the opening event of a series of observances to mark the bicentennial year of Lee Boo in London. The exhibits called attention to several of Rotherhithe's historical and ecological features, including especially those related to Lee Boo and the Wilsons. In July, the schools of the area participated in a major Lee Boo observance, under a project coordinated by Mr. Paul Woodhead of the Inner London Education Authority. (This took the form of a musical drama created and performed by people who live and work in the Rotherhithe area.) A handsome commemorative booklet was published to coincide with these events.

Lee Boo on British television. The bicentennial did not go unnoted by the London media. On 24 May, BBC1's twice-weekly program Blue Peter featured a twelve-minute segment entitled "Lee Boo, the Stranger in Rotherhithe" in which original artwork was combined with footage filmed at the tomb and elsewhere along the Thames to tell the story of Lee Boo to the young people of Great Britain.

London does not forget. Because it does not forget, London is a paradise for researchers. The Southwark Local Studies Library is the place to begin a research project involving Lee Boo, the Wilsons, and Rotherhithe. The picture library at "The Wharf" adjacent to St. Mary's can also be of help. In Belau the place to begin is the Belau National Museum, Koror. After years of collecting under the original curator, Hera Owen, it is well stocked with items of a type familiar to Lee Boo and the current curator, Tina Rechucher, is a descendant of some of those who knew Lee Boo.

22 POSTSCRIPT TO LEE BOO

It must be said that my vision of a troop of players visiting Belau is somewhat fanciful. Not that it could not happen on Koror as I have described it, but, sad to say, it is becoming increasingly difficult to find a traditional *bai* in which to hold such a "shew" somewhere within the old stronghold of Artingall. Employing a bit of dramatic license of my own, I have tried to set a scene that would be familiar to Lee Boo and in so doing I recalled my own experiences in Belau in the 1950s.

The "Prince Lee Boo" playbills. It is surely significant in the historical annals of the Pacific that not just one but two plays were performed as a result of Lee Boo's visit to London following the wreck of the *Antelope*. The production staged at the Surrey Theatre was the first to come to my attention. I obtained a copy of the playbill at the Mitchell Library in Sydney, Australia. When I sent a photocopy to my friend Nevil Dickin in London he, in turn, went to the Victoria and Albert Museum, where he found another playbill for an entirely different production staged at the famous Theatre Royal in Drury Lane. Both productions were staged in the Fall of 1833.

In "Dickin's" Drury Lane production, Lee Boo was played by one Mademoiselle Celeste, a recent émigrée from France, who later starred in such productions as *Paris and Pleasure* and *The French Spy*. Included in the cast of this version of Lee Boo's adventures was one "Ulva" who was billed as a "Pelewese, betrothed to Prince Lee Boo." The production included a "Chorus of the Pelewese," and on the second night, added a troop of "Pelewese Dancers."

The Drury Lane production had Act I open with a "Sea View on the Island of Pelew, with Yawl on the Stocks, and the Wreck of the *Antelope* in the Distance." Also, somehow, the audience was to see "A Mangrove in the Island of Artingal, [and] Exterior of the Palace of Abba Thulle, [with] the setting Sun, and Mode of Pelewese Worship"! Act II was set in "Captain Wilson's Apartment in London" and included in its scenery "A Villa on the Thames [and the] Gardens of Captain Wilson's House." And, on the Thames an "East Indiaman in Full Sail [plus] Storm, and Clearing-up of Mist to a Bright Moonlight."

This production was performed as an "after piece" at the Drury Lane theater, following, on Friday, 1 November 1833, for example, *Macbeth;* on Saturday, *As You Like It;* and on Monday, Shakespeare's *Henry the Fifth.* One might have thought the most appropriate companion piece would have been *The Tempest.*

But what further honor can one wish for Lee Boo than that he appear on the same bill as Shakespeare? Good night, Sweet Prince.

SOURCES
AND BIBLIOGRAPHY

Before preparing this list of sources and the bibliography that follows, I weeded out more than half of the works consulted. Only those I considered most germane to this book have been included, and, where appropriate, I have noted specific details.

SOURCES: UNPUBLISHED MATERIAL

NOTE: Items are identified first by the institution or private collection in which they were found, secondly by the reference number of the holding institution, and thirdly by a very brief reference to specific data found in them.

British Library Manuscript Department
ADD MS 854: "Collection of Views of Headlands, England to China," by A. W. Devis.
ADD MS 19,301: McCluer's Journal.
ADD MS 31,981D: "Plan of Antelope Bay, Patagonia, 1782," by A. W. Devis.
ADD MS 33,979 (pp. 153–154) and ADD MS 33,982 (p. 252): contain the letters from Captain Cummings to Sir Joseph Banks re the Pelewan canoe brought to England from Macao for Banks. [McCluer had the canoe from Pelew to Macao.]

British Museum Map Library
Fol. Maps 148e.7: "Plan of the Cities of London and Westminster, the Borough of Southwark and parts adjoining . . ." by Richard Horwood, 1792–1799.
Maps C.21.c.12 (pp. 78–82): McCluer's Charts and sketches of the Pelew Islands, 1791–1794.

Guildhall Library, London (Manuscript Department)
MS 12, 818A-45-146: Presentation Paper for Robert White requesting that he be admitted to Christ's Hospital School at the age of "7 years upwards" there "to be educated and brought up among other poor children."

MS 12, 818A-48-6: Presentation Paper for John Wedgborough requesting that he be admitted to Christ's Hospital School at the age of "nine years upwards" there "to be educated and brought up among other poor children."

MS 12, 818/11: Christ's Hospital School Register, 1771–1783, pp. 65 and 115: Robert White and John Wedgborough are shown to have been "discharged" in care of Captain Wilson "to be trained in the Service of the E. I. Co."

India Office Library and Records, London
Bombay despatches
IOR: E/4/1006: Vol. 11, 5 Nov. 1789 to 3 June 1790, pp. 129–158. The EIC Directive sent from London to Bombay authorizing the Expedition to Pelew under McCluer.

Bombay public proceedings
IOR: Range/342
Vol. 12, 1790, pp. 447 and 455. McCluer at Bombay prior to Expedition. [His letter requesting better pay for his officers.]
Vol. 16, 8 July to 31 Dec. 1793, p. 806. McCluer's letter of 10 Feb. 1793.
Vol. 19, 6 Jan. to 24 April 1795, pp. 397–403. McCluer's letter to "the Government General" re his having left Belau, his meeting with Hayes, etc., dated 23 July 1794, Macao.

Factory records, China and Japan
IOR: G/12/77 1783: [Consultation Book "by" E. C. Pigou] pp. 42–55. Covers period from 5 June 1783 when "The *Antelope* . . . arrived from England . . ." to 20 July 1783 when "The *Antelope* sailed from hence," and includes correspondence between the Company's agents and the Chinese officials.
IOR: G/12/79 1784–85, p. 2: Captain Wilson "with all his people" . . . "safely arrived at Macao"; the *Oroolong* sold, money divided among crew, Devis paid, etc.
IOR: G/12/103 1792–93, p. 244: Proctor to Chief, Select Committee, Canton, 15 Feb. 1793 re McCluer "whom I expect in about twenty days at Macao." Also McCluer's letter to Harrison dated 12 Feb. 1793 explaining that he would remain in Belau.
IOR: G/12/108 1794–95, p. 42: McCluer's arrival at Macao in small boat noted on 4 May 1794.
IOR: G/12/119 1797–98, pp. 45–159: Snook's arrival at Macao aboard the *Warley* with Captain Wilson and three Belauan women. "I have a house" while awaiting passage to Belau. Purchases *Diamante* and sails for Belau.
IOR: G/12/122 1798–99, pp. 147–235: Snook at Macao after his voyage to Belau; his report and sale of *Diamante*.
IOR: G/12/125 1799, p. 39: Further to Snook at Macao.

Marine records, miscellaneous
IOR: L/MAR/1/36:
28 Dec. 1781: Henry Wilson appointed to command the *Antelope*.
18 Jan. 1782: H. Wilson and his officers "allowed Gratuities in lieu of Private Trade."

Marine records
IOR: L/MAR/B 480E: Log of the *Morse,* 6 Aug. 1781 to 6 Sept. 1784.
IOR: L/MAR/B 570A: Log of the *Antelope,* 31 Dec. 1781 to 4 June 1783.
IOR: L/MAR/B 570C: Ledger Book for the *Antelope.*
IOR: L/MAR/B 570(2): "Impress" book for the *Antelope.*
IOR: L/MAR/B 570(3): "Absence" book for the *Antelope.*

National Library of Scotland
MS 1068: Melville Papers, pp. 86–92. Dalrymple's comments on McCluer's route: China to Pelew through the Philippine Islands.

Royal Society Library, London
Blagden Letters, 29: Banks' letters to Sir Charles Blagden, 22 Sept. 1784, and 12 Oct. 1784 re Lunardi's flight.

SOURCES: MISCELLANEOUS

The Nevil Dickin Private Collection
   I am particularly indebted to Nevil Dickin for his many letters, for information from his files, and for data he has shared with me regarding Captain Wilson's family, his home on Paradise Row, and the Oroolong House in Devon, as well as for information on the life and works of the artist A. W. Devis and for details concerning the lives of McCluer and Snook (particularly Snook's Sword) and for information relating to Banks and Dalrymple (now at the Museum of Mankind, London).

Letters
   Howard I. Chapelle, (then) Senior Historian, Department of Science and Technology, Smithsonian Institution. Letter to author dated 24 February 1969: "I am quite sure your *Antelope* was built at Newbury (now 'Old Newbury'), Massachusetts."
   Philip Chadwick Foster Smith, Curator of Maritime History, Peabody Museum, Salem, Massachusetts. Letter to author dated 3 June 1969: "I think it is most certain that the marking of 'Nwbry' refers to Newbury or Newburyport, Mass."

Playbills
The Mitchell Library, Sydney, F792E: English playbills relating to Australia. Of these, 3 are for "Prince Lee Boo" as performed at the Surrey Theatre, London, in November of 1833. Others in this collection include "Omai, or A Trip Round the World," and "The Pirates: Or, The Calamities of Capt. Bligh."
The Victoria and Albert Museum Library: "Prince Lee Boo" as performed at the Theatre Royal, Drury Lane in October and November of 1833.

SOURCES: PERIODICALS AND NEWSPAPERS

Country Life
   (London) 1 October 1964, p. 840: Snook's Sword.

The Friend
(Honolulu) June 1862, pp. 42–43: An article entitled "The Manuscript of Rev. S. Greatheed" details the visit of the ship *Lee Boo* to Honolulu along with the ship *Jackall.*

Gentleman's Magazine and Historical Chronicle
Vol. 54, 1784, Part 2, Supplement for the Year 1784. Contains an anonymous letter describing the shipwreck of the *Antelope,* important in that it tends to confirm much of what Keate later wrote—especially the crew's high regard for Captain Wilson.
Vol. 58, no. 1, Part 2, July 1788, pp. 629–631: unsigned review of Keate's *Account of the Pelew Islands . . . ,* first edition.

The Journal of Pacific History (Canberra)
Vol. 4, 1969, pp. 83–104: "Alexander Dalrymple and New Guinea" by Howard T. Fry. This article describes Dalrymple's interests in McCluer's survey of the northwestern coast of New Guinea. The journal always features articles of interest and importance to Pacific Island researchers.

Literary Magazine
Vol. 2, no. 12, 1757: Dr. Johnson's statement re his addiction to tea.

London Chronicle
1–3 Nov. 1791, p. 426: "the African Prince . . . named John Nambana, Prince of Robana . . ." His reaction to the "great guns, and other objects of curiosity . . . at Plymouth."

London Gazette
Various issues, August through November, 1784.

Micronesian Reporter
Vol. 10, no. 5, pp. 26–29: Prince Lee Boo.
Vol. 22, no. 1, pp. 38–43: Rupack Street and Lee Boo.
Vol. 25, no. 2: Koror-Babeldaob bridge.

The Morning Post and Advertiser (London)
24 March to 31 Dec. 1784. Various issues containing such bits and pieces of information as the arrival of the *Morse,* advertisements of Lunardi's "Grand Aerostatic Machine" when it was on display and when the "Aerial Journey" was to be launched. Also pineapples and turtles advertised for sale.

The Quarterly Review (London)
June and October, 1844. In an article on children's books, *Prince LeBoo* [sic] is listed fourth among those recommended, following *Nursery Songs of England, Aesop's Fables,* and *Persian Tales,* and ahead of the fifth placed *German Popular Tales Translated from Grimm.* The writer said of Prince LeBoo, "We wish this beautiful character to live in the hearts of children."

BIBLIOGRAPHY: PUBLISHED MATERIAL

Abeel, David. *Journal of a Residence in China and the Neighboring Countries . . .* 2nd ed. New York: J. A. Williamson, 1836.
Pp. 57–58 describe the Belau Islanders' canoes "feathering the ocean, and advancing in pursuit . . . they come dancing over the waves like 'fairy sprites,' and with a velocity, which demands a stiff breeze . . . for a ship to equal."

The Adventures of Madiboo. London: T. & R. Hughes, 1809.
  A novel inspired by Keate's *Account.*

Alexander, Michael. *Omai "Noble Savage."* London: Collins & Harvill Press, 1977.
  Omai before, during and after his time in London. Well packaged and written—
  just enough for most readers. For those inspired to want more there is McCormick's more thorough treatment.

Annual Register. 1784 and 1785. London: Dodsley, 1787.

Annual Report to the United Nations (for) *The Trust Territory of the Pacific Islands.* Washington, D.C.: U.S. State Department, various years.
  Useful in this context for statistics of the educational pursuits of the various islanders including the Palauans.

Apple, Russell. *Micronesian Parks, A Proposal.* Saipan, Mariana Islands: Trust Territory
  of the Pacific Islands, 1972.
  The "Englishman's Island" of Oroolong is included within proposals.

Archenholz, Johann Wilhelm von. *A Picture of England.* London: "Printed for the
  Booksellers," 1797.

Archer, Mildred. *India and British Portraiture, 1770–1825.* London: Philip Wilson Publishers for Sotheby Parke Bernet Publications, 1979.
  The *Antelope*'s own artist, Arthur William Devis, became one of the "British Portrait Painters in India" and the author devotes 36 pages to his work, including
  some 30 illustrations. "Unlike most British portrait painters who went to India
  by choice, Arthur William Devis arrived there almost by accident." The accident
  was the wreck of the *Antelope* that gave him the opportunity to go to India.

Auchmuty, James J., ed. *The Voyage of Governor Phillip to Botany Bay.* Sydney: Angus
  & Robertson, 1970. (Originally published in London: John Stockdale, 1789.)
  Contains an account of Captain Shortland's visit to Belau (offshore) aboard the
  Alexander, 1788, pp. 142–144.

Barnard, Edward C. *Naked and a Prisoner: Captain Edward C. Barnard's Narrative of
  Shipwreck in Palau, 1832–1833.* Edited by Kenneth R. Martin. Sharon, Mass.: The
  Kendall Whaling Museum, and The Trust Territory Historic Preservation Office,
  Saipan, Mariana Islands, 1980.

Barnett, H. G. *Being a Palauan.* New York: Holt, Rinehart & Winston, 1960.
————. *Palauan Society.* Eugene, Oregon: University of Oregon Press, 1949.

Barrett, Charles. *The Island World: An Anthology of the Pacific.* Melbourne: Oxford
  University Press, 1944.
  "Prince Lee Boo," pp. 113–119, is a brief retelling of the conventional Lee Boo
  story.

Barry, Florence V. *A Century of Children's Books.* London: Methuen, 1922. (Reissued
  by Singing Tree Press, Detroit, Mich., 1968.)
  A reference to "The History of Prince Lee Boo" is made on p. 239.

Bates, Alan. *Directory of Stage Coach Services, 1836.* New York: A. M. Kelly, 1969.
  Lists the stops the stage coach made on the road from Portsmouth to London.

Baudet, Henri. *Paradise on Earth: Some Thoughts on European Images of Non-Euro-
  pean Man.* Translated by Elizabeth Wentholt. New Haven: Yale University Press,
  1965.

Beaglehole, J. C., ed. *The Journals of Captain Cook on His Voyages of Discovery.* 3 vols.
  London: Hakluyt Society (Extra Series no. 35), 1955–1967.

"A landmark in historical scholarship" for which students of Cook owe "an immeasurable debt": R. A. Skelton.

Beck, Edward Josselyn. *Memorials to Serve for a History of the Parish of St. Mary, Rotherhithe* ... Cambridge: Cambridge University Press, 1907.
Provides background about Rotherhithe and information from church records concerning Lee Boo and the Wilsons.
Besant, Walter. *London in the Eighteenth Century.* London: Adam and Charles Black, 1903.
Bingham, Hiram, Jr. *Story of the Morning Stars, the Children's Missionary Vessels.* Boston: The American Board, Congregational House, 1907.
Bissell, Benjamin. *The American Indian in English Literature of the Eighteenth Century.* New Haven: Yale University Press, 1925.
Bligh, William. *The Log of the Bounty.* 2 vols. Introduction and Notes by Owen Rutter. London: Golden Cockerel Press, 1937.
————. *A Voyage to the South Sea Undertaken by Command of His Majesty ... and an Account of the Mutiny on Board H.M.S. Bounty* ... New York: New American Library, 1961.
Blue Peter Book Twenty-Two. London: BBC-TV, 1985.
Pp. 64–68 contain a pictorial section on the Lee Boo story, written by Dorothy Smith and illustrated by Robert Broomfield. The same illustrations were used in the BBC1 television presentation of 24 May 1984 as a segment of the Blue Peter program for young people.
Boast, Mary. *The Mayflower and Pilgrim Story: Chapters from Rotherhithe and Southwark.* London: The Council of the London Borough of Southwark, n.d.
————. *Southwark, A London Borough.* London: The Council of the London Borough of Southwark, n.d.
————. *The Story of Rotherhithe.* London Borough of Southwark Neighbourhood Histories no. 6. London: The Council of the London Borough of Southwark, 1980.
Excellent 28-page local history booklet with a page devoted to "Prince Lee Boo."
Boswell, James. *The Life of Samuel Johnson.* Selected and abridged by Edmund Fuller. Laurel Classic edition. New York: Dell, 1960.
Bridge, Admiral Sir Cyprian. *Some Recollections.* London: John Murray, 1918.
P. 300: "In my early schooldays most English boys were given to read a book called *The History of Prince Lee Boo.*" And on pages 300–302 Bridge records how he brought about a peace treaty between "Abba Thuol" and "his enemy 'king' Aracklye."
Broughton, William Robert. *A Voyage of Discovery* ... London: Cadell & Davies, 1804.
P. 39: Reference to the *Prince Lee Boo* and the *Jackall* in Hawaii.
Bryan, E. H., Jr. *Guide to Place Names in the Trust Territory of the Pacific Islands.* Honolulu: Pacific Scientific Information Center, B. P. Bishop Museum, 1971.
Buck, Peter H. *Explorers of the Pacific.* Bernice P. Bishop Museum Special Publication 43. Honolulu: B. P. Bishop Museum, 1953.
Butts, Miriam, and Patricia Heard. *The American China Trade: "Foreign Devils to Canton" 1783–1843.* Jackdaw No. A22. New York: Grossman Publishers, n.d.

A collection of reproduced documents which, with the descriptions supplied, are very helpful to an understanding of the foreign trade at Canton.

A Catalogue of the . . . entire Collection of Natural History, comprising the most choice and curious specimens of shells, corals, ores, minerals, agates . . . etc. of the late George Keate, Esq. . . . which will be sold by auction, by Mr. King at his Great Room, King Street, Covent Garden . . . London: Printed by Barker & Son, [1802].
The sale was to extend over a period of twelve days. A few items to be sold were from "Palos" (presumably Belau). For one of the 120 items or lots to be sold on the eighth day of the sale, the description reads: "A braided trochus, from the South Seas, Spiked mulberry, beaked snail, lesser chorny pyrum, from Palos . . ." See also my entry for Thomas Martyn.

Chancellor, E. Beresford. *The XVIIIth Century in London: An Account of Its Social Life and Arts.* London: B. T. Batsford, 1920.
Mentions Nando's Coffee House at No. 17 Fleet Street, p. 133, and has print of Lunardi's balloon on exhibit at the Pantheon, p. 118.

———. *The London of Charles Dickens . . . Setting of His Novels.* London: Grant Richards, 1924.
The settings include areas around Rotherhithe, especially those in *Oliver Twist.*

Chatterton, E. Keble. *The Old East Indiamen . . .* London: T. Werner Laurie, [1914].
On p. 250 there is a full-page sketch of the *Panther* as taken from the Journal of William Henry, entry for 15 August 1794, at Suez Harbour.

Cheyne, Andrew. *A Description of Islands in the Western Pacific Ocean . . .* London: J. D. Potter, 1852.

Christian, F. W. *The Caroline Islands. Travel in the Sea of the Little Lands . . .* London: Methuen, 1899.

Clark, Thomas Blake. *Omai, First Polynesian Ambassador to England.* Honolulu: University of Hawaii Press, 1969. (Facsimile reproduction of original edition printed by Colt Press, San Francisco, 1940.)

Coffin, Edward M. "Merrimac River Shipping." Paper read before the Historical Society of Old Newbury, 27 May 1926. Newburyport, Mass.: Historical Society of Old Newbury, 1926. (Pamphlet.)

Collinder, Per. *A History of Marine Navigation.* Translated by Maurice Michael. New York: St. Martin's Press, 1955.

Colquhoun, Patrick. *A Treatise on the Police of the Metropolis.* Montclair, N.J.: Patterson Smith, 1969. (Reprint of 1806 edition.)
A mine of information on London crime in the late 1700s and early 1800s including much on convicts in hulks: "Convicts, under sentence of Transportation, put on board hulks on the River Thames, from 11th January, 1783, to 12th December 1795." (Some of the hulks were at Woolwich where Lee Boo might have seen them if he made a trip down the river to Greenwich.)

———. *A Treatise on the Commerce and Police of the River Thames.* London: Printed for J. Mawman, [1800].
Classifies and describes the "River Plunderers," "River Pirates," "Light Horsemen," etc.

Connolly, James B. *Master Mariner, Life and Voyages of Amasa Delano.* New York: Doubleday, 1943.

Unfortunately lacking in helpful information about Delano's experiences in Pelew.

Cook, James. *The Three Voyages of Captain James Cook Round the World.* 7 vols. London: Longman, Hurst, Rees, Ohme, & Brown, 1821.

Cotton, Evan, and Charles Fawcett. *East Indiamen: The East India Company's Maritime Service.* London: Batchworth Press, 1949.
This is the useful sort of book one wishes to encounter early in research rather than late which was, unfortunately, my fate.

Cowper, William. *The Poetical Works of William Cowper.* Edited by H. S. Milford. London: Oxford University Press, 1934.
The reference to Omai appears on p. 43, lines 633 through 677 of "The Task," Book 1.

Cox, Edward Godfrey. *A Reference Guide to the Literature of Travel including Voyages . . . Shipwrecks and Expeditions.* Vol. 2. Seattle: University of Washington, 1938.

Cranmer-Byng, J. L., ed. *An Embassy to China, Being the Journal kept by Lord Macartney during His Embassy to the Emperor Ch'ien-Lung, 1793–1794.* Hamden, Conn.: Archon Books, 1963.
Mentions some of the post-Pelew voyages of Captain Proctor.

Dalrymple, Alexander. *A Collection of Views of Land in the Indian Navigation.* London, 1783.
"They were taken by Mr. Ephraim Welsh in the voyage of the Fox Packet to and from China 1781 & 1782 . . . where they saw the Palos Islands which are delineated as also part of the Bashees and Formosa" (p. 14).

Dalyell, Sir John Graham. *Shipwrecks and Disasters at Sea . . .* Edinburgh: Archibald Constable & Co., 1812.
"Wreck of the Antelope Packet, 1783" appears on pp. 59–117 as, presumably, abstracted from Keate.

Danton, George H. *The Culture Contacts of the United States and China . . . 1784–1844.* New York: Columbia University Press, 1931.
Provides a brief but authoritative account of the first Americans at China including Amasa Delano in whose views of China and the Chinese he found "much misinformation."

Dapp, Kathryn Gilbert. "George Keate, Esq., Eighteenth Century Gentleman." Ph.D. dissertation. University of Pennsylvania, Philadelphia. 1939.
Indispensable and only work on Keate.

De la Mare, Walter. *Desert Islands and Robinson Crusoe.* London: Faber & Faber, 1930.

Delano, Amasa. *A Narrative of Voyages and Travels . . . in the Pacific . . .* Boston: E. G. House, 1817.

De Maré, Eric. *London's River, the Story of a City.* New York: McGraw-Hill, 1965.
———. *London's Riverside: Past, Present and Future.* London: Max Reinhardt, 1958.

De Munilla, Martín. *La Austrialia del Espíritu Santo.* 2 vols. Translated and edited by Celsus Kelly. Cambridge: Cambridge University Press, 1966.
The "opinion of Fray Jeronimo de Valera" re taking islanders to "territories inhabited by Christians" is found on p. 316.

Dening, Greg. *Islands and Beaches: Discourse on a Silent Land, Marquesas 1774–1880.* Melbourne: Melbourne University Press, 1980.

The Dictionary of National Biography. London: Oxford University Press, [1921–22].

Dodge, Ernest S. *Islands and Empires . . .*, Vol. 7 of *Europe and the World in the Age of Expansion* series. Minneapolis: University of Minnesota Press, 1976.

A chapter entitled "Tourists from the Islands" includes "the Prince of Palau"—Lee Boo.

DuBose, LaRocque. *Aye, Aye, Sir!* New York: Lothrop, Lee & Shepard, 1958.

A juvenile novel centered on the relationships between Captain Wilson and his son Henry. Based on the wreck of the *Antelope* and limited to the events at Pelew.

Dunlop, Andrew. *The Memoirs of a Bombay Mariner, Being the Story of Captain John McClure of the the Bombay Marine—Hydrographer, (1767–1792)*. Salisbury, Rhodesia: M. O. Collins, 1975.

Drumond, J. C. and Anne Wilbraham. *The Englishman's Food: A History of Five Centuries of English Diet*. London: Jonathan Cape, 1958.

A good idea of what the men of the *Antelope,* aside from officers, ate when at home is given for 1762: "The diet of this Suffolk labouring family, living 'as do the poor,' consisted of dried pease, pickled pork, bread, cheese, milk, and small beer." Drop the milk and cheese and substitute ship biscuits for bread and add the livestock carried by EIC ships and you have an approximation of the diet of the *Antelope* men at sea.

Eagle, Dorothy, and Hilary Carnell, eds. *The Oxford Literary Guide to the British Isles.* Oxford: Oxford University Press, 1977.

The East Indian Chronologist. Calcutta: Hircarrah Press, 1801.

P. 64: Wreck of the *Antelope* recorded under "1783" and Lee Boo's death and his epitaph under "1784."

Ehrlich, Blake. *London on the Thames.* Boston: Little, Brown, 1966.

Ellis, William. *Polynesian Researches, During a Residence of Nearly Six Years in the South Sea Islands . . .* 2 vols. London: Dawsons of Pall Mall, 1968.

Re Omai: "The individual who had been brought from the ends of the earth, and shewn whatever England could furnish, adapted to impress his wondering mind, returned, and became as rude and indolent a barbarian as before" (p. 101).

Fairchild, Hoxie N. *The Noble Savage: A Study in Romantic Naturalism.* New York: Columbia University Press, 1928.

Fairley, W. *Epitaphiana or the Curiosities of Churchyard Literature . . .* London: Samuel Tinsley, 1873.

It is noted that the Romans often wrote "Sta, Viator!" on their tombs "to attract attention of passers-by, which expression is to this day imitated by the English, who commence many of their verses with the words, Stop, Reader!" (As does Lee Boo's epitaph.)

Fletcher, Geoffrey S. *The London Nobody Knows.* London: Penguin, 1966.

———. *London's River.* London: Hutchinson, 1966.

Force, Maryanne T. "The Persistence of Precolonial Exchange Patterns in Palau . . ." Ph.D. dissertation. Walden University, 1976.

Force, Roland W. *Leadership and Cultural Change in Palau. Fieldiana Anthropology* vol. 50. Chicago: Chicago Natural History Museum, 1960.

Force, Roland W., and Maryanne Force. *Just One House: A Description and Analysis of Kinship in the Palau Islands.* Bernice P. Bishop Museum Bulletin 235. Honolulu: Bishop Museum Press, 1972.

Forster, E. M. *Two Cheers for Democracy.* New York: Harcourt, Brace, & World, [1951].

Foster, William. *The East India House, Its History and Associations.* London: John Lane, The Bodley Head, 1924.

Fry, Howard T. *Alexander Dalrymple (1737–1808) and the Expansion of British Trade.* London: Frank Cass, 1970.

Chapter 6, "The British in the East Indies, 1761–1805," provides background for McCluer's mission to the New Guinea area and the relationship that Dalrymple had to the mission.

Furnas, J. C. *Anatomy of Paradise.* New York: William Sloane, 1937.

Furber, Holden. *John Company at Work* . . . Cambridge: Harvard University Press, 1948.

Gardiner, Leslie. *Man in the Clouds: The Story of Vincenzo Lunardi.* Edinburgh: W. & R. Chambers, 1963.

Gibson, Charles E. *The Story of the Ship.* New York: Henry Schuman, 1948.

Appendix 1 provides "Wage Rates of English Able Seamen from 1375–1943."

Gill, Conrad. *Merchants and Mariners of the 18th Century.* London: Edward Arnold, 1961.

Gillilland, Cora Lee C. *The Stone Money of Yap, A Numismatic Survey.* Smithsonian Studies in History and Technology, Number 23. Washington, D.C.: Smithsonian Institution Press, 1975.

Glascock, William Nugent. *Naval Sketch Book, or, The Service Afloat and Ashore.* London, 1826.

Goldenberg, Joseph A. *Shipbuilding in Colonial America.* Charlottesville, Va.: University Press of Virginia, 1976.

Gunson, Niel, ed. *The Changing Pacific: Essays in Honour of H. E. Maude.* Melbourne: Oxford University Press, 1978.

Contains "The Role of the Beachcomber in the Carolines," by Father Francis X. Hezel, in which Madan Blanchard and John McCluer, among others, are featured.

Hardy, Charles. *A Register of Ships, Employed in the Service of the United East India Company, from the Year 1760 to 1810* . . . London: Black, Perry, & Kingsbury, 1811.

Harper, C. G. *The Portsmouth Road.* London: Chapman & Hall, 1895.

Hatanaka, Sachiko. *A Bibliography of Micronesia Compiled from Japanese Publication, 1915–1945.* Occasional Papers, no. 8. Tokyo: Research Institute for Oriental Cultures, Gakushuin University, 1977.

Hawaii Architects and Engineers, Inc. *Cultural Considerations for Planning in Micronesia.* Saipan, Mariana Islands: Trust Territory Planning Division, 1968.

Henderson, Daniel. *Yankee Ships in China Seas: Adventures of Pioneer Americans in the Troubled Far East.* New York: Hastings House, 1946.

"Amasa Delano Sees a Commodore Go Native," pp. 73–86.

Herbert, Admiral Sir Richmond. *The Navy in India, 1763–1783.* London: Ernest Benn, 1931.

Herz, Michael J., ed. *Palau and the Superport: The Development of an Ocean Ethic.* San Francisco: Oceanic Society, 1977.

Hezel, Francis X. *The First Taint of Civilization: A History of the Caroline and Marshall Islands in Pre-Colonial Days, 1521–1885.* Pacific Islands Monograph Series no. 1. Honolulu: University of Hawaii Press, 1983.

This excellent history includes the *Antelope* episode, Blanchard, McCluer, Delano, and all of those who entered the scene at Belau prior to 1885. (Published after I had completed my research.)

———. *Foreign Ships in Micronesia: A Compendium of Ship Contacts with the Caroline and Marshall Islands, 1521–1885.* Saipan, Mariana Islands: Trust Territory Historic Preservation Office, 1979.

Hezel, Francis X., and M. L. Berg, eds. *Winds of Change: A Book of Readings on Micronesian History.* Saipan, Mariana Islands: Trust Territory Bureau of Education, 1981.

The History of Prince Lee Boo, A Native of the Pelew Islands. Brought to England by Captain Wilson. 10th ed. London: Printed for J. Harris, Corner of St. Paul's Church Yard, 1806.

Published in the manner of a chap book, this little volume ran to at least 20 editions in London alone, not to mention printings elsewhere. Editions vary, especially in format. Several have their own illustrations by artists employed to illustrate by use of their imagination without reference, apparently, to the authentic artwork within Keate's *Account.* None of these "histories" makes a clear statement of authorship, but all of them are extracts, sometimes with rephrasing and embellishments, of Keate's original work. The British Library's copy of the "Twentieth Edition" was published in 1850, thus demonstrating that there was demand for the book sixty-six and more years after Lee Boo's death. A Dublin edition of 1820 was reprinted by Mnemosyne Publishing Company of Miami, Florida in 1969.

Hockin, John Pearce. *A Supplement to the Account of the Pelew Islands; Compiled from the Journals of the Panther and Endeavour, Two Vessels Sent by The Honourable East India Company to Those Islands in the Year 1790; and from the Oral Communications of Captain H. Wilson.* London: G. & W. Nicol, 1803.

Holden, Horace. *A Narrative of the Shipwreck, Captivity and Sufferings of Horace Holden and Benj. H. Nute . . .* Boston: Russell, Shattuck, & Co., 1836.

Holden's experiences were in the Belaus of the early 1830s but not in the same area of the islands known to the *Antelope* crew.

Horsburgh, James. *The India Directory or Directions for Sailing to and from the East Indies, China . . .* London: Black, Purbury, & Allen, 1817.

———. *Observations on the Navigation of the Eastern Seas.* London, 1797.

"If a ship leaves China in June, July, or August, in my opinion she ought to go out, between Formosa and the Bashee Islands, into the Pacific; and then proceed, between the Philippine Islands and the Peeloo Islands, to the Southward, where she will find Variable Winds, but mostly from the Westward, after past to the southward of the Peeloos, she ought to keep in Longitude about 132 or 133 East till near the Equator, to be able to fetch into Dampier's Strait."

Hughes, Thomas. *Tom Brown's School Days.* London: J. M. Dent, 1944.

Huntress, Keith, ed. *Narratives of Shipwrecks and Disasters, 1586–1860.* Ames, Iowa: Iowa State University Press, 1974.

244 · *Sources and Bibliography*

Keate's *Account* is included in this annotated list of books in which shipwrecks are described.

Jefferies, Greg. *The Port of London.* Jackdaw no. 81. London: Jackdaw Publications, n.d.

Johannes, R. E. *Words of the Lagoon: Fishing and Marine Lore in the Palau District of Micronesia.* Berkeley, Calif.: University of California Press, 1981.

Keate, George. "The Alps." (Poem.) London, 1763.

————. *An Account of the Pelew Islands . . . Composed from the Journals and Communications of Captain Henry Wilson and some of his Officers, who, in August 1783, were there Shipwrecked in the Antelope, a Packet belonging to the Honourable East India Company.* London: G. Nicol, 1788.

This was the first of the five editions printed by Keate's publisher. Other editions, including pirated editions, are too numerous to be listed here. Keate's fifth edition is recommended because it includes Hockin's *Supplement,* added in 1803.

————. *Nachrichten von den Pelew-Inseln in der Westgegend des Stillen Ozeans.* Leipzig: Brockhaus, VEB, 1977.

This is a partial reprint of the 1789 translation done by D. Georg Forster. Chapters 23–26 and the introductory material were omitted while numerous illustrations of a later period were added. It is included here whereas the numerous other translations have been omitted simply because it is the only translation currently in print.

————. *A Short Account of the Ancient History, Present Government, and Laws of the Republic of Geneva.* London: Printed for R. & J. Dodsley in Pall Mall, 1761.

————. *Sketches from Nature . . .* 2 vols. London: Dodsley, 1779.

Kelly, Samuel. *An Eighteenth Century Seaman Whose Days Have Been Few and Evil, to Which Is Added Remarks, etc., on Places He Visited during His Pilgrimage in This Wilderness.* Edited, with an introduction, by Crosbie Garstin. New York: Frederick A. Stokes, 1925.

References to the *Antelope* are on pp. 57 and 260.

Kesolei, Katherine, project director. *Palauan Legends, No. 1.* Koror: Palau Community Action Agency, 1971. (In English and Palauan.)

In a note with reference to "The Story of Dugong" on pp. 15 and 16 it is explained that "when a dugong is killed, one of its vertebrae is taken and used as a bracelet for a favorite son of a royal family." (*Palauan Legends, No. 2* was published in 1975 by the same agency.)

Kingston, W. H. G. *Shipwrecks and Disasters at Sea.* London: George Routledge & Sons, 1873.

Chapter 10 is entitled "Wreck of the *Antelope,*" which is described as "an armed ship of 300 tons" that had sailed from Macao "on the 20th of July, 1783," with "despatches for the Company's Settlements in the East Indian Archipelago," (p. 214).

Kipling, Rudyard. *Captains Courageous.* Garden City, N.Y.: Sun Dial Press, 1937.

Reference to the vessel named for Prince Lee Boo appears on p. 65: "There's the *Prince Leboo;* she's a Chat-ham boat."

Klingman, Lawrence, and Gerald Green. *His Majesty O'Keefe.* New York: Scribner's, 1950.

Kuykendall, Ralph S. *The Hawaiian Kingdom, 1778–1854, Foundation and Transformation.* Honolulu: The University of Hawaii, 1938.

Pp. 45–46 refer to the ship *Prince Lee Boo* which, along with the *Jackall*, was in the Hawaiian Islands from 21 November 1794 to mid-January 1795, during which time both were captured by the Hawaiians and both the captains killed. (The captain of the *Prince Lee Boo* was a Mr. Gordon.)

Labaree, Benjamin W. *The Boston Tea Party.* New York: Oxford University Press, 1964.

———. *Patriots and Partisans: The Merchants of Newburyport, 1764–1815.* Cambridge: Harvard University Press, 1962.

On p. 6 the author notes: "Many of the ships built in Newburyport sailed for England where they were sold to merchants eager to purchase American vessels whose cost was far below English-built ships. The protective arm of the British colonial system, requiring that all vessels engaged in empire trade be of English or colonial construction, made this possible."

La Rochefoucauld, F. *A Frenchman in England, 1784.* Translated by S. C. Roberts. Cambridge: Cambridge University Press, 1933.

Latourette, Kenneth Scott. *The History of Early Relations between the United States and China, 1784–1844.* (Transactions of the Connecticut Academy of Arts and Sciences, Vol. 22, August 1917.) New Haven: Yale University Press, 1917.

Contains, on p. 22, a description of the procedures required of a ship approaching Canton via Macao and a quotation: "No ships were admitted without a cargo of some sort aside from specie," which is attributed, by footnote, to "Snow to Sec. of State, Jan. 24, 1801, Consular Letters, Canton, I."

Lee, Ida (Mrs. Charles B. Marriott). *Commodore Sir John Hayes, His Voyages and Life, 1767–1831.* London: Longmans, Green, 1912.

Describes McCluer's assistance to Hayes.

Lessa, William A. *Drake's Island of Thieves: Ethnological Sleuthing.* Honolulu: University Press of Hawaii, 1975.

Lewenhak, Sheila. *The Voyages of Captain Cook.* Jackdaw no. 20. London: Jackdaw Publications, n.d.

Lewis, Michael Arthur. *The History of the British Navy.* Fair Lawn, N.J.: Essential Books, 1959.

Contains much data that is applicable to East India ships, the merchant service, etc.

Lewis, Wilmarth S., ed. *Three Tours through London in the Years 1748, 1776, 1797.* New Haven: Yale University Press, 1941.

———. *The Yale Edition of Horace Walpole's Correspondence.* New Haven: Yale University Press, 1937– .

P. 447 of Vol. 33 contains the quotations "I smile at the adoration paid to these aerial Quixotes . . ." and "I smile too at the stupidity that pays a guinea . . ." in a letter Walpole wrote to Lady Ossory dated 23 October 1784.

Lindsay, W. S. *History of Merchant Shipping and Ancient Commerce.* 4 vols. New York: AMS Press, 1965. (Reprint.)

Lips, Julius. *The Savage Hits Back.* Introduction by Bronislaw Malinowski. New Haven: Yale University Press, 1937. (Translated from the German.)

P. 213 provides an illustration of a Belauan carved storyboard in which the anthropologist Hambruch is shown "busy measuring a native's height."

Lloyd's Register of Shipping, 1782. (Originally published serially in London; reprinted by the Gregg Press.)

The entry for the *Antelope* is found alphabetically among the A's.

London Missionary Society. *Sermons Preached in London at the Formation of the Missionary Society.* London: Printed and sold by T. Chapman, 1795. (Bound with: *Four Sermons Preached in London at the Second General Meeting of the Missionary Society.* London: T. Chapman, 1796.)

Contains the Sermons and "Memorial . . . respecting the establishment and first attempts of that Society."

Loss of the Antelope Packet, in the Service of the British East-India Company, Henry Wilson, Commander . . . London: Printed for Thomas Tegg, n.d.

Lovett, Richard. *The History of the London Missionary Society, 1795-1895.* 2 vols. London: Henry Frowde, 1899.

Confirms that the first meetings were held at the Castle & Falcon, Aldergate Street.

McCluer, John. *An Account of the Navigation between India and the Gulph of Persia . . .* London: Published at the Charge of the East India Company, by Dalrymple, 1786.

Dalrymple provides an introduction in which he says, "The Young Man, to whom the Publick are indebted for this valuable Work, is self-taught, and therefore it cannot be supposed that, in acquiring the more useful attainments, he should have found leisure to study grammatical precision of language."

———. *Continuation of the Description of the Coast of Malabar from Bancoot, downwards 1789-1790.* London: G. Bigg, 1791.

———. *Description of the Coast of India, 1787-1788.* Published for the East India Company by Dalrymple. London: G. Bigg, 1789.

McCormick, E. H. *Omai: Pacific Envoy.* Auckland: Auckland University Press, 1977.

The definitive work on Omai, disappointing in this context only in that Lee Boo is not treated although other Pacific Island visitors to Europe are.

McKnight, Robert K. *Mnemonics in Pre-Literate Palau.* Anthropological Working Papers, no. 9. Guam, Mariana Islands: Office of the Staff Anthropologist, Trust Territory of the Pacific Islands, 1961.

The knotted twine is one of the mnemonic devices described, although not in the context of Lee Boo.

———. "Nanyo Paradaisu: Images of Life in the Western Carolines." In *Toshi Maruki Exhibition, Island Ways: Impressions from the Micronesia of 1940.* Koror, Palau: Palau Museum, 1978.

McManus, Edwin G., L. S. Josephs, and Masa-aki Emesiochel. *Palauan-English Dictionary.* Honolulu: University Press of Hawaii, 1977.

Margeston, Stella. *Journey by Stages . . .* London: Cassell, 1967.

Markham, Clements R. *A Memoir on the India Surveys.* Amsterdam: Meridian Publishing Co., 1968. (Reprint of 1878 [2nd] ed.)

Pp. 5-6 briefly describe McCluer's survey work prior to the "Pelew expedition" and the expedition itself, including McCluer's decision to remain in Belau. However, this respected author may have been a little carried away when he wrote, "McCluer married natives and lived contentedly for 15 months" and referred to the ladies stranded in Bombay as McCluer's "wives." But he praised McCluer's work, stating that he "was far in advance of his time in his ideas of surveying."

Marryat, Captain. *Jacob Faithful.* London: Dent, 1912.

P. 18: "Everything appeared to me foreign, strange and unnatural, and Prince Le

Boo or any other savage never stared or wondered more than I did. Of most things I knew not the use, of many not even the name. I was literally a savage, but still a kind and docile one."

————. *Newton Forster or, The Merchant Service.* London: Dent, 1895.

Marshall, Dorothy. *Dr. Johnson's London.* New York: Wiley, 1968.

Describes something of Rotherhithe: "There were the men who built the ships at Rotherhithe . . . carpenters, shipwrights, sailmakers, rope yard workers, gun-smiths, etc.

————. *English People in the Eighteenth Century.* London: Longmans, Green, 1956.

Martyn, Thomas. *The Universal Conchologist.* 4 vols. London, 1784. ("at his Academy for illustrating and painting Natural History, No. 16 Great Marlborough St., London . . . sold at his house—No. 26 King St. Covent Garden.")

In the introduction to these unusual volumes of shell illustrations, the author states: "For elegance and brilliance in effect perhaps no museum exceeds that of George Keate, esq. . . . of Charlotte Street, Bloomsbury." (The author is refer-ring to Keate's private collections of shells, gems, and miscellany—but principally shells—which, although not featured in the illustrations of these volumes insofar as I could determine, are described to some extent in a catalogue issued at the time of their sale after Keate's death. The sale catalogue can be seen at the library of the Natural History Museum, London. Although a few of the shells listed were from the "Palos," one can only speculate as to whether they had been brought home to London by the officers and crew of the *Antelope* or by those who had dealings at Belau at a somewhat later date.)

Maude, H. E. *Of Islands and Men.* Melbourne: Oxford University Press, 1968.

In his chapter entitled "Beachcombers and Castaways," Maude briefly relates the *Antelope* story; refers to Blanchard as "the prototype of many later beachcombers throughout the South Seas" because he was "master of the ordnance" for Abba Thulle; and names McCluer "the first of the gentlemen beachcombers."

Mavor, William, ed. *Historical Account of the Most Celebrated Voyages, Travels, and Dis-coveries . . .* Vol. 9. London: E. Newbury, 1797.

Volume 9 opens with the "Voyage of Capt. Henry Wilson, Principally relating to his Shipwreck on the Pelew Islands, and subsequent Proceedings."

Meares, John. *Voyages Made in the Years 1788 and 1789 from China to the North-West Coast of America.* Compiled by W. Combe "from the papers of J. Meares." London, 1790.

Includes the voyage of Captain William Douglas in the *Iphigenia Nubiana* which passed by the "Pelews" in 1788.

Melville, Herman. "Benito Cereno" in *Piazza Tales.* Putney, Vt.: Hendricks House, 1962.

Meredith, J. C. *The Tatooed Man.* New York: Duell, Sloan & Pearce, 1958.

A retelling of the Horace Holden story of "Shipwreck, Captivity, and Suffering" in the Belaus of the early 1830s.

Milburn, William. *Oriental Commerce or the East India Trader's Complete Guide . . .* "Compiled by William Milburn of the Honorable East India Company's Service." London, 1825.

Contains such items as "The river is somewhat broader than the Thames at London Bridge" (at Canton), and exports to China: "cotton wool; sandalwood, shark's fins, and a few others" (including opium).

Ministry of Works. *The Tower of London.* London: Her Majesty's Stationery Office, 1957.

Mitchell, Roger. "The Palauan Story-Board: The Evolution of a Folk Art Style." *Midwestern Journal of Language and Folklore* 1 (Fall 1975): 41–51.

Moorehead, Alan. *The Fatal Impact: An Account of the Invasion of the South Pacific, 1767–1840.* New York: Harper & Row, 1966.

Morand, Paul. *A Frenchman's London.* Translated by Desmond Flower. London: Cassell, 1934.

Morison, Samuel Eliot. *The Maritime History of Massachusetts, 1783–1860.* Boston: Houghton Mifflin, 1961.

Moritz, Karl Philipp. *Journeys of a German in England in 1782 . . .* New York: Holt, Rinehart, & Winston, [1965].

Morrell, Benjamin. *A Narrative of Four Voyages to the South Seas . . .* New York: n.p., 1832.

Morrell, W. P. *Britain in the Pacific Islands.* Oxford: Clarendon Press, 1960.

Morse, Hosea Ballou. *The Chronicles of the East India Company Trading to China, 1635–1834.* 4 vols. Taipei: Ch'eng-Wen Publishing Co., 1966. (Reprint of the 5-volume Oxford University Press edition of 1926–1929).
A rich resource derived from East India Company Records. Volume 2 of the 4-volume work I have used describes the Chinese attitude toward non-cargo-carrying vessels, their suspicions of opium, and a documentation of the *Antelope*'s difficulties upon trying to enter Canton.

Morse, Hosea Ballou and Harley F. MacNair. *Far Eastern International Relations.* Boston: Houghton Mifflin, 1931.
Chapter 4, "Conditions of Intercourse at Canton Prior to 1842" was especially helpful. It contains, for example, a list of "Regulations . . . made for the control of the foreigner, his ships, his trade . . ." on p. 60 and a description of the English and the Dutch India Company factories on p. 61.

Murray, H. *Adventures of British Seamen in the Southern Ocean . . .* Edinburgh: Constable, 1827.

Ngirairikl, Daniel. *The Story of Captain Wilson: Keate's "Account of the Pelew Islands."* Palauan translation by Daniel Ngirairikl. Koror: Palau Office of Adult Education, 1966.

Nicol, John. "The Life and Adventures of John Nicol, Mariner." In *Robinson Crusoe's Own Book; Or, The Voice of Adventure . . .*, edited by Charles Ellms, pp. 144–195. Boston: J. V. Pierce, 1843.
Nicol was sailing in the Pacific shortly after the *Antelope*'s voyage and was at Canton circa 1787. His descriptions of Canton and his observations in general have a ring of authenticity. He was a cooper as his father had been before him, and he knew how to be useful in other ways—in making candles, for example.

O'Gorman, Edmundo. *The Invention of America.* Bloomington, Ind.: Indiana University Press, 1961.
Profoundly pursues such themes as "Columbus himself was not responsible for the idea that he 'discovered America.' Where then did it originate?" Has relevance for

those who would set about determining who "discovered" the various Pacific islands.

O'Keefe, John. *A Short Account of the New Pantomime called Omai, or a Trip Round the World* . . . London: Printed for T. Cadell, 1785.

Osborne, Douglas. *The Archaeology of the Palau Islands.* B. P. Bishop Museum Bulletin 230. Honolulu: B. P. Bishop Museum, 1966.
The author included the Englishmen's island of Oroolong as a part of his archaeological explorations.

Owen, David Edward. *British Opium Policy in China and India.* New Haven: Yale University Press, 1934. Archon Books reprint, 1968.
The *Nonsuch* affair is explained on pp. 53–59. Chapter 1, "A Historical Introduction," is highly recommended to those interested in the subject of the East India Company's role in the opium trade.

Paine, Ralph D. *Lost Ships and Lonely Seas.* New York: Century, [1920].
"The Noble King of the Pelew Islands," pp. 393–412, is a brief abstract of Keate's *Account.*

Palau Community Action Agency. *A History of Palau.* 3 vols. Koror, Palau: Palau Community Action Agency, 1976.
This 3-volume history of Belau to 1947, the only history of its kind, is largely the product of a Belauan effort headed effectively by Katherine Kesolei of Koror, Belau.

Pan, Shü-lun. *The Trade of the United States with China.* New York: China Trade Bureau, 1924.
Re the "new people": "Samuel Shaw, the Supercargo of that ship *(Empress of China),* says in his *Journal:* 'The Chinese were very indulgent toward us. They styled us the new people . . .' " (p. 6).

Parkinson, C. Northcote. *Portsmouth Point: The British Navy in Fiction, 1793–1815.* Cambridge, Harvard University Press, 1949.
No fewer than six novels of Captain Marryat are represented, with excerpts to illustrate one facet or another of life aboard a naval vessel. Parkinson points out that much can be learned from the fictional works of men who knew the sea: Marryat, for example, "served from 1806 until his retirement as Captain in 1830." A delightful little book with a useful glossary and index.

————. *Trade in the Eastern Seas, 1793–1813.* Cambridge: Cambridge University Press, 1937.
I found this book to be an invaluable resource. On pp. 310–316, for example, Parkinson gives an account of the friction that sometimes existed between the Royal Navy and the East India Company's officers. In this context Henry Wilson and his ship the *Warley* are specifically mentioned—that Wilson, either as an act of mischievousness or because of impatience with naval escorts, sometimes failed to comport his ship in precisely the manner advised by the naval commander. Parkinson appears to side with Wilson although allowing for the risks involved.

————. *The Trade Winds: A Study of British Overseas Trade during the French Wars, 1793–1815.* London: Allen & Unwin, 1948.
Includes maps illustrating the Eastern Passage—the passage that took EIC ships between the Philippines and Palau (as the *Antelope* had attempted at an earlier date).

————. *War in the Eastern Seas, 1793–1815*. London: Allen & Unwin, 1954.
Parkinson devotes several pages to a description of "The Battle of Pulo-Aur," in which a fleet of East Indiamen, including Henry Wilson's *Warley*, beat off a French fleet under Admiral Linois. The fact that neither Wilson nor the *Warley* is mentioned in this account is evidence enough that they did not play a major role in this event, although Parkinson does mention both in a somewhat different context in his *Trade in the Eastern Seas*.

Pavière, Sydney H. *The Devis Family of Painters*. Leigh-on-Sea: F. Lewis, [1950].
Includes the *Antelope*'s Devis.

Peacock, Daniel J., and Paul Woodhead. *Lee Boo, A Prince in Rotherhithe*. London: Rotherside Books, 1984.
This twenty-page publication was a contribution to Rotherhithe's Lee Boo Bicentennial. Using an essay I wrote for that purpose, London educator Paul Woodhead added a foreword describing the Rotherhithe of his boyhood and enlisted the talent of artist Robert Tedman who designed the booklet and created several of its illustrations. An introductory letter was contributed by Ibedul Y. M. Gibbons.

Pevsner, Nikolaus. *The Buildings of England: London (Except the Cities of London and Westminster)*. London: Penguin, 1952.
Includes Rotherhithe.

Philips, C. H. *The East India Company, 1784–1834*. Manchester: University of Manchester Press, 1961.

Phillip, Arthur. *The Voyage of Governor Phillip to Botany Bay*. Sydney: Angus & Robertson, 1970. (Originally published in 1789.)
Pp. 142–144 contain an account of Lieutenant John Shortland's visit to Belau aboard the transport *Alexander* on 10 September 1788. Also the *Friendship*.

Piper, John. *The Companion Guide to London*. New York: Harper & Row, 1965.

Poe, Edgar Allen. *The Narrative of Arthur Gordon Pym*. Introduction by Richard Wilbur. Boston: D. R. Godine, 1973.

Price, A. Grenfell. *The Western Invasions of the Pacific* . . . Oxford: Clarendon Press, 1963.

Price, Willard. *Pacific Adventure*. New York: John Day, 1936.
Chapter 19, pp. 214–219, "Mishap of the Antelope," is a brief retelling by one of the very few American authors to visit Belau during the period of Japanese administration.

Pritchett, V. S. *London Perceived*. New York: Harcourt, Brace & World, 1962. (Harvest Book paperback edition.)

Pudney, John. *Brunel and His World*. London: Thames & Hudson, 1974.

Rasmussen, Steen Eiler. *London: The Unique City*. Introduction by James Bone. Cambridge: MIT Press, 1967. (Reprint of 3rd ed., 1947.)
An excellent source. Used in this work primarily for its references to St. James's Park and the Adam brothers' Adelphi.

Rawson, Geoffrey. *Pandora's Last Voyage*. New York: Harcourt, Brace & World, 1963.

Rees, Abraham, ed. *The Cyclopaedia: or, Universal Dictionary of Arts, Sciences, and Literature*. 39 vols. London: Longman, 1819.

Robinson, Howard. *The British Post Office, A History.* Princeton: Princeton University Press, 1948.

———. *Carrying British Mails Overseas.* New York: New York University Press, 1964.

Contains a footnote that might have applied to the *Antelope:* "It cost about £600 to copper a bottom, and took at least six weeks. The copper plates measured 4 feet by 14 inches" (p. 52). (The context is 1778.)

Rodgers, Stanley. *The Pacific.* London: Harrap, 1931.

Chapter 10, entitled "Pacific Shipwreck," begins with a 6-page abridgment of the *Antelope*'s story.

Rolt, L. T. C. *The Aeronauts: A History of Ballooning, 1783–1903.* London: Longmans, 1966.

Roosevelt, Hall, and Samuel Duff McCoy. *Odyssey of an American Family: An Account of the Roosevelts and their Kin as Travellers, from 1613 to 1938.* New York: Harper, 1939.

Chapter 7, pp. 74–87, entitled "Letter from Canton," has "Cousin Amasa Delano" telling his "Dear Cousin" what he had seen on repeated visits to Canton. In the preface, the authors explain that they have "pieced together from various letters" the one letter herein referred to. (Amasa was a cousin of Franklin Delano Roosevelt's grandfather, Warren Delano.)

Rosenbach, A. S. W. *Early American Children's Books.* New York: Kraus Reprint Corp., 1966.

The History of Prince Lee Boo . . . is mentioned as "an extremely popular book, frequently reprinted." (The specific edition cited was published in 1802 by B. Johnson & J. Johnson in Philadelphia.)

Runden, John P., ed. *Melville's Benito Cereno, A Text for Guided Research.* Boston: D. C. Heath, 1965.

The brief story of Franklin Delano Roosevelt's effort to borrow a copy of Amasa Delano's book is told on page v of the preface.

Sandstrom, Gosta E. *The History of Tunnelling . . .* London: Barrie & Rockliff, 1963.

Includes the Brunels' Rotherhithe-Wapping Tunnel: "The first subaqueous tunnel in the world since the 3,045-ft. tunnel under the Euphrates . . . became nothing more than a pedestrian pathway and a favourite shelter of the numerous homeless generated by the Victorian Age . . ."

Sharp, Andrew. *The Discovery of the Pacific Islands.* Oxford: Clarendon Press, 1960.

Shineberg, Dorothy, ed. *The Trading Voyages of Andrew Cheyne 1841–1844.* Honolulu: University of Hawaii Press, 1971.

Contains references to the *Antelope,* Captain Wilson, and Abba Thulle both in Shineberg's scholarly introduction and in Cheyne's text, with numerous references to Palau throughout in that Cheyne made a major effort to establish himself as the principal trader serving the area.

The Shipwreck of the Antelope East-India Packet, H. Wilson, Esq. Commander . . . in August 1783. By one of the Unfortunate Officers. London: D. Brewman, for R. Randall, 1788.

Dapp says, "a clear case of a publisher's pirating the *Account of the Pelew Islands*

. . . a palpable steal from Keate and in spite of all the touches designed to give it an authentic air, could have fooled very few persons." Dapp also quotes the review in the *Analytical Review* 2 (Sept. 1788): 32, "it is evidently nothing more than a short abridgment of that performance (Keate's) calculated to answer the purpose of popular information and pecuniary advantage to the editor, who in general, has closely followed Mr. Keate's narrative."

Simmons, Jack, ed. *Journeys in England, An Anthology.* Newton Abbot, Devon: David & Charles, 1969. Reprint of Odhams Press edition of 1951.
A useful collection with an excellent 21-page introduction.

Sitwell, Edith. *English Eccentrics.* New York: Vanguard Press, 1957.
Alexander Selkirk qualified as one of the eccentrics.

Smith, Bernard. "Coleridge's 'Ancient Mariner' and Cook's Second Voyage." In his *The Antipodean Manifesto, Essays in Art and History,* pp. 168–207. Melbourne: Oxford University Press, 1976.
The relationships between the poet's experiences as a boy at Christ's Hospital (school) and his "Ancient Mariner" are examined and Prince Lee Boo is again mentioned, if rather parenthetically, in the context of Coleridge's poem "To a Lady . . ." pp. 190–191.

—————. *European Vision and the South Pacific 1768–1850, A Study in the History of Art and Ideas.* London: Oxford University Press, 1960.
An essential work of engrossing interest in which the artistic efforts of the *Antelope*'s Devis receive more than casual mention and in which some of Devis' Pelew Island work is exhibited.

Snow, Edward Rowe. "Loss of the Packet Antelope" in *The Vengeful Sea,* pp. 26–40. New York: Dodd, Mead, 1956.
Another retelling based on Keate's *Account.*

South Pacific Commission. *The Koror Community Center.* Technical Paper no. 46. Noumea, New Caledonia: South Pacific Commission, 1953.

Spoehr, Florence Mann. *White Falcon, The House of Godeffroy and its Commercial and Scientific Role in the Pacific.* Palo Alto: Pacific Books, 1963.

Staunton, George. *An Authentic Account of an Embassy from the King of Great Britain to the Emperor of China.* 2 vols. London: G. Nicol, 1797.
McCluer and Proctor are mentioned: "it was the *Endeavour* brig, commanded by Captain Proctor . . . the *Endeavour* belonged to the EIC and had been employed under the command of a gentleman of science of the name of McCluer . . ." (McCluer's stay in Pelew is related) Vol. 1, pp. 451–452. "Captain Proctor confirmed, in many instances, the favorable accounts given of the Pelew Islands by Capt. Wilson" (p. 453).

Stevenson, Mrs. Robert Louis. *The Cruise of the Janet Nichol . . .* New York: Scribner's, 1914.

Stevenson, Robert Louis. *In the South Seas.* London: Chatto & Windus, 1900. (Reprinted, Honolulu: University Press of Hawaii, 1971.)

Stroven, Carl, and A. Grove Day, eds. *The Spell of the Pacific: An Anthology of its Literature.* New York: Macmillan, 1949.
Pp. 826–831: "The King of Palau Visits Captain Wilson" is a 6-page excerpt from Keate.

Sutherland, Lucy S. *The East India Company in Eighteenth-Century Politics.* Oxford: Oxford University Press, 1962.

————. *A London Merchant, 1695–1774.* Oxford: Oxford University Press, 1933. (Reprinted, London: Frank Cass, 1962.)

Tamarin, Alfred, and Shirley Glubock. *Voyaging to Cathay: Americans in the China Trade.* New York: Viking Press, 1976.
Published "for young people," but useful to the serious researcher as well. Contains, for example, excellent descriptions and illustrations of Macao and Canton circa 1783–1850.

Teller, Walter. *Five Sea Captains.* New York: Atheneum, 1964.
One of them is Amasa Delano.

Tetens, Alfred. *Among the Savages of the South Seas: Memoirs of Micronesia, 1862–1868.* Translated by Florence Mann Spoehr. Stanford, Calif.: Stanford University Press, 1958.
Includes illustrations from Keate's *Account* and, although concerned with the German period, has references to earlier times.

Tinker, Chauncey Brewster. *Nature's Simple Plan . . .* Princeton: Princeton University Press, 1922.
Delightfully readable treatment of, among other things, the Noble Savage.

Tompson, Richard S. *Classics or Charity? The Dilemma of the 18th Century Grammar School.* Manchester: Manchester University Press, 1971.

Tristram, W. Outram. *Coaching Days and Coaching Ways.* London: Macmillan, 1924.
Tells the story, on pp. 179–184, of the "Murder by the Smugglers" (in the late 1700s) and reports the murder of a sailor in 1786 to illustrate the hazards of travel along the Portsmouth Road.

Trumbull, Robert. *Paradise in Trust: A Report on Americans in Micronesia, 1946–1958.* New York: William Sloane Associates, 1959.

Turberville, A. S. *English Men and Manners in the Eighteenth Century.* 2nd ed. London: Oxford University Press, 1929.

Uchetemel a Llach er a Beluu er a Belau (Constitution of the Republic of Palau). Koror, Palau: Palau Constitutional Convention, 1979.

Villiers, Alan. *Monsoon Seas: The Story of the Indian Ocean.* New York: McGraw-Hill, 1952.

————. *The Way of a Ship.* New York: Scribner's, 1953.

Ward, R. Gerard, ed. *American Activities in the Central Pacific, 1790–1870.* 8 vols. Ridgewood, N.J.: Gregg Press, 1967.

Webb, Sidney, and Beatrice Webb. *English Local Government from the Revolution to the Municipal Corporations Act.* Vol. 2: *The Manor,* and Vol. 3: *The Borough.* London: Longmans, 1908.
Provides background on the London of Lee Boo's time, e.g., very poor sanitation, deplorable conditions in and around slaughter houses, the worst prisons in England, etc. Neglect of the Thames was so bad that "in 1798 National Government took in hand what the City Corporation had neglected, and established a marine police."

Webster, John C. *Sir Brook Watson.* [Sackville, New Brunswick: 1924]

A 25-page pamphlet describing Watson's early life, especially the time he spent in Nova Scotia before his rise to prominence in London.

Wellsman, John. *Panorama of London, 1749.* From an original engraving made by the Buck Brothers in 1749; contemporary notes by John Wellsman. London: Sidgwick & Johnson, 1972.

West, Jane. *Poems and Plays.* London: Longman & Rees, 1799.
The poem "Pelew" is on pp. 258–266 of volume 4, published in 1805.

Wheatley, Henry B. *London Past and Present: Its History, Associations, and Traditions.* 3 vols. London: John Murray, 1891.

Whitney, Lois. *Primitivism and the Idea of Progress in English Popular Literature of the Eighteenth Century: Contributions to the History of Primitivism.* Baltimore: Johns Hopkins Press, 1934.
Pp. 115–118 contain references to Lee Boo much in the same manner as Fairchild's more extensive treatment of the same subject matter.

William, Harry. *South London.* London: Robert Hale, 1950.

Williams, C. A. S. *Outlines of Chinese Symbolism and Art Motives.* Shanghai: Kelly & Walsh, 1941.
The section entitled "Dragon," pp. 132–141, provides some confirmation of Per Collinder's "Ching Lung—the blue-green dragon." (*Ching Lung* is translated Green Dragon.)

Wilson, Francesca M. *Strange Island: Britain through Foreign Eyes, 1395–1940.* London: Longmans, Green, [1955].
Includes excerpts from "A Journey through England and Scotland in 1784" by Faujas de Saint Fond.

Wilson, James. *A Missionary Voyage to the Southern Pacific Ocean.* Introduction by Irmgard Moschner. Graz, Austria: Akademische Druck -u. Verlagsanstalt, 1966. (Also, New York: Praeger, n.d.)
Comments on "Pelew" are on pp. 306–308.

Wilson, Mary F. *Between Bridgers.* London: Copyprints Ltd., n.d.
59-page local history booklet on Rotherhithe.

Wonderful Escapes. Dublin: Printed for J. Charles, 1819.
Contains the *Antelope* story as abstracted from Keate.

Wright, Charles, and C. Ernest Fayle. *A History of Lloyd's: From the Founding of Lloyd's Coffee House to the Present Day.* London: Macmillan, 1928.

Zimmerman, Elwood C. "Nature of the Land Biota." In *Man's Place in the Island Eco-system,* edited by F. R. Fosberg, pp. 57–64. Honolulu: Bishop Museum Press, 1963.
". . . most Europeans would probably have found the islands dietetically monotonous if not difficult places in which to live." (Although reference is primarily to Polynesia, with some variations the same might be said of Micronesia.)

INDEX

Abba Thulle, 2; as "king" of Pelew, 33; visits Oroolong, 39–41, 50, 54; requests armed assistance, 43; entertains Henry Wilson, 49; and launching of *Oroolong*, 54–55; requests Lee Boo be taken to England, 56; bids farewell to the English, 67–68, 134, 258; awaits word of Lee Boo, 195, 222; learns of Lee Boo's death, 128; encounters with McCluer, 128–129, 132–134; death of, 142; Delano's appraisal of, 143; London street named after, 176. *See also* Ibedul

Abercromby, Robert, 130

Account of the Pelew Islands, An, 2, 31, 120, 181, 215–216; translations of, 3, 215

Adam, Robert, 100

Adventures of Madiboo, The, 177, 225

Adze, 184

Alcohol: aboard *Antelope*, 17, 199; after shipwreck, 26, 37, 45, 46; Lee Boo and, 75; in East Indies, 135

Alexander (ship), 222

Amboyna (Moluccas), 135–136

Americans: at Canton and Macao, 72, 207, 208; in Belau, xiv, 184–185, 227

Animals, aboard ships, 23, 127–128, 139; taken to Belau, 129, 139, 151. *See also* Dogs; Horses

Antelope (ship), 9–10, 196–197; owners of, 11; voyage of, 13–21, 31, 197, 200–210; log of, 14, 17–21, 197; boats of, 17, 26, 27, 54; wreck and salvage of, 25–28, 30, 35; replica and model of, 184, 196; remains of, 187, 228; search for origins of, 196; provisioning of, 199

Aoutourou, 165–166

Apple, mountain, 68

Ariel (ship), 121

Arra Kooker, 33, 35, 38, 57

Art and artists, 14–15, 46, 101, 107, 131. *See also* Belau, art of; Devis, A. W.; Wedgebrough, J.; White, R.

Artingall (Melekeok), 45, 47, 49, 133, 191

Aye, Aye, Sir!, 225

Bai (houses). *See* Belau.

Balloon flight, 104–105. *See also* Lunardi, Vincenzo

Banks, Sir Joseph, 105, 163–164, 187

Barker, Peter, 14, 17, 43, 49

Beck, Rev. Edward J., 3, 176

Belau (Palau/Pelew/Palou), xiii–xiv, 25, 26, 50–51, 180; foods of, and feasting, 38–39, 46, 48, 53, 67, 180, 190, 192; canoes of, 31, 39, 45, 47–48, 50, 129, 135, 180, 187, 217, 226; art of, 130, 191; *bai* (houses) of, 60, 130, 191; agriculture of, 130; causeways and piers of, 46, 191; postage stamps of, 229. *See also* Coorooraa; Oroolong

Belau islanders, xiv, 32, 38–39, 180, 184; mimicry of, 38, 96; dancing of, 46, 48, 49; warfare and weapons of, 45, 202, 203; music, 49, 132; "compassionate people," 134; progressiveness of, 228. *See also* Abba Thulle; Arra Kooker; Ibedul; Kockywack; Lee Boo; Phymoo; Qui Bill; Raa Kook; Reklai; *rubak*

Benger, Philip, 14, 17, 25

Bermondsey, 86, 176

Besant, Walter, 81, 211

Betel nut, 32, 39, 132, 184, 191

Bible, 165, 172

ABOUT THE AUTHOR

Daniel J. Peacock was born in Amityville, New York, but grew up on a small Indiana farm. After attending Richmond, Indiana, public schools, he graduated from Earlham College in 1948. Peacock first went to Micronesia in 1953 to join the U.S. Trust Territory's Education Department. The islands' appeal led him to pass the next twenty-six years there, except for a year spent at Drexel University in Philadelphia to obtain a master's degree in library science. His Micronesia experience included five years in the Belau Islands where he first heard of Lee Boo, seven years on Pohnpei, where he was a teacher-librarian at the Pacific Islands Central School, and thirteen years on Saipan as supervisor of library services for the Trust Territory. During his stay on Pohnpei, he was a frequent contributor to the weekly *Ponape-Per,* in which an early part of the Lee Boo story first appeared. He has also published articles in the *Micronesian Reporter,* the *South Pacific Bulletin, Pacific Islands Monthly,* and other Pacific area periodicals. Since his retirement in 1980, Peacock has devoted himself to the completion of Lee Boo's story. Final research for the book, conducted in both Hawaii and England, stretched over a period of three years.

▦ **Production Notes**

This book was designed by Roger Eggers.
Composition and paging were done on the
Quadex Composing System and typesetting on
the Compugraphic 8400 by the design and
production staff of University of Hawaii Press.

The text and display typeface is Compugraphic
Bembo.

Offset presswork and binding were done by Vail-
Ballou Press, Inc. Text paper is Writers RR
Offset, basis 50.

www.ingramcontent.com/pod-product-compliance
Lightning Source LLC
Chambersburg PA
CBHW070756270326
41927CB00010B/2166